A structural analysis of small groups

A Structural Analysis of Small Groups is concerned with the emergent properties of groups as systems, where those properties arise from, but where such properties are equivalent neither to those of individuals nor their interactions.

First, an examination of group theory is presented. Particular emphasis is placed upon processes of group integration, identity and leadership, using the theories of Freud, Bion, Winnicott, and Lacan. Methodological problems of group research are examined, including problems of definition and measurement, e.g. transindividual processes are defined, described and appropriate measurement methods are discussed. Finally, within a framework of systems, psychoanalytic and social psychological theories, five small groups are analysed to determine their structural and dynamic properties.

The book aims to extend and develop ideas on group dynamics within the psychoanalytic group psychology tradition. In so doing it emphasises the role of unconscious processes in the nature of collective life. In addition to the more traditional analytic ideas about groups the book draws on the work of Lacan.

The book will be of interest to all those concerned with group dynamics, leadership, psychoanalysis, systems theory and social psychology.

Susan Long is Senior Lecturer in Organisation Behaviour at the Swinburne Institute in Melbourne, Australia, and Chairperson of the Australian Institute of Social Analysis established in 1983 to develop in Australia work pioneered at the Tavistock Institute of Human Relations in London. She also works as a psychotherapist and is a group and organisational consultant in private practice.

A structural analysis of small groups

Susan Long

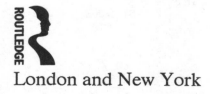

London and New York

First published in 1992
by Routledge
11 New Fetter Lane, London EC4P 4EE

Simultaneously published in the USA and Canada
by Routledge
a division of Routledge, Chapman and Hall, Inc.
29 West 35th Street, New York, NY 10001

© 1992 Susan Long

Typeset from the author's wordprocessing disks by
NWL Editorial Services, Langport, Somerset

Printed and bound in Great Britain by
Mackays of Chatham PLC, Chatham, Kent

British Library Cataloguing in Publication Data
Long, Susan
    A structural analysis of small groups.
    1. Psychoanalysis
    I. Title
    150.195

Library of Congress Cataloging in Publication Data
Long, Susan, 1948–
    A structural analysis of small groups / Susan Long.
    p.   cm.
    Includes bibliographical references and index.
    1. Small groups.   2. Group psychoanalysis.   I. Title
    HM133.L73   1991   91–14208
    302.3'4 – dc20   CIP

ISBN 0–415–06501–1

To my parents Marjorie and Leonard who provided me with my first group

Contents

List of figures and tables   ix

Acknowledgements   x

1 Overview   1

Part I   Theoretical framework

2 A systems framework   9

3 Group psychology   17

4 Integration in groups   49

5 Identity, leadership and authority   57

6 Research methodology for group systems   75

Part II   The cross-sectional study

7 Group 1, session 1   91

8 Group 2, session 1   107

9 Group 3, session 1   120

10 Comparison of groups 1–3 from the cross-sectional study   131

Part III   The longitudinal qualitative study

Introduction to Part III

11 The longitudinal qualitative study   139

12 Conclusions and implications for future research   175

Appendices

Appendix A   Leadership and authority   179

Appendix B   A report on a study of group members'
             perceptions of each other   183

References   189

Name index   200

Subject index   202

Figures and tables

FIGURES

1   Spatial representation of elements (group 3 members) high
on dimension 3, in the 1x2 plane of the three-dimensional
group space   185

2   Spatial representation of elements (group 3 members) low
on dimension 3, in the 1x2 plane of the three-dimensional
group space   186

TABLES

1   States inferred from the observation of the first session of
three different self-study groups   133

2   Summary of the first major episode in the longitudinal study   156

2.1 The group structure (social syntax) in terms of episode,
actions and acts   156

2.2 The social semantics (the meaning of the episode, actions
and acts)   156

3   Summary of the second major episode in the longitudinal study   161

3.1 The group structure (social syntax) in terms of episode,
actions and acts   161

3.2 The social semantics (the meaning of the episode, actions
and acts)   161

4   Summary of the third major episode in the longitudinal study   166

4.1 The group structure (social syntax) in terms of episode,
actions and acts   166

4.2 The social semantics (the meaning of the episode, actions
and acts)   167

Acknowledgements

This book has involved me in years of study and preparation and there are many people who have helped and influenced me through those years.

I want to thank my husband, Michael Long. In addition to the emotional support and domestic load that he has carried over these years, being a social researcher himself was invaluable to me. He was especially helpful during the processing of the data for the multidimensional scaling study reported in Appendix B. Without his aid I would not have been inspired to master the statistical methods that proved best for this task.

I want also to thank Dr Charles Langley who guided me in the research, provided stimulating discussions and, through many careful readings of the manuscript, aided me in its preparation; also Mr Leonardo Rodriguez and Dr Russell Grigg for their seminars held at Prince Henry's Hospital, Melbourne. Without these seminars my reading of Lacan would have proceeded with much more difficulty. I also thank the other members of the Melbourne Centre for Psychoanalytic Research who took part in this 'Lacan seminar'. Their contributions to many enlivening discussions made my theoretical explorations in this area a most pleasant task. Another group to thank are members of the Australian Institute of Social Analysis, especially Alastair Bain, but also others, too numerous to mention by name, with whom I have worked on many occasions and who continue to provide me with a space in which to think mutually with others about groups, including all those who have been members of AISA working conferences on group relations which enable the exploration of group phenomena to occur. My thanks also to other colleagues who have read portions of the manuscript in earlier form and provided me with useful comments. These include Richard Bell, Huguette Glowinski, Alastair Bain and Ross Williams. Thanks also to Dr Loren Borland who mentored me in my early years of psychoanalytic study.

My deepest appreciation is extended to the group members whose interactions and behaviours are the data for this research.

Finally, I would like to point out that much of Chapters 4 and 7 were originally published in a slightly different form as: S. Long (1984) 'Early integration in groups: A group to join and a group to create', *Human Relations* vol. 37, no. 4, pp. 311–32. A small section of Appendix B has been published as: S. Long (1989) 'Leadership and gender: A psychoanalytic approach', *Analysis* vol. 1, no. 1 (a publication of the Centre for Psychoanalytic Research, Melbourne, Australia). I would like to acknowledge permission given by the publishers to include this material in the book.

Chapter 1

Overview

The field within which this work is set is that of group psychology. As such it is concerned with the emergent properties of groups as systems, where those properties arise from, but are not equivalent to either the properties of individuals or of their interactions. The group properties of cohesion and schism, for example, may be described only in terms of the total group as a system, not in terms of any one particular individual, or particular individuals and their interactions.

The human individual, however, stands in a reciprocal relationship to the groups which s/he helps constitute. The lessons of social psychology stress social determination, humans presumably being largely derived from social process. However, humans at the same time are creating their social environments. To focus on the individual in the group requires a perspective that both places the human subject as emergent from a social nexus, and also implies the importance of individual as well as socially derived identity (Harré, 1979; 1983).

A discussion of the relations between different systems helps to resolve the dilemma of 'reciprocal' causation within human systems, i.e., with the seeming paradox of humans who both create and are the result of social processes. This remains paradoxical only when we regard the system 'individual' as enclosed within, or subordinate to the system 'group'. A different view is presented when the group (or several groups) is regarded as enclosed within, or subordinate to the individual. This question will be considered more fully in Chapter 2 where the relationships between systems will be considered. It is perhaps sufficient here to say that it is up to the observer to decide how a system is best conceptualized for his or her specific purposes. It is for the observer to decide whether the group is understood primarily as composed of individual roles, or whether the central focus should be the individual, seen as a complex of elements, uniquely organized, yet also derived from roles experienced in many different groups, or, indeed, as both.

STYLE OF THE PRESENT WORK

The present work involves much that is 'exploratory, clinical and impressionistic' (Mann, 1974, p. 14) as well as more conventional empirical approaches. This calls for a style of rigorous definition (Rychlak, 1977), and for the use of ideographic research methods (Allport, 1962). For example, one reason why research into group phenomena is difficult is because the concepts used often seem to be counter-intuitive. Not least of the problems involved is the creation and use of *transindividual* concepts that identify processes of the group-as-a-whole (Stock and Lieberman, 1962; Wisdom, 1970). These concepts rely on a careful and intensive description of individual behaviours and interactions within the group because it is the *patterning* of these that provides the data upon which 'group' concepts are predicated. That is, group data are constituted from specific individual behaviours evoked by other specific behaviours in particular patterns. Case study methods seem most appropriate in identifying these patterns. This seems to be the case for one section of small group research which has been strongly influenced by research into group psychotherapy (Bion, 1961; Foulkes, 1964; Kissen, 1976b, Schlachet, 1986), for experiential learning groups (Back, 1972; Gibbard et al., 1974; Smith, 1982), and for organizations (Etzioni, 1961; Miller, 1976; Katz and Kahn, 1978), all of which areas have emphasized observational and clinical methods of research. Individual case studies are frequently used (Clark, 1972; Gibbard et al., 1974; Kissen, 1976a; Lawrence, 1979), and are appropriate for the exploration of uniqueness in systems (Allport, 1962).

ORGANIZATION OF THE BOOK

Part I Theoretical framework

This consists of Chapters 2–6. Chapter 2 will consider the choice of a 'systems' framework. This will require describing the nature of systems, the relationships of systems to their environments, and the complex relations that may be described as existing between systems. Such a discussion provides a background to an argument for the unique and specific place of group psychology within the social sciences, presented in Chapter 3.

Chapter 3 will also survey some theories relevant to this task. In anticipation it might be said that understanding reciprocal relations between individuals and groups is difficult. Within the field of social psychology, the available conceptualizations have often centred on interpersonal relations (e.g., Thibaut and Kelley, 1959). Even recent formulations that argue for the group as a psychological reality in itself (e.g., self-categorization theory, Turner et al., 1987), maintain the primacy of the individual insofar as the individual self becomes identified with a particular cognitive category, which constitutes the group.

The idea of reciprocal relations and constraints on the coming-into-being of both groups and individuals, that is, the idea that human groups and human individuals are emergent entities standing in a systemic relation to one another (albeit a system at a logical level different to both individual and group systems understood separately), is an idea difficult to comprehend. However, in the end it is Lacan (1977) who provides one of the most useful theories. This theory places the psychological subject as emergent from the social nexus. Moreover, this subject is understood as split and difficult to identify, i.e., as emergent from many *different* sources, and yet this subject can find more or less a constant place in the social order, in that area of symbolically ordered human experience that underlies social life. The symbolic systems of the group, e.g., the linguistic and other value systems employed by members, provide a basis for the examination of those structural properties of the group from which the member/subject emerges. Another way of stating this is to say that Lacan's theories provide a framework for understanding the nature of some transindividual phenomena where 'transindividual' refers to the group process as beyond the individual and his/her interactions yet embodied in the individual.

A useful starting point for the group researcher is to understand those processes that enable a collection of individuals to become a *psychological entity*, that is, a psychological group. Winnicott (1945; 1951), for example, provides the specific details of a psychological unity forged from the inner chaos experienced in early infancy and immanent in adult life. In particular, his work most usefully addresses the psychology of the individual as emergent from the mother/child pair, itself a dyad set in a social scheme (Davis and Wallbridge, 1983). Moreover Winnicott's work can be adapted to guide the observation of larger systems. In studying the emerging individual, he identifies three major processes: 'integration', 'personalization' and 'realization'. These are processes commensurate with a more general view of the development of *any* living unity, e.g., of small groups or, perhaps, of larger organizations or nations. Such processes map the development of new entities or systems as they emerge from an older order. These ideas will be elaborated in Chapter 4, where the ideas of Winnicott (1945) and Mahler (1968; Mahler et al., 1975) are applied to an understanding of the integrative processes present early in the life a group.

Chapter 5 introduces the ideas of identity and identification as major transindividual group processes. Following the ideas of Freud (1921), identification is regarded as a prime factor in group cohesion and as a basis for the structuring of group roles around the group's primary tasks (Freud, 1914; Rice, 1965). Theories of identification, leadership, authority and power are presented as a theoretical framework for the studies that follow. Firstly, the nature of identification is explored through the theories of Harré (1979; 1983), Erikson (1950; 1968), Lacan (1977) and Freud (1914; 1921). In particular, the vicissitudes of narcissistic libido are regarded as forming a basis for identifications in groups. Secondly, the nature of power, authority and leadership is explored. This is done by reference to modern social psychological literature (e.g., Hollander, 1985, Appendix A), as well as to psychoanalytic theory. Several dimensions of leadership and authority are suggested. In concluding this chapter, a view is proposed of identification as a transindividual process linking the group members to their symbolic leaders through the group power and authority structures.

A systems framework presents specific methodological problems to the researcher. These problems largely result from the complex nature of systems, with their many interrelated parts. This complexity often makes it difficult to apply traditional experimental methods, particularly when it is the *changing pattern* of systemic organization, rather than the independent effects of specific static variables, that is to be observed. Furthermore, systems research is often based on non-temporal causal models (Rychlak, 1968; 1977; Clark, 1972; Watzlawick et al., 1974). That is, causes are explained in terms of form, or in terms of the system's anticipation of the future implications inherent in present forms. These explanations provide an alternative to explanations in terms of deterministic, antecedent (and non-'reciprocal') causes. Because of the stress on 'formal' explanations, the methodological problems are largely those involved in 'naturalistic observation'.

Chapter 6 discusses such methodological problems (encountered by the researcher working in a systems framework) as (a) defining the 'system' or 'entity' to be examined, (b) deciding the attributes to be measured, and (c) describing and interpreting the data of the research. Chapter 6 also describes some methods appropriate for research in a systems framework. Forgas (1979) argues that a combination of several research strategies, including naturalistic observation, structural analysis and the analysis of member perceptions, enables the researcher to more validly analyse social interactions than any one method taken alone. These form the basis of the particular research methods to be used in the empirical studies to be reported.

Part II The cross-sectional study

Chapters 7–9 present the first of the empirical sub-studies reported in this book. The focus of this research is on integrative processes in groups. The dialogue of members during the first meeting of each of three different groups is examined in detail in order to determine underlying group structures. In turn these structures are considered to form group 'states'. Each group is examined in terms of these states and a summary and conclusions are provided in Chapter 10.

Part III The longitudinal qualitative study

A longitudinal study of a group is presented in Chapter 11. This study analyses some major events or episodes from the 14 weekly meetings that took place. These episodes are viewed as 'structural organizers' in that they organize the group structures through the interactions that take place between members, and through the meanings that members attribute to them (Harré, 1979; 1982). These interactions are seen both to constitute the episodes and to structure the group's responses to the episodes. This is because they are viewed as symbolic and self-reflexive. They constrain structure, meaning and subsequent action much as linguistic processes act to constrain (rather than strictly determine) linguistic structure and semantics (Saussure, 1959; Jakobson and Halle, 1956; Chomsky, 1965; 1968; Bateson, 1973). From this analysis, an attempt is made to define the particular structures of the group studied. In so doing, leadership, authority and power are related to the group processes. An associated study of group member perceptions of themselves and other members is presented in Appendix B.

The final Chapter 12 provides some general conclusions and implications for future study.

Part I

Theoretical framework

Chapter 2

A systems framework

In this chapter, a systems theory framework is presented as a general context to the theories and studies that are described in the later chapters. It is a framework intended to orient the reader towards a number of basic pragmatic issues. These include problems of:

1 defining the *entities* which are to be researched (e.g., defining boundaries);
2 defining the *attributes* of entities to be examined (i.e., deciding which observations to make and how to make them);
3 deciding which *relationships* are to be examined, and deciding how these relationships are to be understood (e.g., as strictly determined through antecedent/consequent relations, as elements in a formal pattern, as relations dependent on some symbolic order, or in any other way);
4 *articulating differences* that occur within the system when, for example, the system is relating to other systems, or is in a changing environment.

It is also a framework intended to help the reader to discern differing interpretations about the nature of the entity or relations under consideration. These interpretations include those made from within the system (e.g., the perspective of a group member or the perspective from a particular role), and those made, seemingly, from without the system (e.g., the perspective of an observer).

It is the *group as a system* that is the basis of the present investigation. Consequently, this chapter will introduce some ideas about the nature of systems and their interactions.

THE NATURE OF SYSTEMS

A classic definition of a system is given by Hall and Fagen (1955, p. 18) who state that, 'a system is a set of objects together with the relationships between the objects and between their attributes'.

Implied in this definition is the notion that, not only should the elements that constitute the system be taken into account during work with that system, but so too should the internal patterning, which itself is an element of a further order. Consequently, change to any one part of the system should, at least theoretically, affect all other parts of the same system, even when the systemic organization includes internal boundaries and inhibitions.

It is interesting that the given definition poses a definite boundary to a possibly infinite set. That is, a set of 'objects' may be delimited though their relationships may be infinite; or, conversely, the relations pertaining to the internal organization of a system may be strictly limited whilst the possible objects are not. The lexicon and set of syntactical rules of a natural language provide an example of the former (i.e., a limited but structured vocabulary may be infinitely combined to form new sentences, Chomsky, 1965; 1968). The rule of addition in the number system instances the latter case (any number may be added although the rules of addition are strictly defined and limited). Hence the term 'system' refers to an abstraction of relations between items, which in themselves may be abstractions.

This conception of 'systems' has led to a new tract of scientific discourse (Emery, 1969). For example, after considering some basic properties derived from an examination of Prigogine's work on entropy in open systems, Von Bertalanffy (1950) considered the possibility of a 'general systems theory' which crossed disciplinary boundaries.

> Conceptions and systems of equations similar to those of open systems in physiochemistry and physiology appear in biocoenology, demography and sociology. The formal correspondence of general principles, irrespective of the kind of relations or forces between the components, leads to the conception of a 'General Systems Theory' as a new scientific doctrine, concerned with the principles which apply to systems in general.
>
> (Von Bertalanffy, 1950, pp. 83–4)

The literature on systems is broad and stems from a variety of different sources. Emery (1969) comments on the contributions of philosophy, physics, chemistry and biology. The systems approach is not so much a unified theory, as a paradigmatic approach to the description of observations and theoretical issues within the particular sciences mentioned (Kuhn, 1962). In the biological and social sciences this approach has been taken variously by Von Bertalanffy (1950), Sommerhoff (1969) and Maturana and Varela (1980) within biology, by Emery and Trist (1965), Katz and Kahn (1978) and by the 'Tavistock' school (e.g., Rice, 1969; Miller and Rice, 1967; Miller, 1976; and Lawrence, 1979) from within social and organizational psychology, and, in the fields of communication and family therapy, by Bateson (1968; 1973), Minuchin (1974; 1981), Hoffman (1971), Dell and Goolishian (1981) and Dell (1982).

Open and closed systems

Systems differ according to the degree of permeability they have to their respective environments: the more open the system, the greater the number and/or kind of boundary transactions. An example is the living cell itself. The cell is bounded by a semi-permeable membrane which selectively allows materials to pass. Certain biochemical principles manage this process. Similarly, organization management groups may be considered as boundary regulators, functioning to select the transactions that the organization will have with the environment (Katz and Kahn, 1978).

From these examples, it can be seen that the openness of a system is not necessarily fixed. At any one time a system may be considered as relatively open or closed, depending upon the boundary regulation emanating from the system itself, with aid from environmental feedback.

This idea of boundary is essential to the distinction between system and environment, and consequently enables the observation of the system as a unit. In a basic sense, the relationship of system to environment is one whereby the system inputs, processes and outputs elements of the environment, and is responsive to certain forms of feedback input for system regulation. The simplicity of this formulation is apparent, however, when the relationships between systems are considered. Take the following definition from Hall and Fagen:

> For a given system, the environment is the set of all objects, a change in whose attributes affect the system, and also those objects whose attributes are changed by the behaviour of the system.
>
> (Hall and Fagen, 1955, p. 20)

It follows, then, that systems may act as environments for other systems, and, in fact, a simple relation of system to random elements in an unsystematized environment would be rare, if not implausible. Understanding system/environment relations, therefore, requires an understanding of system/system relations. Watzlawick et al. (1974) formulate a theoretical framework suitable for discussing the relationships *between* systems by adapting two theories from the field of mathematical logic, i.e., the theory of groups and the theory of logical types (Whitehead and Russell, 1963). Three points that they make are relevant:

1 The distinction between *member* and *class*. This distinction is crucial to a systemic analysis. The two concepts should not be confused, as this would constitute a violation of the law separating logical types (Whitehead and Russell, 1963). The difference between individuals as members and humankind as a class is instanced. The latter cannot be described by reference to particular individuals nor to their simple aggregation.

The Theory of Logical Types makes it clear that we must not talk about the class in the language appropriate for its members. This would be an error in logical typing and would lead to the very perplexing impasses of logical paradox. Such errors of typing can occur in two ways: either by incorrectly ascribing a particular property to the class instead of to the member (or vice versa), or by neglecting the paramount distinction between class and member and by treating the two as if they were of the same level of abstraction.

(Watzlawick et al., 1974, p. 27)

2 Systems, like groups, may be explained only in terms external to themselves, i.e., by 'metasystemic' concepts. In clarifying this point it could be said that attempted explanations from within the system are better seen as *definitions* (or descriptions), insofar as the systemic elements are explained by reference to other elements much as a dictionary provides definitions by reference only to other words. Only a metalanguage of linguistics, for example, can attempt to *explain* natural languages. Similarly, rules that govern a system may often be considered as 'meta' to the system proper and may then be able to provide explanations.

The idea that definitions (descriptions) are made from within the system has a parallel idea in the work of Merleau-Ponty (1962). His phenomenology states that meaning is present through our ongoing presence in a real world. 'Because we are in the world, we are condemned to meaning, and we cannot do or say anything without its acquiring a name in history.' (p. xix) This 'meaning' is apparent only through its being lived (i.e., from within the ongoing system). To Merleau-Ponty, the phenomenological method involves a transcendental stepping back in order to look at the real world 'for what it is as a fact for us, before any thematization' (p. xv). There is, for him, a self-evident 'real' that must be reconsidered and rediscovered. Language is removed from this and can provide explanations only from outside the phenomena. Consequently language is seen to remove us from our experience. It involves a 'meta' experience.

3 System change may be effected either from inside or outside. The former type of change Watzlawick et al. term first order change. This is the type of change that occurs 'within a system that itself remains invariant' (Watzlawick et al., 1974, p. 10). Group theory, they state, gives a framework for such change. The latter type of change, termed second order change, is understood not by reference to what occurs inside a class between members, but by reference to those changes that affect the nature of the system itself. The theory of logical types, they claim, 'gives us a frame for considering the relationship between member and class and the peculiar metamorphosis which is in the nature of shifts from one logical level to the next higher' (p. 10). In this type of change the member is changed as a consequence of a systemic shift.

HIERARCHICAL ORDERING

For Watzlawick et al., the relationships that exist between systems are clear when systems are hierarchically ordered, and where a class becomes an element in a system at a logical level 'meta' to its own elements. A simple example given by these authors concerns some systems involved in an automobile. They describe the driver's ability to change the performance of the engine as occurring in two different ways: by supplying more or less fuel (by operating the accelerator pedal), or by changing gears. The idea of first order change is applied to the changes within each gear. Second order change is seen as analogous to the gear change itself:

> Let us strain the analogy just a little and say that in each gear the car has a certain range of 'behaviours' (i.e., of power output and consequently of speed, acceleration, climbing capacity, etc.). Within that range (i.e., that class of behaviours), appropriate use of the gas pedal will produce the desired performance. But if the required performance falls outside this range, the driver must shift gears to obtain the desired change. Gear shifting is thus a phenomenon of a higher logical type than giving gas, and it would be patently nonsensical to talk about the mechanics of complex gears in the language of the thermodynamics of fuel supply.
>
> (Watzlawick et al., 1974, p. 9)

The order implied in the example is hierarchical. Each gear is a system in itself. Within that system a certain order prevails, where output depends on the elements within the system. The gear in question itself, however, is an element in a system of gears. This system of gears is, conceptually, a superordinate system.

NON-HIERARCHICAL RELATIONS

In the abovementioned example, Watzlawick et al. are concerned with establishing the differences between members and classes in hierarchical situations. However, not all relations between systems must be of this kind. Different relations may be envisaged, some of which may at first seem illogical. They begin to make sense when the *focus of the observer* of the system is made clear. The examples which follow illustrate this:

1 *Relations between systems of a similar logical type*
   (a) Systems may be independent and form part of the environment of each other, e.g., two liver cells, or two family units living in suburbia.
   (b) Systems may share some common elements, e.g., two different discussion groups may have some common members and some unique members.
   (c) Two systems may share common elements that are related differently in each of the systems, e.g., two different committees may share a common

membership, but have separate functions. Bion's (1961) examples of the co-existence of 'work' and 'basic assumption' groups, operating within the same set of people, may fit this category of systemic relations.

Each of the abovementioned types of relations involves two or more systems that are not related to one another in an hierarchical manner.

2 *Relations between systems of a different logical type*
   (a) A system may be a sub-system of another system, e.g., the marketing division of a large organization. Hierarchically, the organization is super-ordinate to its marketing division, yet the representatives of these two systems may have to communicate, discuss, and reach decisions of import to both systems, i.e., they must have an organized form of relationship. This is the case even in the situation where one man 'wears two hats', as may be the case in a small organization when the general manager also manages marketing.
   (b) Two systems may seem to share common elements yet have different functions, as in the relationship type 1(b). Further, the systems may also stand in a superordinate/subordinate relation to each other. An example would occur in the unusual, but not impossible case of common member-ship of a county court and a higher court of appeals.

3 *Reciprocal relations between systems*
   This is the most difficult set of relations to describe, and seems to pose the logical paradox that Watzlawick et al. warn of. These relations between systems are such that one system apparently is an element in another system, that in turn is an element of the first system. That is, the systems involved seem each to be an element of the other. For example, my family may act as an (introjected) element in my character, and yet I am an element in my family system.

This relationship of reciprocity can be fully examined only when we consider the nature of the words and concepts used to examine social life. Words that seem to stand for identical units are deceptive. Take for example the word '*me*'. This may refer to *me* as an individual system, or to *me* as an element in a social system. What may seem to be a total system and also an element of another system, may be confused by the terms used. Watzlawick et al. (1968) refer to the paradoxes created by this confusion of terms as 'paradoxical definitions' or 'semantical antinomies'.

> Perhaps the most famous of all semantical antinomies is that of the man who says of himself, 'I am lying'. On following this statement to its logical conclusion, we find that it is true only if it is not true; in other words, the man is lying only if he is telling the truth and, vice versa, truthful when he is lying. In this case the theory of logical types cannot be used to eliminate the antinomy, for words or combinations of words do not have a logical type hierarchy.
>
> (Watzlawick et al., 1968, p. 193)

They claim that such semantic antinomies, unable to be analysed within the language that expresses them, may be understood when one has available a second language specifically utilized for the analysis of the first. Another language may then analyse this second language, each language standing in an hierarchical relation to the one that it considers.

> This suggestion was developed, mainly by Carnap and by Tarski, into what is now known as the theory of levels of language. . . . It postulates that at the lowest level of language statements are made about objects. This is the realm of the *object language*. The moment, however, we want to say something *about* this language, we have to use a metalanguage, and a metalanguage if we want to speak about this metalanguage, and so forth in theoretically infinite regress.
>
> (Watzlawick et al., 1968, p. 193)

This theory (of levels of language) enables the hierarchical ordering of linguistic systems, at least theoretically and when the position of the observer (of the linguistic system) is clear. Bateson's distinction between communication and meta-communication is relevant here. Whereas communication involves the transmission of a message, meta-communication involves the *relationship* between communicators (Bateson, 1968). Also relevant is Wilden's concept of the 'frame' of a communication and the logical relations of analogue and digital organization (Wilden, 1980; 1987).

This brings us to a more general consideration of the relationships described above. It can be seen that understanding the relationship involved requires a clarification of the manner in which the elements of a system are defined. Take example 1(c) above. Here one must consider the committee member as having separate roles within the different committees. In this sense the *person* is the common element, yet this commonality is apparent rather than real if we consider the *role* as the appropriate element. Taken in this sense, no two systems can have common elements because the elements are defined *from their place in the system*. The role of son, for example, is somewhat different in every family. It is only the signifier 'son', located within the symbolic linguistic system, that renders all these sons identical. This signifier is part of a system 'meta' to the particular family systems that contain the living sons.

The relationships between systems, described previously, help us to clarify matters when common parlance is employed. This is important for understanding the everyday use of descriptions and their pragmatic consequences, as Watzlawick et al. (1968) point out. It must always be remembered, however, that systemic elements cannot strictly be defined from outside the system itself, and a scientific description of systems and their behaviours must take great care in clarifying semantic paradoxes.

What has been referred to as a reciprocal relationship between systems seems, then, a semantic problem. The *person* who is created by social process, i.e., a socialized human person who operates as an individual, is different from the person who is a member of a group, i.e., who has a *role*. Yet, in pragmatic terms this is still problematic. The subject, who experiences him or herself both as *person* and as *role*, is at pains to unite this confusion. It seems that human subjectivity is necessarily split, at least between, on the one hand, the aspect of being a systemic totality shaped largely by social process, and, on the other hand, a role within that social process. The living of this paradox cannot be denied simply by referring to it as a semantic paradox. Perhaps, as Lacan (1977) attempts to demonstrate, semantic paradox is itself a basic constituent of the human psyche. Nonetheless, in describing the relationship between the individual and the group, it is incumbent upon the observer to maintain the distinction between person and role, and to observe the effect of the paradox entailed in a subjectivity that attempts to unite these aspects.

Another way of viewing the aforementioned paradox is by way of stressing the relationships within systems. Bachelard does this when he states: 'in reality there are no simple phenomena, the phenomenon is a tissue of relations' (Bachelard, 1934, cited in Lecourt, 1969, p. 39). The relations he refers to are those that hold between scientific concepts. Words, he says, tend to give the impression that these concepts refer to entities, whereas he holds that concepts are better understood from their function within a system of concepts. Taking this view, it is the *relations* between members that may be seen to define the group, not the members themselves in any independent fashion, nor even their conscious face to face *relationships*. It may be that only when the individual attempts self-definition without reference to a specific group (or, as is more likely, with reference to more than one particular group) is confusion of identity experienced. Understood in this way, some 'inner' conflicts may be the expression of internalized 'intergroup' conflicts.

The discussion so far has attempted to establish a systems framework for a further discussion on the nature of group psychology. Indeed, an explication of what shall now be termed the 'paradox of reciprocal systemic relations' underlies and informs much of the observational material to be discussed in this work. This framework provides a conceptual space for group members to be regarded both as individuals and as members. A related duality is explored by Turquet (1975), who refers to 'membership individuals' and 'individual members' of groups. Furthermore, the framework allows us to consider both the 'individual' and the 'member' positions as co-existing in persons in an intricate manner. The person may experience him or herself as a number of members, each as elements of separate systems. In order to experience 'wholeness' as an individual, these somehow require integration.

Chapter 3

Group psychology

This chapter aims to outline those theories within psychoanalysis that have aided the establishment of 'group psychology' as an area of study separate from the areas of individual and social psychology. This separateness seems to be required because the system 'group' occupies a conceptual space distinct from that of individuals or their immediate interactions. It is also separate from the space occupied by the sociological concept of 'aggregate' (i.e., a combination of non-interactive parts) such as 'blacks', 'whites', 'labourers' or 'smokers', etc. The group is a 'gestalt' with properties other than those of its constituent parts. Moreover it is a developing and changing system.

Before detailing the relevant theories, some conceptual problems are worth raising as a context to the field and to aid in the focus on the group as a system.

Human systems containing many individuals pose a conceptual problem for researchers and those who wish to study group phenomena. For example, the tendency to conceptualize super-individual complexity as the addition of discrete entities, and the associated tendency to reductionism, has often been a problem for social psychology (Billig, 1976; Turner et al., 1987). This discipline cannot simply be defined as the study of individuals in a social context, for that is what psychology itself examines. Yet the defining of a social psychology of interactions, with a logic of social determination, still has its difficulties when the psychology of groups remains indistinct; and an understanding of the structures and dynamics of groups, in terms other than the addition or even the interaction of individuals, requires a linguistic and conceptual territory of its own. What then are the systems available to study that might aid in the study of groups?

TYPES OF SYSTEMS AVAILABLE FOR STUDY

At least three distinct levels of systems are relevant and conceptually available: the individual, the interpersonal and the social or *transindividual* levels (Billig, 1976; Wisdom, 1970). Each provides a different type of explanation for human behaviours.

Although spoken of as 'levels', it should be remembered that the hierarchical status of these groupings (of systems), that is, their ability to conceptually subsume each other in a systematic and ordered manner, depends on the focus of the observer and the manner in which they are constituted as entities (Maturana and Varela, 1980). There is no inherent hierarchy; so the nature of human subjectivity involves the experience of being in systems located at *all* of these levels. Any explanation of large-scale social processes, for example, involves all three levels of explanation.

The individual level

Explanations in terms of individual processes include the effects of genetic, physiological and psychological differences. They may include the effect of a particular individual combination of traits or internalized propensities. These explanations do, however, tend to 'derive the ultimate causes of social events from constitutional processes common to all human beings' which tendency 'makes certain assumptions about a pre-social "human nature" which is basic to all individuals' (Billig, 1976, p. 8).

Billig includes, at this level, reference to some aspects of the work of Freud, the work of Roheim, Money-Kyrle, Glover and Menninger, whom he regards as dogmatic in their reductionism of social behaviour to the individual; and to the work of Lorenz and Storr, who are basically concerned with the immutability of the aggressive instinct and its consequent role in the shaping of human social behaviour. His critique of these authors is not aimed at the validity of an examination of individual processes per se, nor on the whole at the empirical substantiations provided. It is the applicability of this level of analysis to social phenomena that is questioned.

The interpersonal level

Here explanations are couched in terms of interactions between individuals. The interactions are examined as they present themselves, with little reference to a general underlying symbolic system that constrains the interactions.

> At such a level, the causes of social phenomena are sought in the face-to-face interaction between persons. The individual per se is no longer the unit of explanation, but instead the focus is on the relation between individuals.
>
> (Billig, 1976, p. 8)

Traditionally, the discipline of experimental social psychology tends to examine the interpersonal level and its effects on the individual. For example, Allport (1985) writes that social psychology is 'an attempt to understand and explain how the thoughts, feelings and behaviours of individuals are influenced by the actual, imagined or implied presence of others'. This definition has influenced many social psychologists, and many modern texts take it as a starting point (e.g., Lindzey and Aronson, 1985). It implies that the proper focus for social psychology is the psychological consequences of interpersonal interactions.

Billig regards most psychoanalytic explanations of social phenomena as consisting of this and the individual processes level. His examination of Freud's group psychology, for example, acknowledges its attempts to deal with a social analysis at all levels, but is resolved into a critique that places Freud's theory squarely at the level of the interpersonal, i.e., the analysis of social phenomena as it proceeds from the oedipal complex, seen as an interpersonal phenomenon; that is, a playing out of the interpersonal dynamics of the family upon a wider social arena.

Billig's critique will be challenged in the present work by reference to Lacan's reading of Freud. Lacan attempts to show that subjective experience is registered not only at the level of interpersonal interactions (the Imaginary register), but also at the level of social value (the Symbolic register). Value is largely seen in linguistic processes and Lacan regards the basic processes of the unconscious, i.e., condensation and displacement, as structured in a similar manner. This position will be elaborated later in this chapter. However, Billig's critique may be applicable to the work of the American neo-Freudians and to the social learning theorists in those cases where social analysis tends to proceed by the analysis of interactions alone.

The social or transpersonal (transindividual) level

The third level of analysis is the *social level* at which, Billig says, 'large scale processes are not reduced to smaller units, but are analysed in their own terms' (Billig, 1976, p. 8). Here 'cultural or societal variables are brought into prominence.' Analysis at this level requires that observations of behaviour be set in their specific social contexts. These include group ideologies and identities, together with societal variables such as economic and political conditions. Billig's point is made clear in his critique of Rainwater (1966) who describes the social misfortunes of a black man in the USA. Through time, this man became unemployed, was deserted by his wife, and radically changed his political views. Rainwater's statement that 'again and again in his [the black man's] comments one can see the displacement into a public, race relations dialogue of the sense of rage, frustration and victimization he had experienced in his illfated marriage' (Rainwater, 1966, p. 382) is taken by Billig as an ill-conceived reduction of a social to an interpersonal conflict.

Rainwater in fact argues for a larger 'systems' view than Billig admits. Nonetheless Billig's point remains valid. Any imputation that political beliefs are simply a reflection of interpersonal relations, in work or marriage, is absurd. An explanation of frustration leading to aggression in purely individual terms is also unsatisfactory, even if evidence of an 'aggressive nature' were available. The behaviour makes more overall social sense if we see it as related to the broader aspects of ingroup identity and intergroup relations. (In fact Rainwater suggests this: 'White cupidity creates structural conditions highly inimicable to basic social adaptation . . . to which negroes adapt by social and personal responses . . . which results in suffering directly inflicted by negroes on themselves and on others' [Rainwater, 1966, p. 365].)

Although it seems that modern social psychologists are increasingly using explanations at one or all of these levels (Doise, 1978), the focus on the group as such is rarely central. Turner et al. (1987) review the work of social psychologists in the 1940s and 1950s and conclude that their emphasis on individualism, despite being an attempt to understand group formation with reference to interdependence (following the classic work of Asch, Lewin and Sherif), was due to an inability to sustain a social level of inquiry. As soon as group constituents were examined the individuals became as if isolated persons. 'The idea that the relations between group members might be mediated *psychologically* by their membership in a joint unit seems to have been lost or more accurately simply not found necessary' (Turner et al., 1987, p. 24). Turner's own work attempts to reverse this trend and return to the idea of the social group as an antecedent rather than a consequent of interdependence. His self-categorization theory presents an analysis of the relation between individuals and groups that is not located simply at the interpersonal level. In this theory self-categories (a form of self-concept) are understood to be derived from self/other comparisons and similarities at different levels (individual, interpersonal, group, national, etc.) and individuals utilize those categories most salient to them at a particular moment. Hence a self-categorization as a group member may be more salient than an individual self-categorization when involvement in the group is high and when the member is highly identified with other group members. Nonetheless, the individual (person) and group (role) categorizations are still regarded as separate alternative modes or reference categories in this theory.

However, to review comprehensively the work of modern social psychology is not the task of this book. The field of group psychology has grown through reference to many different paradigms of research including social psychology and psychoanalysis (as might be seen in Billig's references to both of these). The psychoanalytic paradigm will be explored more fully here. In particular, a theoretical schema of transindividual processes arising within the field of Lacan's 'Symbolic' register and located in individuals will be advocated.

DISCIPLINES AND PARADIGMS

Consider the experiments of Stanley Milgram (1974). These experiments were conducted in order to study obedience to authority. Milgram arranged a situation where subjects, designated as teachers, were convincingly led to believe, in the name of research, that it was necessary for them to administer mild to severe electric shocks to fellow subjects, designated as pupils. The administration of shocks was to be completed even in the face of strong protests from the pupil. The convincing 'authority' was dressed in a white laboratory coat, and was continually present throughout the experiment to instruct the subject. In fact the shocks were never administered, although in some variations of the experiment, cries of pain and pleas to stop could be heard through an intercom system. Many variations of this basic situation were employed by Milgram. His results indicated that substantial proportions of normal subjects were prepared to 'shock' their fellow subjects when given instructions by someone whom they believed to be a responsible authority.

These experiments enable a variety of observations, including observations relevant to different disciplines. For example, the phenomena of 'authority' and 'responsibility', which seem to arise from certain role distinctions, are best regarded as *group* phenomena. The authority held by certain roles is due to the interrelatedness of roles in the relevant system, in this case the relations between scientist, teacher and student. Moreover, the observations that individual differences occurred in, for example, the level of shock that a subject was willing to administer, despite changes in some experimental conditions, traditionally belong to the province of *psychology*. Finally, the observation that certain particular institutionalized roles, e.g., 'scientist' or 'doctor', have an effect on the behaviour considered, is perhaps best explained in terms of *sociological* theory.

Consequently we can see that a particular method, in this case a set of experiments involving people in a social setting, will not necessarily give rise to observations and explanations set within a single discipline. The social psychology experiment (as exemplified in the work of Milgram) is better regarded as a paradigm of research (i.e., able to be substituted within many ongoing disciplines) rather than the means by which a discipline is delineated. It is, however, a paradigm that may allow for observations described and explained by concepts developed in a variety of areas, including that of group psychology. (For another example of such a paradigm see Turner's discussion of the 'minimal group paradigm', Turner et al., 1987, pp. 26–8.)

Although particular 'scientific paradigms' (Kuhn, 1962) often develop within a discipline, it is also the case that such 'paradigmatic' explanations across disciplines may have more in common than different paradigms within a discipline. For example, structuralist approaches in sociology, anthropology, education and psychology share concerns that are very different in many regards from, say, the concerns of behaviourism in these same disciplines.

In contrast to an emphasis placed on methods, Allport's definition of social psychology, i.e., 'an attempt to understand and explain how the thoughts, feelings and behaviours of individuals are influenced by the actual, imagined or implied presence of others' (Allport, 1985), centres on the dominant substantive interest and the modes of explanation employed by many experimental social psychologists. It may be that scientific disciplines are better defined in terms of their object of study than in terms of their methods (Bachelard, 1934). This enables the establishment of a variety of theoretical and explanatory models. Allport's central concern is for psychological (individual) theory, because it is the basic psychological processes within the individual that he wishes to explain. Nonetheless the 'influence' he mentions is from sources other than the individual, and these require some explanation.

In Allport's terms, social psychology is really a discipline with permeable conceptual boundaries. Disciplinary permeability operates according to the substantive areas that the researcher will allow. Allport indicates that his interest lies in the effects on the individual. He believes that the study of the 'individual in culture' is preferable to formulations in terms of the group mind (Allport, 1985, p. 29). However, to those concerned with groups, the effects of and on the group primarily need to be distinguished and considered, and the group as a system cannot be dismissed as a vague analogical idea. Several paradigms, originating perhaps in the methodological and conceptual spawning grounds of a variety of disciplines, may be applicable.

Establishing a particular method of research, or a particular paradigmatic approach to explanation, may not then lead us to a particularly clear definition of group psychology. One needs, perhaps, to look for a substantive area of difference, that is, an area that defines the group as an entity in itself with its own distinctive properties. Such a substantive area might be termed the 'syntagmatic' dimension of science. This tends to emphasize the connections between the defined elements of a particular scientific system, much as the syntagmatic dimension of language refers to contiguous relations between signifiers (Jakobson and Halle, 1956).

Discussion will now turn to this task of defining group psychology. It would seem that the task includes finding a conceptual framework that emphasizes effects on groups as well as on individuals, and that concentrates on trans-individual phenomena (Wisdom, 1970) that arise from within a social matrix. The following attempts to do this within the framework of psychoanalysis, which has a substantive basis in the study of psychic experience, both conscious and unconscious.

GROUP PSYCHOLOGY

A linguistic and conceptual territory for group psychology is emerging through the efforts of those who come after Freud's work on *Group Psychology* (1921). Important in this tradition are Bion (1961), Foulkes (1964) and Slater (1966). Their efforts are set within the psychoanalytic paradigm with its complex methods of clinical observation. Whereas Doise, Billig and Allport struggle to delineate the boundaries between individual and group (or interpersonal and intrapersonal), the works of the psychoanalytic group theorists call for a radical upturning of the individually autonomous psychological subject. To these theorists, the subject is not a simple unit (or system) that interrelates with other units, but a multifaceted social element. Moreover, the psychoanlytic perspective allows a review of the problematic of individualism vs. the group. In the discussion to follow this issue is not addressed by postulating separate modes of functioning that are alternatively operated under different social conditions (as in Turner's view, Turner et al., 1987). More complexly, the individual is to be regarded as the locus of semi-independent integrations in the social field. This in turn requires the view of human subjectivity as an experience of uneasy compromise – a view central to psychoanalysis.

This modern subject may be understood, for example, as existing within several spheres of influence which are themselves organizers of a variety of group forces. Religion is one such organizer (Slater, 1966; Rieff, 1982), as are politics (Rieff, 1966). Another example is the sphere of the 'social' as defined by Donzelot (1979). His analysis of the 'social' sector is a good example of analysis at the *social level* mentioned earlier. In his terms, the 'social' has a psycho-historical aspect and has arisen as a 'particular sector in which quite diverse problems and special cases can be grouped together; a sector comprising specific institutions and an entire body of qualified personnel', and which 'cuts across and reshapes previously existing or independent divisions, providing a new field for the forces already present' (Deleuze, in the Foreword to Donzelot, 1979). Hence, to Donzelot, the 'social' is regarded as a converging point for many forces and, as such, it is reflected in those subjectivities that emerge within the influence of this sector (cf. the economic, religious, judicial, etc. sectors). Donzelot argues that the family, in particular, is now located in the 'social' which, consequently, takes a major part in the shaping of private subjectivities.

Following Foucault (1966), Donzelot argues that psychoanalysis is yet another one of these sectors. These authors claim that psychoanalysis, as a theory of human behaviour and as a technique of psychotherapy, has prominently structured modern thought about human nature, and has affected many modern human institutions. However, the present work regards psychoanalytic theory as containing an understanding of the emergence of subjectivities within a variety of sectors that collectively organize human strivings: political (Rieff, 1966), religious (Slater, 1966), economic (Fromm, 1970), private (Lasch, 1979) and the 'social' (Donzelot, 1979). Each writer contributes to an overall view which tends to substantiate the emergence of a number of subjectivities, each present, at the same time, in the individual who is variously *subjected to* the different sectors of group and organizational life.

In taking this multiple view of subjectivity, psychoanalysis breaks into the long-cherished psycho-physical parallelism prevalent in modern psychology which assumes that a unitary skin-bound body is a container for a parallel individual unitary psyche. Certainly psychology regards this psyche as complex and multifaceted, and each facet itself is seen as complex and even fragmented or contradictory. Yet a belief in unity seems paramount, and personality theory has always had a plethora of concepts that describe an internal structure that integrates all of these aspects and processes: e.g., of selves (Rogers, 1967), cardinal traits (Allport, 1961), source traits (Cattell, 1965; Cattell and Kline, 1977) and actualizing tendencies (Maslow, 1977). Integration may be a pre-requisite of psychological health for the individual, but to postulate a primary overarching unity in the individual as a basis for observable transindividual processes is unnecessary, and could be misguided.

What occurs when we reject a simple psycho-physical parallelism, as do Freud and Lacan (Muller and Richardson, 1982), and contemplate the possibility of the co-existence of several kinds of (un)consciousnesses within the one person? Can a psyche essentially divided and split in the individual be understood as unitary in terms of its many currents and circuits in the social field? The implications are for a view which recognizes the presence of *several semi-independent psychic systems within the individual each having strong systemic links at a group level.* That is to say, an element of a group system may operate in the individual such that it is systemically linked to similar or complementary elements in other individuals and yet is relatively inde- pendent of other intraindividual elements (which themselves are elements in other social systems). Put another way, elements of 'mind' or 'self' may be viewed as specific (individual) locations for aspects of a general social process (Harré, 1984). Such a view does not deny the importance of other unifying systems within the individual, e.g., the integrating internal structures of personality, without which the present view would simply be an illustration of multiple personality; it simply stresses and brings to the fore transindividual systems. As Slater (1966, p. 251) says, 'Unless we are to remain utterly fixated on physical bodies, it is apparent that a group is not a collection of individuals at all but only of pieces of them.' He suggests that the unit of group analysis must embody 'that segment of an individual's instinctual life which he commits to a group'.

So, to Slater, groups can be understood neither by reference to individuals seen collectively nor in terms of disembodied roles that have no link to 'the needs, the motives, the feelings which, however group-specific they may be, nonetheless derive from a breathing organism' (Slater, 1966, p. 251). Somehow, we require a manner of conceptualizing the group that allows an understanding of the vitality inherent in transindividual or interdependent systems. That is, we need to know how the 'pieces', referred to by Slater, are connected in the group other than through the individual's unifying processes.

The following presents a brief overview of the ideas of some relevant theorists. These are: Freud, Klein, Bion, Slater, Foulkes and Lacan. The focus is on this need to find an adequate manner of conceptualizing transindividual group phenomena, not by a study of individuals alone, nor through their interactions without reference to overall social constraints, values, etc., nor through aggregate statistics. The group is not an aggregate but a living system which draws on and, simultaneously, creates the richness found in the individual psyche.

FREUD

Freud (1921) arrives at a definition of a primary group after considering the question of changes in mental functioning brought about by membership in groups that have a leader. He says (p. 80), 'A primary group of this kind is a number of individuals who have substituted one and the same object for their ego ideal and have consequently identified themselves with one another in their ego.' So, a mechanism exists whereby individuals share in a common structure that has its origins outside of each member (i.e., the leader), and members are also identified within a common structuring of mutually influencing egos.

Freud describes the processes by which these transindividual vinctures occur in the light of identificatory processes in general. Three sources of identification are proposed:

First, identification is the original form of an emotional tie with an object; secondly, in a regressive way it becomes a substitute for a libidinal object tie, as it were by means of the introjection of the object into the ego; and thirdly, it may arise with every new perception of a common quality shared with some other person who is not an object of the sexual instinct.

(Freud, 1921, p. 65)

Although the first two types of identification described may be important for the relations between group members under some circumstances, it is the third form that Freud invokes as a major explanation for the ties between group members, the important shared quality being their relationship with the leader. This relation to the leader is considered to be identical with the relation that exists between hypnotist and subject, and similar to the relation of being in love. In all these relations the object (leader, hypnotist, beloved) comes to take the place of the ego-ideal of the subject(s). This occurs through the process of introjection, which, simply stated, is the process of incorporating an external structure into the psyche. This internal structure is consequently isomorphic with the external structure, or with the individual's perception of that outer structure.

Freud's work on groups will be considered further later when the concept of identity is examined (Chapter 5). It is important to note here, nonetheless, that he also introduces into his analysis the myth of the primal horde. This is a quasi-historical *social level* account, and is important for an understanding of the cultural and symbolic relevance of what might otherwise have remained a libidinal explanation at the interpersonal level. The role of the symbolic leader in the genesis of group and individual psychology will also be taken up more fully later in this work.

Freud's followers have elaborated and extended different aspects of his work on groups. For example, Redl (1942) has developed the idea of 'central person', which redefines the role of the leader in a broader context of centrality. To Redl, central persons, through identification, become the focus of group processes. These latter include ego-control processes, such as those operating when a central person becomes a 'good example' for other members, and libidinal release processes, such as those operating when a central person becomes the 'ringleader', or the one who is first able to express the forbidden desires of other members. By this analysis, central persons need not be 'leaders' in the traditional sense. That is, they need not be consciously authorized leaders.

Slater and Rieff have developed the ideas contained in the primal myth, particularly focussing on concepts of sacred authority in the culture at large. Slater's approach is through the study of these processes as expressed in small groups (Slater, 1966). His work will be discussed in more detail later in this chapter. Rieff's approach is through an examination of the effect of the role of psychoanalysis on modern culture (Rieff, 1959; 1966). His work will be discussed in Chapter 5.

KLEIN

Klein and her followers have placed particular emphasis upon the processes of identification through projection and introjection (Segal, 1979). Although Klein does not directly discuss group phenomena, her concepts are elaborated by some who do (e.g., Bion, 1961; Miller and Rice, 1967; Main, 1975). Furthermore, her ideas provide another way of viewing transindividual processes.

Melanie Klein developed some of Freud's ideas, particularly those related to the concept of introjection and its role in superego formations. In contrast to Freud, she worked directly with children and came to a somewhat different view of the processes involved in the establishment of the superego (including the ego-ideal), and also believed that these processes occurred in the first year of the infant's life (Klein, 1946). They occur in two major phases described as 'positions'.

The paranoid schizoid position

In Klein's view, the infant's early experience is structured by the primitive ego defence of 'splitting'. This splitting acts to separate experience into 'good' and 'bad' aspects and is originally instituted in order to defend a fragile ego against its own aggressive impulses. These impulses are felt to be too strong and destructive to be contained within the ego. Their fate is to be projected outward and into external objects. These objects are then experienced as persecutory. The mechanism of splitting, and the resultant paranoid anxiety, is seen as basic to the paranoid schizoid position. Klein regards this structuring of the psyche as a natural part of early development. She considers it pathological only if it dominates in later childhood or adult experience.

Klein understands the processes described as occurring at an unconscious phantasy level, and the objects described, whether internal or external, as phantasy objects. As such, they form structures within the psyche that act to structure the infant's relations with his or her reality. This reality contains within it real satisfactions and deprivations that become associated with the phantasy object world. Consequently the breast, that both satisfies and, in its absence, deprives the infant, becomes a phantasy object of great importance. Because of the splitting process that affects both the ego and the external objects, the breast comes to be experienced as two objects: one 'good' and one 'bad'. Klein believes both 'good' and 'bad' external objects are introjected. As introjects they serve to strengthen the existent structures created by the original splitting process.

The depressive position

Klein sees the depressive position as the result of a gradual maturation that allows the infant to reintegrate both the split off parts of the ego and external objects. At the physical level, the child's perceptual and cognitive skills have developed. These now enable the child to recognize his or her caretaker as a whole person. At the instinctual level, the aggression, felt earlier as uncontainable, is now experienced as less dangerous. This is partly due to the strengthening of the libidinal urges and their expression in direct object love (towards the whole mother or mother substitute). Both these changes bring about changes in psychic organization. In relating to a mother perceived as a whole person, the child comes to see that the 'good' and 'bad' are aspects of a totality to whom he or she is libidinally tied. This results in a weakening of the split in the ego. The internal 'good' and 'bad' objects are no longer isolated. The child is more able to experience aggressive urges and to feel guilt about them. This guilt in turn leads to a wish to repair the phantasized damage done by the aggression. The depressive position is, then, characterized by 'love, guilt and reparation' (Klein, 1937).

Klein's concepts were formulated to explain her observations of young children during play therapy sessions (Klein, 1955) and her observations of older children and adults during psychoanalysis. They refer to processes within the person that structure the inner phantasy world. Importantly, however, this structuring is seen to influence relations in reality. Her elaboration of the concept of *projective identification* illustrates this importance.

The concept comes originally from the work of Ferenczi (1916) although this is rarely recognized by post Kleinian theorists (De Board, 1978). In

Kleinian theory it refers to a process where phantasied, split off parts of the self are projected into others, so that those others are seen to possess these parts, and so that the individual becomes identified with the other (Segal, 1979).

Although Klein saw projective identification as a mechanism with many effects (e.g., ridding oneself of unwanted parts, control of the recipient, protecting 'good' parts by safely projecting them into an idealized other), Kleinian analysts have developed the concept even further (Sandler, 1989). Ogden (1979) refers to it as a dual process. In its first (projective) aspect, a person rejects a portion of his or her own experience (e.g., a feeling, thought or attitude), and acts to induce it in another. The second (identificatory) aspect of the total process involves the reincorporation of the rejected portion of experience. This is done through an identification of the ego, with the recipient of the projection. The identification is partial, and centres on the original projection and the manner in which the other is able to deal with the thoughts and feelings induced throughout the course of the interactions (between projector and recipient), and their consequences. Bion (1965) believes that the projective identifications of analysands leave them feeling closer to (i.e., more identified with) the analyst, but also leave them with a feeling of impoverishment. Malin and Grotstein propose that projective identification 'seems to be the way in which human beings are able to test their own inner psychic life by projecting psychic contents out into the environment and perceiving the environment's reaction to these projected parts of oneself' (1966, p. 31). They suggest a receptive attitude to these projections on the part of the analyst.

The concept of projective identification emphasizes the effects of phantasy on real social relations between individuals. Moreover, it emphasizes a view of interactions between individuals occurring at an unconscious level. Many of these interactions are seen to be occurring not only without the awareness of the participants, but in an unconsciously collusive manner (Ogden, 1979; Grotstein, 1981; Bain, 1981; Horwitz, 1983; Gilmore and Krantz, 1985; Morrison, 1986). Klein's formulations seem to contain an implicit transindividual quality at the point where the intrapersonal and the interpersonal are regarded as mutually interdependent, and, more importantly, where the functional relations between, say, mother and child, are constrained by these processes. This quality, not explicit, nor fully at the social level in Klein, is developed in the work of Bion.

BION

Bion believed that when a group of people act as a psychological group, that is, when they are interacting together to work on a common task, not one, but two groups are operating. In simple terms these groups are recognized as either the work group or as a form of basic assumption group. The work group (often referred to as the sophisticated work group) comprises those group structures and dynamics that operate to work on the chosen conscious task of the group. The basic assumption group may take one of three forms: dependency, fight/flight and pairing. This group operates at a largely unconscious level, and comprises those group structures and dynamics that operate when the group has met as if for purposes other than the consciously stated task. This underlying assumption guides an unconscious collusive process based on projective and introjective identifications (Main, 1975). The basic assumption dependency group (Ba.D.), for example, acts as if the members have met in order to be led by a powerful and dependable leader. The fight/flight group (Ba.F.) acts as if the members have met in order to fight an enemy or to flee from danger. To witness a sexual pairing which will result in a new 'messiah' is the major underlying assumption of the pairing group (Ba.P.).

Bion believes that acting in line with an unconsciously held collusive belief often leads the group members to abandon their agreed task whilst rationalizing this step in the light of the assumption. For example, a classroom group may cease actively working on a problem (its primary task) in order to demonstrate (unconsciously) the superior (or inferior) abilities of the teacher. Students may be tempted, for example, not to think problems out for themselves. Their belief that the teacher is the only one with knowledge prevents them from testing their own abilities, and consequently from experiencing possible failure. On the other hand, they also risk being more creative or knowledgeable than the teacher and hence risk his or her possible wrath. To challenge the teacher's knowledge directly may then express a variety of uncomfortable feelings, including anxiety, guilt and fear of reprisals. These feelings are avoided by the unconscious group solution (defence) of dependency and belief in the teacher's omniscience.

The basic assumption group does, however, provide much of the group's energy, possibly due to its power of representing certain instinctual strivings that operate within an interpersonal context, or because it represents shared fantasies that have roots in more widespread societal myths (Shambaugh, 1986).

Because of this, Bion believes that the sophisticated work group situates its work upon one or two basic assumptions and that the energy for the work is derived from the underlying group. As with Freud's analysis of the church and the army, Bion sees the work of such groupings as due to a basic assumption that links the members to their leaders, to their leading ideas, and to each other. He terms this dynamic the group valency, and also proposes that individual members and leaders have valencies for particular basic assumptions (Rioch, 1970).

In Bion's descriptions, there are some important differences that should be noted between the basic assumption groups and the work group. One of these is that in the work group members are more differentiated, and able to operate in a more autonomous fashion, than in a Ba. group. A Ba. group operates so that differences between members are minimized. It is as if members are all units in one collusive system, unable to access other aspects of themselves. Ba.D. members act as if they are unable to use knowledge that they obviously have in other contexts; it is as if only the leader has any abilities. In basic assumption pairing (Ba.P.), the members act as if they have gathered to witness the pairing of two individuals for the purpose of producing a new messiah or messianic idea. The abilities of those other than the selected pair, or abilities seemingly irrelevant to the pairing process, are ignored. Faith in the dependable or messianic leader is continued at a mythical or fantasy level; real individuals are seldom able to fit the role for any lengthy period of time.

The observations made by Bion, and others who have used his methods, lend support to the idea of *semi-independent systems within the individual that have strong systemic links at the group level*. The members of the Ba. group may usefully be thought of as elements in a system operating at the unconscious collusive level. The behavioural results of the group operating at this level, together with the nature of the psychological processes operating within the individual, suggest that there is greater commonality between the Ba. role of the individual and this same role in other individuals, than between the Ba. role of the individual and those other aspects of the individual that operate in different contexts, even within the same group of people. Slater's 'pieces' have a greater commonality across – than within – subjects, for this particular aspect of psychic functioning, in this particular setting. During the operation of the Ba. group, the individual is unable to access or act on aspects clearly accessible at other times.

During basic assumption group functioning, individuals seem to find themselves saying things that they normally would disagree with or would modify, and behaving in a manner that they later experience as alien to themselves. This occurs in extreme forms during mass crowd situations where a true psychological work group is not formed, yet basic assumptions are acted on. In these situations the distinctive boundaries between individuals, even if present for some functions, are not recognizable within the emotion or assumption prominently displayed in the crowd.

Neither work nor basic assumption groups occur simply and purely by themselves. They are abstractions which explain a tendency towards particular forms of group life. In terms of the present work, the idea of basic assumption groups clearly indicates transindividual phenomena, i.e., those systems that occur across individuals. During the operation of the work group these transindividual systems are less apparent because individual systems, and the individual aspects of the group system (i.e., differentiated roles), are more apparent.

Before leaving Bion's work a critique that locates it solely at Billig's interpersonal level should be mentioned. It is apparent that Bion does refer to interpersonal dynamics in terms of face to face interactions and in terms of interpersonal unconscious Kleinian constructs such as projective identification.

Lacan (1977) for one regards such formulations as lacking a Symbolic explanation and thus pertaining only to the Imaginary field, itself an effect rather than a cause. But the theory of basic assumptions in groups goes beyond this. The basic assumption is a cultural concept; a conjunction of value, in the Saussurian symbolic sense, with emotion. It is not simply an assumption held between particular persons, although any particular group may express and live the assumption in a unique manner; it is a group position held in relation to the question of authority. This will be explored more fully in Chapter 5.

SLATER

Slater (1966) brings together ideas from the work of Freud, Bion and Neumann (1954) to support an approach to the evolution of groups in an historical–cultural framework. His clinical observations involve a close examination of small group discussions. The groups met for the purpose of allowing members to learn about group processes as they occurred. Slater's first concern was to learn about the dynamics of small groups. He found, however, after many years of working with these types of groups, that the processes so examined had parallels to many large scale social phenomena. Moreover, he discovered that group members frequently referred to the processes and emotions experienced in terms that alluded to mythical, literary and religious experiences in the larger social arena. These and other impressions led him to look at the small group as a microcosm of larger social processes, particularly those expressed in social myths, fantasies and religions.

The descriptions of group development that he presents are strongly influenced by Freud's analysis of group life. In particular, he carefully traces the relations that develop between group members and the designated group leader, relying heavily on the themes of deification, death, revolt and fraternity. The primal horde myth, as outlined by Freud, centres on these themes, and it is this myth that Slater elaborates, extends and operationalizes in terms of the small group.

For example, Slater examines the process of what he terms the 'group revolt' against the original group leader. In the groups under consideration, this usually culminated in the form of asking the leader to leave the room so that the group might operate independently. Seemingly a simple request, the decision-making processes leading to its occurrence were painstaking, and involved heated discussions and disputes between a variety of sub-groups or factions. In terms of the emotions experienced, this request, which eventually became a group demand, frequently represented an act of rebellion against formal authority. In the extreme it represented the idea of murder, insofar as the leader was to be deposed and replaced by a new regime. Not surprisingly, everyday terms used in such situations include: 'giving him the chop' and 'axing her'. Additionally, the group member chosen to attempt the deposition may be named the 'hit man'. For Slater, all these terms reflect the underlying fantasies examined in his analysis.

So Slater attempts to illustrate the importance of the fantasies, associated within social actions, that may be pointers to the structural elements that are common to a variety of social situations that, on the surface, seem very different. For example, the offering of a sacrifice in certain religious practices, and the selection of a group member for discussion in a therapy group, seem very different social actions. However, if fantasies of appeasement of a powerful figure are present in both situations (i.e., the god in the former instance; the therapist in the latter), then an important common feature is discernible.

Bion's influence is also strongly present in Slater's work. Not only does Slater examine the evolution of groups in terms of the basic assumption groups and their implications, but he also employs Bion's Kleinian perspective with respect to translating ideas of pre-oedipal individual development into the group context. His major framework for discussing the evolution of groups is phrased in terms of boundary differentiation, a process somewhat akin to the development of a separate consciousness in the developing individual. Tracing its development allows Slater to attempt to integrate Bion's ideas. The scheme he proposes places the basic assumption groups into two 'different levels of conceptualization', described in the following manner:

> (1) There is a continuum of group evolution, involving the increasing awareness of individual and group identity and separateness; (2) there are several defence mechanisms – fight, flight, pairing, dependency – which periodically become a shared property of the group – a group culture. Specific mechanisms are especially appropriate to particular points on the continuum, presumably points of actual or incipient transition.... This paradigm would fit Bion's suggestion that the basic assumptions 'may not be fundamental phenomena, but rather expressions of, or reactions against, some state more worthy of being regarded as primary' (Bion, 1957, p. 456).
>
> (Slater, 1966, pp. 169–70)

Slater is suggesting a schema whereby the basic assumptions are placed on a developmental continuum of increasing boundary differentiation. Each basic assumption is seen to give rise to a particular type of culture. The importance of the culture emanating from each basic assumption rests, however, on the group defence against the specific anxieties generated at particular points along the suggested continuum. The fight/flight group, for example, is seen as the major defence against the blurred boundaries typical of poor differentiation between an individual and the group itself.

> [The member] will experience a sense of envelopment, which, unless he can somehow translate the unconscious material into something pleasant or at

least familiar, will induce a feeling of incipient terror. . . . Fight and flight are both mechanisms for warding off this state when it arises. . . . Fighting is a way of saying, 'this is me. I am different (in fact opposite) from you'. . . . Flight, of course, simply removes the individual from the morass altogether.

(Slater, 1966, p. 179)

There is the obvious analogy here with the undifferentiated boundaries that Klein sees as typical of very early infancy. Her discussion of the paranoid/schizoid defence against anxiety (Klein, 1946; 1975) clearly forms a conceptual basis for descriptions such as those given by Slater about the fight group, in particular. Also in keeping with Klein are his later descriptions of the seductive nature of the state of undifferentiation, alongside its anxiety provoking features.

The other basic assumption groups are also seen to generate defensive cultures associated with anxieties and seductions pertinent to other points on the differentiation continuum. In summarizing his ideas Slater states:

The dependency group seems to be concerned with a somewhat more advanced stage, in which individuality is at once acknowledged and denied, through an attempt at symbiotic union with authority after the fashion made classic by Frommian theory. The pairing group is an attempt to make palatable full individuation and separateness by maintaining a disembodied fantasy of mystical unity and immortality in the form of a distant future messiah.

(Slater, 1966, p. 181)

There is an inherent contradiction in an approach that combines a theory of defence patterns (associated with particular structural configurations) with a developmental schema. Psychoanalysts have run into the same problem of finding a defensible developmental sequencing of defence modes. Different theorists have proposed different chronological orderings of the emergence of defensive structures at the level of individual development. Klein escaped the problem partially by referring to her prime defence modes as 'positions' rather than stages, hence allowing for the possibility of each of the positions to re-emerge under different conditions after their first appearance. Freud considered defensive patterns in conjunction with particular histories and was less apt to order them developmentally than his disciples were. Furthermore, it may be argued that Freud emphasizes synchronic shifts more than diachronic developmental processes (Zukier, 1985). Nonetheless, theoretical attempts to maintain developmental sequencing are numerous (e.g., Abraham, 1927). Similarly a variety of developmental sequences have been proposed for groups (Bennis and Shepard, 1956; Martin Jr. and Fawcett Hill, 1957; Tuckman, 1965; Hartmann and Gibbard, 1974).

The contradiction alluded to in Slater's work expresses itself as this: if defence mechanisms are acquired in a specific genetic developmental sequence, then observations of such sequencing should be unequivocal and be shown to be the same in a vast majority of cases. This would substantiate their generality. Further, if these same mechanisms or modes are also seen to be structurally linked to internal structures of the individual or group, then the conditions associated with the internal structures need also to be developmentally linked, which implies a specific chronology. Without this, the concept of regression is required.

However, the problem of the individual is not our concern here, but Slater's sequencing of group development is. Implied in his theory is that, except for the first few moments of a group, evidence of a fight group indicates a group regression, and that this regression is more severe than that involved in the dependency and the pairing groups. If this means 'formal (i.e., structural) regression' (Freud, 1900, p. 699; Scheidlinger, 1976), then this is just as easily construed as a structural change involving more diffuse boundary differentiation than other structural changes, i.e., Slater's continuum reflects structural positions rather than a specific chronology. If it means 'temporal regression' (Freud, 1900, p. 699) or 'developmental regression' (Fenichel, 1945), then something different is implied. The continuum becomes a set sequence of defences. Without this distinction between types of regression, absurdities are engaged. In fact Slater goes on to interpret the group structural myth of the primal horde in strictly developmental terms, according to his theory of the occurrence of basic assumption groups. He postulates socio-historical events, such as the emergence of kingship, strictly according to these principles, which parallel his ideas of small group development (Slater, 1966, pp. 240–1).

Such developmentalist reconstructions encounter difficulties when they aim at a general reconstruction from theoretical developmental schemas, rather than from researching the unfolding of specific group histories. Such difficulties are increased by a failure to understand that historical reconstructions are themselves social behaviours made from within a social structure that already defines 'maturity' (i.e., the culmination or 'end product' of development). But, to take an example from biology, a rainforest tree may develop abnormally if the mature forest canopy and undergrowth are not present, because it makes its internal changes within a specific ambience. This is because the genetic system does not code information about an absolute maturity. 'The genetic and nervous systems are said to code information about the environment and to represent it in their functional organization. This is untenable; the genetic and nervous systems code processes that specify series of transformations from initial states, which can be decoded only through their actual implementation' (Maturana, 1970, p. 53). In optimal environmental conditions, the genetic code seems to anticipate maturity only because that maturity is already present in the environment.

Closer to the present point, a child may not develop through normal psychological stages if a mature and relatively stable individual is not available to interact with, that is, another individual who has some mature internal objects in the Kleinian sense. The social environment, in this case, seems to contain the anticipation of maturity. Similarly, a group of people will have some access to, and be influenced by, ideas of group maturity, when they enter a new, structurally primitive group. The observation of such a group should not neglect regarding this as a major shaper of the group. (The idea of 'anticipation' as an influence on structure will be examined in Chapter 6 when methods of research are considered.)

The primitive stages of socio-cultural history are not easily reconstructed They are imagined from within the context of present maturity, i.e., they are reconstructed by means of concepts established in the present. In this sense they are ethnocentrically derived reconstructions. Two points are relevant: (a) a group examined in our culture begins its life with an 'anticipation' of 'maturity' as experienced in our culture. Group members may expect their groups to develop along certain predictable lines. These expectations form part of the structure of the group as a whole. That is, present expectations constrain future behaviours. Past cultures, in contrast, may have anticipated other forms of maturity and hence have had a different context within which members operated. For example, many modern Australian family members expect to live in a household with only their immediate nuclear family. This structures the interactions of many young people embarking on marriage, and also structures the new family grouping established by marriage and childbearing (Richards, 1978). Families established in other cultures or the past did not have the same expectations (Shorter, 1975). (b) Once a group has reached the stage defined as 'mature', fluctuations in its structure or forms of defence are not necessarily developmental regressions. An established group that is able to work well may employ flight defences under certain conditions of extreme stress. It becomes perhaps no more identical to a group during formation than a psychotic is to a normal baby. If the important point of coincidence is a particular internal structure or a particular intersystemic relation, then that is the point to identify. Reference to a mystical developmental regression may unneccessarily complicate the matter. Kingship may share properties with authoritarian leaders of groups; the two are not necessarily identical.

In the simplest possible terms the problem is one of generalization. Can the observation of particular groups give rise to predictable developmental sequences? More complexly, it is a question of the use of the concepts of 'development' 'or 'history', when dealing with socio-cultural phenomena. Slater makes the mistake of directly transferring the structures discovered in a study of group histories to a general developmental schema, as if history were precoded. The alternative is to see the group in a process of continuous modification, of states from former states.

These problems can be understood more clearly if we make reference to the work of Maturana and Varela (1980). Their densely argued work employs and requires a new conceptual framework. Their description of the place of the observer in scientific endeavours is profound, whilst deceptively simple. Basically, they state that all descriptions are made by observers who interact descriptively with the entities that they create through their observations. These descriptive interactions lie within the cognitive domain of the observer, being 'a system that through recursive interactions with its own linguistic states may always linguistically interact with its own states as if with representations of its interactions' (Maturana and Varela, 1972, p. 137). To these authors, concepts of time, development, information transmission, memory, etc. are all within the descriptive domain of the observer, not in the phenomenology of the system described, which phenomenology can only arise through the interactions of its systemic components, not through the descriptions of an observer.

Insofar as groups themselves are constituted of (a) independent physical unities and (b) linguistically interacting observers, they operate in a variety of non-reducible domains including the descriptive domains of the participating observers. An observer making comment upon the group may describe the changing states so observed as developmentally preordained, or precoded in the initial states of that group. However, this is possible only because the observer is able to describe the group in relation to its distinction from other entities, and from a frame of reference outside of the group so described. The ongoing ontogeny of the group, however, may be regarded as the history of its structural transformations from within its own closed organization. Each change is a direct transformation of an existent structure. History becomes the description of this progress and is, thus, in Maturana's terms, within the cognitive domain of the observer, rather than inherent in the structural organization of the group itself. These authors are claiming that 'development' and 'history' are linguistic terms used, from the outside, to describe an entity whose changes are not so much precoded as adaptive ongoing changes of state (Dell, 1982).

Recognizing that individuals both constitute the social system and are observers of it, the anticipation of maturity described earlier is, thus, within the descriptive domain of the interacting observers rather than within the physical domain of the present group structure or within the phenomenology of the group as a social system. According to Maturana (1970), the internal structural changes of living things are attempts to specify a closed organization in response to perturbations that threaten the identity of the system as a self-constituting (or autopoietic) system. Similarly with social systems, internal change is specified by social organization. One organization exerts pressures that act to perturb the group. This leads to a new organization, and so on.

In human groups, however, the components that constitute the group are also capable of observing that group and through this process are able to direct social structural change via an external perspective (Maturana and Varela, 1980, pp. xxiv–xxx). This is necessarily through members' capacities as observers, which are distinct from the social structures of the group as such, and which entail the domain of linguistic descriptions. Developmental schemas are within the domain of descriptions, not the phenomenological domain of the group. Historical descriptions are less misleading as they trace the structural changes of systems rather than imply a precoding towards maturity (or some such concept) in the system itself. This rather difficult problem will be returned to in Chapter 6.

The importance of Slater's work to the present study involves the contribution that he makes to an understanding of the evolution of group consciousness. As consciousness is strictly an attribute of individuals, this understanding is largely by way of analogy. However, in his concept of a slowly emerging boundary differentiation between the individuals and the group, Slater has defined a transindividual phenomenon. When occurring in the life of already established groups, such phenomena are necessarily developmentally regressive (if one takes a developmental perspective, as he does). Other theorists handle the idea of group regression in a non-developmental manner. Foulkes is one.

FOULKES

Foulkes (1964) presents his ideas on groups from within the framework of group therapy. Whilst a traditional Freudian analyst in the practice of individual psychoanalysis he pioneered the practice of analytic group therapy. His observations were influenced by a keen comparison of the similarities and differences between individual and group treatments, specifically with respect to the transference processes that occurred in both situations. In time, he came to reserve the idea of transference proper for the psychoanalytic pair of analyst and patient. However, Foulkes sees the types of interchanges and communications that occur in groups as sharing some characteristics with the transference situation. It is his elaboration of these characteristics that forms the basis of his group psychology that attempts to be purely transindividual.

In order to best understand the concepts adopted by Foulkes, it is useful to realize that they emerged in a very pragmatic manner from modifications necessary to the techniques of individual psychoanalytic therapy. Consider the principle of free association. This principle, which refers to that process whereby the individual attempts to relate all that comes to mind without censorship, is applied to the group. The results are interesting given that free association by individuals is not possible in a group in the same way that it is possible in the atmosphere provided by a more passively receptive analyst. In the group setting, other group members take up points in the communication and respond with their own personal comments, hence influencing and punctuating the flow of the individual's own thoughts. It seems, though, that given the instructions to freely talk in a group, the process of the group as a whole resembles a free association.

Bion's idea of group task is matched in Foulkes' scheme by the idea of a group occupation. Every group has an 'occupation' or reason for coming together. As well as the stated occupation, the group may have one or more latent occupations or 'preoccupations', of which members may be partially or totally unaware, and which are very often masked by the consciously enacted occupation. Foulkes sees that the processes of communication within the group (overt and covert, verbal and nonverbal) serve either to express or to defend against these preoccupations, much as an individual's dream both expresses and defends against his or her own repressed impulses. The more the situation resembles the free association process, as in dreams and individual therapy, the more the group communication processes reflect the group preoccupations.

Further, the whole of the communication network existing in the group may be understood as a system. As such, it forms the frame of reference for its individual parts, whether these be individuals, communications, aspects of individuals and so on. This system Foulkes terms the 'group matrix'. Having such a concept he is able to say:

> Looked at in this way it becomes easier to understand our claim that the group associates, responds and reacts as a whole. The group as it were avails itself now of one speaker, now of another, but it is always the transpersonal network which is sensitized and gives utterance, or responds. In this sense we can postulate the existence of a group 'mind' in the same way as we postulate the existence of an individual 'mind'.
>
> (Foulkes, 1964, p. 118)

Foulkes regards the group matrix as an 'interconnected whole'. It is a mental matrix whose individual elements do not necessarily share a common boundary with physical individuals. He suggests they be called 'psyche-individuals'.

With this transindividual concept of group matrix in mind we can re-examine the idea of group structures and regressive phenomena discussed earlier with regard to Slater. It seems that boundaries between individuals, within individuals, and around the group as a whole, are as important to Foulkes as to Slater. During group phenomena, communications may occur across these boundaries. For example, within the matrix, displacements of symptoms may occur between individual patients; splitting of the group occurs in the form of sub-groups, or the isolation of an individual who is then assigned many of the characteristics that others reject in themselves (Foulkes, 1964, p. 119). Such dynamics involve the restructuring of intragroup boundaries such that different boundaries become more or less permeable, more or less diffuse. Rather than seeing these structural changes as developmentally sequenced, Foulkes invokes a concept of multi-dimensionality. He under-stands the group to be operating on at least four levels simultaneously:

1 *The current level* is where 'the group is experienced as representing the community, public opinion, etc., and the conductor as leader or authority' (Foulkes, 1964, p. 114). The chorus in classical Greek tragedy is seen to reflect this level of the group.

2 *The transference level* 'corresponds to mature object relations'. The group tends to represent the family with the 'conductor' as mother or father, and the group members as siblings.

3 *The level of bodily and mental images (projective level)* corresponds to the level of inner object relations as described by Klein and Winnicott. In this case the group relations are viewed as reflecting inner object relations. Group members may 'mirror' rejected or repressed parts of the self. In fact, the group as a whole may be seen as representing a body, often the mother's, and individual identities may be submerged into this image (Foulkes, 1964, p. 116).

4 *The primordial level* represents that level of functioning where primordial or primitive cultural and collective images predominate. These images are akin to the archetypes of Jung (1954) and reflect the collective experience of the cultures from which the group members come.

These four levels of group experience may operate simultaneously, although the group will most often be preoccupied with one level at any given time. Regression in this scheme may be seen as an intensification of preoccupations within levels in a more undifferentiated state, i.e., levels 1, 2, 3 and 4 respectively.

Within particular cultures, groups will have as members some mature individuals, so all levels may be seen as operating from the group's inception. Indeed, Foulkes asserts the essentially social nature of humans, recognising the emergence of individuals 'as the result of developments within the community' (Foulkes, 1964, p. 109). For him the communal level (the level of social value) is always present, as are the other levels that may seem intuitively to be present within the biographies of individual members. In this regard he follows Freud (1921) who sees collective psychology as predating the development of individual psychology.

Foulkes has given us the powerful transindividual concept of group matrix, within which the structures of the group form and re-form. Additionally, he has supplied us with a view of structural regression in the group that does not rely on developmental concepts. It postulates the primary importance of the group viewed as a community within which the representations of inter-personal relations, of intrapersonal object relations, and of primordial phantasy, all have a place.

LACAN

The theories of Jaques Lacan provide an understanding of transindividual processes that structure the internal dynamics of the individual and give rise to individual subjectivity, albeit experienced as irreconcilably split. Some Lacanian concepts will be extensively adapted to the analysis of groups in later chapters. Consequently, they will be discussed in detail here.

Lacan's subject is not an intuitively apprehended 'individual', but may be understood as a structural position within a configuration held in place by important social signifiers. However, this is a demonstrable, not a theoretical, subject (i.e., the subject is 'found' through an examination of dialogue in the psychoanalytic interview). These ideas of structure, subjectivity and language are interwoven in his theories.

Lacan has consistently stressed the split nature of the psychological subject. This split is in reference to:

1   a subjectivity dominated by an alienated and alienating ego, composed largely through a myriad of libidinal object choices originating in the mother;
2   a subjectivity also dominated by a powerful ego-ideal, created through a series of identifications originating in (the identifications of) the oedipal phase;
3   a subjectivity also at the mercy of an unconscious symbolic order which emanates from a symbolic cultural heritage alongside an individual symbolic heritage (see Lacan, 1959, especially his description of schema R).

These are identifiably the ego, superego and id described by Freud and renegotiated by Lacan who stresses the importance of this tripartite division by setting it within three 'registers' of experience important to the human group. These three registers are the Symbolic, the Imaginary and the Real. Human subjectivity is divided on the basis of these three registers of experience, and a subject is simultaneously registered in all three.

The complexity with which Lacan presents his ideas makes it difficult to render them simply and concisely. This difficulty was seemingly intended by Lacan (Lacan, 1957; Muller and Richardson, 1982) insofar as it also minimizes simple-minded renditions that claim to explain his theories by means of superficial categorizations, a fate that he felt often befell the theories of Freud. More importantly, the experiences and subjectivities with which psychoanalysis deals are themselves multiplex and not easily reduced. Furthermore, the very vehicle used in explanation and communication, i.e., language, is an integral part of the complexity that it attempts to explicate.

In Lacanian theory, language and subjectivity are, if not synonymous, tightly interdependent. This is particularly so with regard to the ego, i.e., a person's self-image built from the images of particular others, and in regard to the general Other (in the Symbolic register). This Other (O), is Lacan's term for the unconscious and serves to remind his readers of his contention that the organization of the unconscious is cultural and beyond the individual. Lacan says:

> The subject as such, is uncertain because he is divided by the effects of language. Through the effects of speech, the subject always realizes himself more in the Other, but he is already pursuing there more than half of himself. He will simply find his desire ever more divided, pulverized, in the circumscribable metonomy of speech.
>
> (Lacan, 1979, p. 188)

Lacan is pointing (amongst other things) to the never ending mirror effect of the discovery of self through interaction with others, who also have the same process to undergo. He also indicates that this is done only in the context of the human symbolic function, which names, describes and creates the human cultural field, and, which, in its refractive, ever referring nature ('the metonomy of speech'), has the effect of dividing the so created subject into a veritable prism.

The symbolic register

The interdependence of the human subject and language may best be approached through a description of the Symbolic register, which is basically the register of language and culture. A human subject, according to Lacan, is introduced to symbolic experience by others, usually parents. However, although particular individuals serve the function of introducing the child 'into' the register, its basis extends beyond them. For example, however employed by its users, a language is essentially a system in itself, decipherable (in the case of ancient languages) even after all its natural users are long dead. So, language has some independence from any particular speaker, if not from speech itself.

Lacan considers that symbolic systems, such as a language or a kinship system, organize and structure experience in a particular way, i.e., they give meaning or signification to experiences. The system of language is perhaps the system *par excellence* for describing those qualities that are physically contained and expressed in individuals, yet gain their meaning and become fully operative only in a system spanning the transindividual dimension (cf. the idea of 'production machines', Deleuze and Guattari, 1983, where the production of desire is seen to lie at a social rather than an instinctual level). Lacan takes the work of the structural linguists, Saussure (1959) and Jakobson and Halle (1956), as his starting point. Their work will be described briefly, as a background to Lacan's ideas.

Saussure understood language to be a system of signs, each of which consisted of a signifier and a signified. Although the signifier is introduced as a 'sound image', and the signified as a 'thought image' or concept, Saussure is clear that he intends no simple nominalism. He prefers the terms signifier and signified, and stresses that the *value* of the signifier is derived from its relations with other signifiers in the linguistic system. 'Language is a system of interdependent terms in which the value of each term results solely from the simultaneous presence of the others' (Saussure, 1959, p. 114). The relation of signifier with signified, he states, is purely arbitrary. He uses an analogy with a sheet of paper. The paper represents the total sign, the opposite sides represent the signifier and signified. The two systems into which the two terms are linked, are seen to be separate. They are the systems of signifiers (language), and of signifieds (meanings/thoughts).

It might be added here that a system of roles within a small group or a large organization may be explained in a fashion similar to the above. The role of leader, for example, has value in a sense equivalent to that of a sign as described by Saussure. It gains value from its relation to the roles of follower, deputy, challenger, rebel, etc. Similarly we might say of a role (or partial object in the Kleinian sense) what Saussure says of a word:

> Its content is really fixed only by the concurrence of everything that exists outside it. Being part of a system, it is endowed not only with a signification but also and especially with a value, and this is something quite different.
>
> (Saussure, 1959, p. 115)

Jakobson and Halle (1956) discuss a view of language that emphasizes the relations between signifiers. They propose that language is structured according to two major axes. These are the axes of paradigmatic and syntagmatic relations. Briefly, the paradigmatic axis represents relations of positional and semantic similarity. Signifiers related along this axis may occupy a similar position in, e.g., a sentence. These signifiers may also be semantically similar.

The syntagmatic axis represents relations of positional and semantic contiguity, i.e., signifiers related along this dimension may occupy contiguous positions and have contiguous meanings. For example, in the sentence, 'the knife lay next to the fork', 'lay' and 'next' occupy contiguous positions and 'knife' and 'fork' are semantically contiguous. The arguments of Jakobson and Halle are similar to Saussure's (1959) arguments of relations 'in absentia' (relations between latent or absent signifiers able to replace the present one) and relations 'in praesentia' (relations between signifiers present in the discourse, Grigg, 1985–6).

Jakobson and Halle view these two axes as being related to two major linguistic processes that each involve substitution. They relate the substitution involved in a metaphor to the paradigmatic axis. We may, for example, substitute 'frame' for 'body' in 'whatever stirs this mortal frame' (Grigg, 1985–6). The metaphoric effect comes from the meanings attached to the substituted signifier's latent presence. The signifiers are related positionally and semantically (the latter being an effect of language not of 'things'). Jacobson and Halle relate metonomy to the syntagmatic axis. This is a process whereby a signifier comes to replace another that is contiguously related. For example 'crown' replaces 'king', or 'turf' replaces 'horse racing'. The displacement has occurred in, e.g., 'he serves the crown'.

Lacan extends and changes the work of Saussure and Jakobson and Halle. He minimizes the importance of the sign in Saussure, and concentrates on the importance of the signifier. Contrary to the relation implicit in Saussure's analogy with the piece of paper, Lacan stresses the transitive nature of the relation between signifier and signified. By this he means that although the relation is arbitrary, the signifier is not tied to any one signification. In a sense it 'resists signification' (Lacan, 1957) by resisting a permanent relation. To Lacan, the relation is one where the signifier 'slides' over the signified such that a signifier may now mean one thing, later another, depending on the signifying chain into which it is inserted. Consequently, it will evoke in the subject a variety of meanings, some of which may not be in his or her conscious experience. Take, for example, the signifier 'bill'. It evokes different meanings in the following contexts: 'the bill was too expensive', or, 'the duck had a damaged bill'. Also note the retrospective attribution of meaning in, e.g., 'the delivery of the bill was delayed by the absence of the parliamentary speaker'.

To Lacan, the totality of the system of signifiers provides an infrastructure for the culture. Three particular signifiers, however, are seen by Lacan as essential to human subjectivity. These signifiers act as cornerstones to the whole Symbolic register; all other signifiers, he claims, are held in relation to one another through their influence. They are the unconscious signifiers that mark out the oedipal configuration: the 'name-of-the-father' (the symbolic father), the 'desire-of-the-mother' (signifying mother's desire), and the 'phallus' (Lacan, 1953b; 1959). To Lacan, these signifiers locate major 'anchoring points' of the system of signifiers in the system of signified experience.

It is important to note that these are signifiers not objects, and that they may represent a multiplicity of significations (due to the 'sliding' relation described above). According to Lacan, symbolic systems are independent of any direct one-to-one correspondence with a 'real' world. They act to structure our experience rather than to set up an inner world parallel to a real outer world. That is, they act to impose order onto experienced disparity (Miel, 1970).

Lacan (1957) illustrates this latter point with reference to the signifiers 'ladies' and 'gentlemen' located above two doors. What is it that these terms signify? In this case they do not 'nominate' a group of females and a group of males. They do indicate a place where certain functions may be carried out, but the signifier 'toilet' may do just as well. Further, the doors, and the two rooms, may be identical in all material respects, so it is not a characteristic of the object that is signified. They specifically signify, however, a social practice of segregation. Furthermore they have meaning only in relation to each other.

In other circumstances the word 'lady' may signify something quite different.

The Symbolic register is organized at an unconscious level, even though individuals may be aware of the meaning of a great number of signifiers. Lacan's famous dictum, 'the unconscious is structured like a language' (Lacan, 1957) denotes the nature of this organization. It refers to his view of the unconscious as a system of signifiers, which are open to signification (i.e., open to new meanings), and which are related to one another through the processes of condensation and displacement (Freud, 1900).

Here the influence of Jakobson is recognizable (Jakobson and Halle, 1956). To Lacan, the unconscious is structured by processes analogous to the linguistic processes of metaphor and metonomy. To reiterate, metaphor (following Jakobson and Halle) operates on the basis of the substitution of signifier for signifier. For example in the poem 'La Belle Dame Sans Merci', Keats uses metaphor to describe the complexion of a young man:

> I see a lily on thy brow,
> With anguish moist and fever dew:
> And on thy cheek a fading rose
> Fast withereth too.

The power of the metaphor derives from the addition of new associations provided by the substitution. In contrast, metonomy operates by a process of contiguous association (Lemaire, 1977, pp. 32–4). For example in the metonymic formation, 'I'll buy you a glass', the speaker means 'I'll buy you a glass (of beer)'. The term 'glass' comes to stand for its contents by way of contiguous association.

Lacan extends Jakobson's ideas by juxtaposing them with Freud's. In so doing, however, Grigg (1985–6) believes that he moves away from Jakobson's position with regard to metaphor. Grigg shows that the substitution metaphor is just one of a series of metaphoric constructions. Others are the metaphoric extension (e.g., 'the mouth of the river, cave, bottle, etc.'), and the appositive metaphor (e.g. 'sea of blood', or 'love is war'). He then goes on to argue that whereas metonomy relies on semantic attributes, metaphor does not. Jakobson misses this point, Grigg says, because he equates metaphor with substitution alone (i.e., to say 'love is war' does not imply semantic similarity between the terms. This is created in the metaphor by a contiguous relation). However, Lacan, as Grigg attempts to demonstrate, illustrates the non-substitutive, non-semantic effects in metaphor. He does this by emphasizing the importance of the relations 'that the latent signifier maintains, not with the signifier that has replaced it, but with the other signifiers in the chain to which it is related by contiguity' (Grigg, 1985–6, p. 20).

The import of these arguments is that Lacan's analysis of metaphor indicates the importance of relations held between the signifiers that remain in a latent form in the discourse. This is crucial to Lacan's analysis of the unconscious.

Lacan views the formations of the unconscious as operating similarly to the linguistic processes outlined. For example, in considering the formation of dreams (following Freud, 1900) he relates metaphor to condensation (i.e., both processes act to condense a set of signifiers by substitution), and he relates metonomy to displacement (i.e., both processes act to displace signifiers from one point in the chain of contiguity, or 'the signifying chain', to another). In considering neurotic symptoms, he considers that the symptom is a metaphor representing an unconscious signifier, or (as indicated in the case of metaphor) the symptom may represent a whole series of latent signifiers each unconsciously related to the others (Lacan, 1957). Further, he views desire, whether conscious or unconscious, as a metonomy. By this it seems he means that whatever it is that we desire, this is a metonymic displacement of another desire, and this other of yet another.

Consequently, Lacan says, whatever the particular content of our unconscious thoughts and associations, the structure is like that of language. Furthermore, although both the linguistic system and the unconscious consist of signifiers that are arbitrary (in the sense of having no inherent and necessary meaning), and that are open to meaning through experience, the structure of the unconscious is culturally 'anchored' in terms of the oedipal structure. These ideas will be taken up later (especially in Chapter 12).

The Imaginary register

In contrast to the symbolic register, the Imaginary register represents the experience of the ego. It is the register of particular images constructed through time. The Imaginary representation of 'father', for example, may be structured for the subject by the symbolic signifier 'father', yet it is built from particular experiences of a particular father. It is also subject to influence from the rest of the subject's Imaginary constructions. The Imaginary is, to Lacan, the realm of the signified, rather than of the signifier. It reflects the effects of the signifying chain of the subject's particular experience.

To Lacan, the ego is not coextensive with the 'subject'. It is deluded, imaginary, illusionary, deceptive and deceived, yet crucially important in the constitution of the psyche. It (the ego) is the focus of 'self' experience. Although the description given is somewhat akin to the descriptions of false-consciousness in the early Marx, in this case it is not just the desires of a malign ruling class that structure the consciousness of the ego. To Lacan, it is inevitable that the ego is structured (unconsciously) by the 'desire of the other' and is consequently removed from the subject's own (original) desire.

The mirror stage is central to the structuring of the Imaginary register (Lacan, 1949) and is quintessentially and unescapably human. It organizes those moments when the child, dependent and subject to instinctual urges, having recognized a possible fulfillment in and through the other (mainly mother), beholds him or herself as another. The human's ability to regard him or herself as an object, despite being the basis, perhaps, of rational thought, science, technology, art and religion, is seen by Lacan to alienate a person from him or herself, forever. This process is illustrated by the myth of Narcissus. Narcissus did not die because he loved his reflection (i.e., himself as object). He died when, after being continually frustrated by the image's elusiveness, he merged with the image by drowning. In this merging his subjectivity was lost.

The subjectivity (or consciousness) of the ego is created by a split and is necessarily alienated from other human subjectivities. Despite, or perhaps because of, valiant, defensive efforts to integrate it temporarily and across situations, the biographical identity of the ego is the sum of a thousand million fragments. These fragments are created from identifications with objective, reflexive and imagined others. The many selves identified by James (1918), Goffman (1971), Laing (1975) and Horney (1939), are, in a sense, conceptual and experiential integrates of the illusory ego, which acts as a kaleidoscope, setting and resetting its pattern in the image of the other. The important others of our experience set the major basis of identifications, yet, as demonstrated by Freud, these identifications are structured by the oedipal situation. We will return to the nature of the ego as described by Lacan at a later stage, when the nature of identification is more fully explored (Chapter 5).

The register of the Real

The register of the Real is not described as thoroughly or unambiguously by Lacan as are the other two registers. The Real is not synonymous with 'reality'. It contains the area of experience that is unsymbolized and hence apprehended in an ineffable or raw fashion. At one time (1959), Lacan talks of these experiences as somehow resisting symbolization, or remaining unsymbolized due to 'foreclosure', a process differing from the defence mechanisms of the ego in that the material so foreclosed is not only never conscious nor able to be so, but is also unconceptualized even at an unconscious level. In this analysis, Lacan sees the foreclosure of certain important social signifiers as constituting the basic aetiology of psychosis. His re-examination of the case of Schreber is in these terms.

At another time (Lacan, 1979, pp. 167–73), the Real is not simply the obstacle to the pleasure principle, as reality is in the usual interpretation of the 'reality principle', but is of that area of human experience that is desexualized. By way of illustration he points out that the complete removal of the sexual object towards the real renders it 'as a parcel of meat' and evokes disgust, as in an hysterical reaction. Unsymbolized and desexualized material may be experienced in an hallucinatory fashion, alien and ineffable to the subject, yet directly and rawly presented. It is a part of inner experience felt to be alien to the subject.

In distinguishing the three registers, it is useful to think of 'reality' as being an Imaginary construction delimited by the Symbolic field whereas the 'Real' is outside these. Each register is, in this sense, defined in its relation to the other registers. The idea of social reality as a construction is not new, and it follows from our acceptance of this idea that the basis of its construction has both individual and group elements, i.e., Imaginary and Symbolic components. What is of the 'Real' is outside of our constructions and our social and group life.

Lacan offers, then, a construction of the unconscious that is trans-individual, not in terms of its content, but in terms of its structure. Here he differs from Jung whose 'collective unconscious' is collective on the basis of common content (i.e., the archetypes, Jung, 1954). To Lacan, common contents (i.e., common signifiers) are due to the cultural anchors provided by the oedipal situation.

He is able to provide us with yet another perspective on transindividual processes. The individual subject is emergent from a social nexus of others to whom he or she relates in a variety of ways, most specifically through the registers of the Symbolic, the Imaginary and the Real. These relations are regulated, in the normal and the neurotic individual, by the cultural heritage passed down and embodied in the Symbolic register.

REVIEW

A review of the argument thus far would be useful. In the search for an adequate territory for a 'group psychology' the distinction between discipline and paradigm was necessitated. It was concluded, temporarily at least, that a particular paradigm, or network of interrelated methodological and conceptual approaches, does not necessarily lead to observations in a particular discipline.

On the other hand Allport's description of what constitutes social psychology as a discipline, for example (Allport, 1985), is not identical with the description of a group psychology constituted from emergent group processes, i.e., the very processes that Doise and Billig indicate. Group psychology, it seems, differs in some distinct ways from social psychology. The identification of these differences may prove valuable for both fields.

The paradigm of psychoanalysis, which may lay claim to being a discipline insofar as it has identified a totally new human subject (Foucault, 1966), offers much to group psychology. It provides the conceptual tools for a theory of transindividual phenomena that are part of a living system rather than a mere description of aggregate phenomena.

Most useful are the ideas of Lacan and Foulkes which may be viewed as standing in a complementary relation to each other. Lacan sees the individual as 'entered' in all three registers of experience. His focus is on the emergent subjectivity of the individual, a subjectivity that is necessarily split because it can come into being only as a reflection of others. Although Foulkes focusses on the group, he also sees the experience of the individual in the group operating simultaneously at four different levels.

However, despite their both examining multidimensional aspects of experience, it is apparent that the group levels that Foulkes employs are not equivalent to the registers described by Lacan. It is more appropriate to see that the relations that Lacan emphasizes are found to operate within the experience of Foulkes' levels. The 'Symbolic' father, for example, who exists in the individual and aids in the ordering of experiences in relation to an 'Imaginary' father (recreated as a reality through experienced relations with a particular man), is present at the Transference Level. Symbolic, Imaginary and Real fathers are also present at the other levels: the leader/king at the Current Level; godlike figures or phallic representations at the Primordial Level; the penis, at the Level of Bodily and Mental Images.

Additionally, the three registers are important at all levels of group experience. A group member may experience another member as a devouring mouth, an imaginary construction at the bodily phantasy level; or as simply greedy, an imaginary construction at the transference level. His/her own personal integration and the general preoccupation of other group members will influence which imaginary construction predominates.

The next two chapters will examine the specific concepts of psychological integration and identity, and attempt to apply them to the area of group psychology. This will serve as a specific theoretical framework for the qualitative studies to follow in Parts II and III.

Chapter 4

Integration in groups

In this chapter, some parallels between the development of individual and group integration will be established in order to provide a theoretical basis for the empirical studies described in Part II. The parallels are best construed within a framework, which itself has the following assumptions: (a) a developing entity does not mature in a vacuum but within an already structured context; further, (b) the structured context of life provides a 'containing' function so that newly differentiated entities are protected and shielded from harm (and possible disintegration) during their development. Also to be included is an impressionistic discussion of some relevant ideas distilled from the author's experiences with groups. These assumptions and impressions provide a basis for the more structured observations presented in Chapters 8–11.

We will begin with some brief statements about groups and infants and will then present some ideas of Winnicott (1945; 1958) and Mahler (1968). These ideas act as a basis for comparisons between individual and group development.

A group does not become an entity capable of doing work (i.e., of functioning at a stated task) simply by virtue of being an aggregate of persons. The parts of the group system, e.g., the roles that people embody in the group, become functionally related to one another whilst group tasks are carried out. In fact roles in themselves would not exist without such relatedness: a mother is not a mother without a child because the two form a dyadic system. Consequently the processes whereby an aggregate of persons integrate and become a psychological group, or a system of interrelated and communicating parts with emergent products, are of great interest. This integration may form a basis for group identity.

Similarly, psychological birth, or the emergence of the individual, is not achieved simultaneously with physical birth. As adults, we see the newborn baby as being a unity separate from others. The baby's acquisition of this vision, however, develops slowly. Winnicott (1945) and Mahler (1968) trace this process.

WINNICOTT

In his paper 'Primitive emotional development' (1945) Winnicott places stress on what he sees as a crucial turning point in the psychological development of the infant. This development takes place at around 5–6 months, although the exact chronology is not important; it is marked most by the infant's recognition of him or herself as a whole person. Winnicott says: 'We can say at this stage a baby becomes able in his play to show that he can understand he has an inside, and that things come from outside' (p. 149). It is at that point of development, tenuously attained but held to with increasing belief as time passes, that the infant seems to conceive of a boundary that identifies things, thoughts and feelings as his or not his or hers or not hers.

Winnicott identifies three processes necessary to the formation of this psychodevelopmental structure: integration, personalization and realization. Integration refers to that process whereby the infant is able to perceive him or herself as existing in one whole piece rather than as many unintegrated pieces. The early experience of non-integration is based on those times when each new sensation may be taken as the basis of an entirely new state of being. The basis of integration, however, lies in the 'acute instinctual experiences which tend to gather the personality together from within' (1945, p. 150), and perhaps more importantly, in the containing action of the mother or infant caretaker who handles and treats the infant as a whole person, matching and fulfilling the infant's needs with mothering responses. The mother acts to draw disparate experiences together and to shield the infant from influences that might disrupt this process. The structural organizers of psychological integration are found, then, in the biological structure of the instincts and in the structured context of the containing mother.

Alongside integrative development comes the process of personalization whereby the infant experiences his or her person as lodged in his or her body. As the infant integrates his or herself, s/he normally comes to see the body as the site of this integration. Although depersonalization and dissociation may be fleeting or minor parts of normal adult life, they represent those phantasy 'out of body' experiences that gradually diminish in the infant as s/he learns to draw into self, or to incorporate, those points of integration that are felt to belong to the self; and to expel, or eject, those aspects of experience that are nonself (Klein, 1946). Once more the mothering and care of the infant body is important. Winnicott believes that, through this care, the infant learns that pleasurable experiences can be kept within, and unpleasure expelled. On the other hand, if the infant experience is one of a body that offers only pain and discomfort, s/he may experience his or her body as an alien thing, not to be associated with his or her (phantasied) self. In such cases an attempt at integration outside the body, perhaps in the mother or some other person, or in a limited portion of the body, may occur.

The third process indicated by Winnicott is that of realization, or reality adaptation. This is achieved to a satisfactory extent when the infant is able to differentiate inside from outside, wishes from objects, and self from mother. Winnicott sensitively explains the process in his discussion of 'the moment of illusion'. Illusion, he says, occurs when the infant's wish, with its hallucinatory fulfillment, coincides with the presentation, in reality, of the object that can actually fulfill the wish.

> I will try to describe in the simplest possible terms this phenomenon as I see it. In terms of baby and mother's breast, the baby has instinctual urges and predatory ideas. The mother has a breast and the power to produce milk, and the idea that she would like to be attacked by a hungry baby. These two phenomena do not come into relation with each other till the mother and child live an experience together. The mother being mature and physically able has to be the one with tolerance and understanding, so that it is she who produces a situation that may with luck result in the first tie the infant makes with an external object, an object that is external to the self from the infant's point of view.
>   I think of the process as if two lines came from opposite directions, liable to come near each other. If they overlap there is a moment of illusion – a bit of experience which the infant can take as either his hallucination or a thing belonging to external reality.

(Winnicott, 1945, p. 142)

Illusory states are the forerunners of the ability to differentiate fantasy from external reality. Without illusion we would never seek reality, nor struggle with its delineation (Grolnick, Barkin and Muensterberger, 1978). We would be left to cling hopelessly to our limited hallucinatory experience, omnipotent and alone.

Again Winnicott is able to demonstrate the powerful function of the containing mother. It is she who is able to present external reality to the child at that moment when a gradually developing inner reality, with its hallucinatory images, will not suffice to fulfill hunger; and when the child's ability to apprehend external reality is optimal. It is then that the infant is able to draw from external reality sustenance not only for physical needs, but also enrichment for inner representations, which in turn allow for more complex illusory material and the possibility of dealing with a more complexly structured external reality. The mothering person, through his or her own personality and actions, is able to provide the structured context whereby, together, s/he and the infant can develop the infant's capacities to integrate, personalize, and adapt to reality. The mothering one is both context (i.e., container) and partner in the process.

MAHLER

Mahler (1968) also describes the processes whereby an infant develops his or her own identity. She refers to these as the processes of individuation. The stages that Mahler sees as important in early development will be briefly outlined for future reference.

Normal autism

This stage occurs in the first few weeks of life and is distinguished by primary narcissism and withdrawal from external stimulation. Perhaps withdrawal is a not quite accurate term, because Mahler explains that the infant has not yet come to invest with energetic interest (cathect) its sense organs, and has no knowledge of external reality. More simply, we can say that the external world is neither identified by, nor important to the infant. This is despite the fact that the external world must, and does, impinge on the infant. Following Freud (1920), Mahler likens this stage psychologically to an egg, where the shell acts as a strong protective barrier against excessive external stimulation. The primacy of sleep ensures the maintenance of this barrier type of boundary.

Symbiosis

Symbiotic union with the mother is built up gradually so that, by the second to third month, this stage is prominent.

> The term 'symbiosis' in this context is a metaphor. It does not describe, as the biological concept of symbiosis does, what actually happens between two separate individuals. It was chosen to describe that state of undifferentiation, of fusion with mother, in which the 'I' is not yet differentiated from the 'not-I', and in which inside and outside are only gradually coming to be sensed as different.
>
> The essential feature of symbiosis is hallucinatory or delusional, somatopsychic omnipotent fusion with the representation of the mother and, in particular, the delusion of a common boundary of the two actually and physically separate individuals.

(Mahler, 1968, p. 9)

Hence the first two stages outlined by Mahler are describing processes similar to those described by Winnicott as pre-integration. Mahler emphasizes a shift from what she calls 'absolute primary narcissim' in the normal autistic phase to the narcissism of the symbiotic phase, where the infant fuses the representations of self and mother. She also indicates the importance of the mothering one as both 'symbiotic partner' and a 'symbiotic organizer'. That is, the mother, through her maturity, is able to act as an auxiliary ego for the infant. Such a function provides a monitoring of the presentations of external reality, and protection of the infant from situations that might overwhelm its developing ego.

Hatching phase

The development of an integrated self is seen to take place during this phase. At first, the self and mother representations are fused, as described above. It is as if the strength of the mother's personality provides a container for the more delicate infant ego. Gradually, however, the process of hatching begins. This is marked by a shift in the attention cathexis of the infant from within the symbiotic orbit towards the outside world. This change in attention fluctuates over time and is exhibited behaviourally in two major ways: (a) more time is spent awake and exploring the environment visually, tactilely, etc.; and (b) the infant displays 'checking back' behaviour, whereby perceptual exploration of not-mother objects is alternated with perceptual exploration of the mother. The infant alternates between gaining sustenance from an already known orbit and enlarging the sphere of experience.

Mahler describes the process of hatching, or developing away from the symbiotic delusion, as taking place through the subphases of separation–individuation (i.e., practising and rapprochement). In these, the infant comes to perceive the self as separate from, although related to the mother. This process is aided by the developing independence that accompanies increased motor performance and perceptual learning. The mother, however, remains a firm contextual basis around which reality may be explored. She acts as a reference point or as a comparison figure. In this sense she represents the 'other' who provides a basis for the ego and the associated realm of the Imaginary (Lacan, 1977).

Mahler's stages emphasize the importance of the mother's role. This role provides a structure that the child can share as a symbiotic partner, and can utilize as a reference point during the processes of hatching and individuation. For Mahler, as for Winnicott, it is clear that the mother acts as both container and partner during the developmental process.

It would seem that the developing identity of the infant occurs optimally when the child enters a context that provides structured containment and mutually responsive partnership. Further, if we are to follow Winnicott's ideas on the place of illusion we might say that, in the earliest stages at least, development will occur when there is a matching of external and internal realities. It is perhaps the human social context that both develops from, and ensures the place of illusion in developing and sustaining the perception of changing realities.

GROUPS

The work of Winnicott and Mahler was introduced to enable a discussion of commonalities between the development of infant integration and identity and the development of group identity. These commonalities are centred in the idea of development within a containing context and the importance of 'the moment of illusion'. Gibbard et al. (1974) demonstrate how illusion, phantasy and myth underlie various accounts of the development of group structures:

> We can regard group fantasy activity – as well as daydreaming and creative and adaptive fantasy – as just this type of intermediate phenomena. As such it is not a true apprehension, a completely veridical perception of reality; at the same time, it is not the kind of distortion that is associated with hallucination, delusion and other such images ... if Winnicott's view is correct, and likewise our application of his views to myth, ritual and shared conscious fantasies in groups, then such activity can be regarded as adaptive if not crucial to group process and structure.
>
> (p. 271)

Here emphasis will be given to a frequent expectation held by members entering a new group, an expectation linked closely to Winnicott's and Mahler's ideas (that new entities are formed within an existing context). The expectation is that members come to join a group, rather than to create or form one. A second and parallel expectation is that leaders are expected to act as both containers and partners in the development of group identity. Such expectations may or may not be consciously formed in the minds of the members. Most likely they are to be located in the area that Gibbard et al. assign to illusion or group myth. It is hoped that the present work will demonstrate that even in groups that form themselves quite self-consciously with regard to tasks and terms of reference, the processes of integrating and discovering identity form an important part of the group's life. These processes include discovering what it is that members have come to join, and what it was that had an existence before they joined it.

Similarly, a group may be leaderless in the sense of having no one person self-consciously designated as leader, yet the leadership functions occurring in that group will be conceived by members as lodged in the overall structure of a containing partnership with members. There is the pressure to be 'one of the boys (girls)' or 'part of the group', alongside the wish and need to be led.

The above factors have been termed expectations, but, as in the case of the infant, it may be that the group must develop its own identity as a part of that process which culminates in an understanding of separation from the 'mother group' or the 'group-which-existed-previously-and-was-joined'. Previous group joining experiences throughout life would, in general, develop the expectation or belief in an identity of the group before it was joined. Consciously or unconsciously this belief apprehends an entity to be joined.

Many groups joined throughout life do, of course, have identities in reality before we join them: school, work, family, church. Yet I wish to explore here the illusion of the group's identity that leads, I believe, to group members eventually coming to terms with their own individuality, the structure of the group, and the roles taken within the group.

Let us term the original group identity (i.e., the group that seemed to be there before we joined it) the illusory 'group-that-is-joined'. A problem for members occurs at a stage somewhat analogous to Winnicott's 5–6 month infant stage. It is a problem that begins to emerge when group members see themselves as constituting a group with definite boundaries; it arises after introductions have been made and group members have tackled one or two issues that have drawn them together. Following Winnicott, we might say that these very early processes in the group consist of integration: the introduction of parts; some work on the 'inside/outside' boundary, or what Schutz (1967) calls inclusion/exclusion issues; and some initial defining of the realities that the group must face. The inclusion/exclusion issue may be dealt with extremely briefly; for example, it may simply be reflected in the group's physical arrangements that denote who is 'in' and who is 'out'. Alternatively someone may simply say, 'Are we all here? Let's get started then.' It may, however, become a very important issue for the group and may take some time to resolve, and in fact be continually returned to throughout the life of the group. Similarly, the initial defining of realities (task, setting, times of meeting, and so on) may be brief or extended.

Beyond these initial developments, a tenuous group identity is formed. This centres around that which the members begin to identify as 'in' their group, and that which is to be excluded. The actual nature of the identity will depend upon the particular issues raised or experienced, and the identity first formed may be tenuous and unstable. However, it is only when such an identity begins to emerge that the group as a whole turns to consider seriously (at whatever level) what it is that they have joined.

This phenomenon, as outlined, seems to come after the development of a tentative and separate group identity, and seems to occur before what Slater (1966) and others have described as the 'rebellion' in self-analytic groups. Such a rebellion occurs when members overtly or covertly attack and attempt to replace the group trainer or consultant. In terms of the present discussion, the members are attempting to replace the leader of the 'group-which-was-joined' with a leader or leaders of the group whose identity they are forming. The rebellion clearly indicates that members have differentiated between the newly formed group identity and that of the group-which-was-joined. This differentiation is enabled by the process of defining the group-which-was-joined.

This process of defining may take many forms. One form is the 'experimenter myth', which reflects the belief that the group is a group to be observed and experimented on by the consultant. The forms of the basic assumption groups described by Bion (1961) are others. Yet another form is the group whose purpose it is to protect and sustain its creators, or alternatively, its creations; family groupings may take such forms. Or we could consider the group that rebels (delinquent groupings), or the groups that actively organize to deceive (criminal groups) or uphold the law (the police).

The identity of the group-that-was-joined may rapidly become apparent to new members, particularly when previous or ongoing members pass on their knowledge. In the case of self-analytic 'laboratory' or 'study' groups, where the trainer or consultant does not present his/her knowledge of such a previous identity, the illusory aspect of its discovery becomes more apparent. Here the identity lies in the wishes, myths, fears and desires of the participants, including the consultant.

The ideas outlined thus far form the basis of a detailed qualitative analysis of the first session of each of three different self-analytic groups. This analysis will be presented in Chapters 7–10 after a discussion of the nature of group identity in Chapter 5, a review of relevant research methods for group systems and a discussion of the specific methods of analysis to be used in the research in Chapter 6.

Chapter 5

Identity, leadership and authority

The last chapter discussed integration in groups. This was considered in relation to Winnicott's views of infant integration, personalization and realization, and Mahler's ideas on individuation. The theories of both these authors seem to form a basis for views on early identity.

The present chapter will attempt, first, critically to explore the nature of identity as presented in the writings of Harré (1979; 1983), Erikson (1968), Lacan (1977) and Freud (1914; 1921). The discussion moves from the more recent formulations back to the original ideas of Freud. This is because the later formulations (e.g., Erikson's) may usefully be considered from the perspective of a transindividual approach, but they encounter problems that may best be overcome by reference back to Freud's early ideas on narcissism.

Following this discussion, the nature of leadership and authority will be examined. It is argued that the process of identification forms the major dynamic between group members because it relates them to the major or primary group tasks. However, this is mediated through the relatedness of members to leaders. By means of the examination of identity, leadership and authority, a perspective will be developed and used as a framework for the qualitative longitudinal analysis to be presented in Chapter 12.

GENERAL COMMENTS ON IDENTITY

Identity presupposes some minimal integration sustained through psychologically meaningful time. To have identity is to have a recognizable wholeness across time and situations. For example, a name, a description, a signature, or a set of mutual belongings may each serve to mark identity in its particular way.

However, identity does not mark a consistent or constant integration. Such unity in an individual is more wished for than felt. Moreover, the inscribing of identity leads to the question of 'identity for whom?', a question the answer to which must be couched in social terms, as it is relevant only in an intersubjective context.

Identity marks the recognizability of a person or group, even if only to him, her or itself. It is this recognizability; this looking at the subject from the outside, or, more correctly, this looking at the subject *as* another, that lies at the heart of identity. This is also what some writers characterize more loosely as the 'self'. However, in using the term 'self', the idea of identification (alluded to in 'identity') is not made explicit. The 'self' comes to have a mystical more than a socially precise meaning. To retain the term identity is to retain the exactness of the aetiology of identity via identifications, and to stress its social embeddedness.

The nature of identity, and the human desire for its presence, are to be examined with the view of understanding further the processes of group identity. Firstly, the work of some authors who have influenced thought on the subject of identity will be examined.

HARRÉ

Harré (1983) distinguishes personal identity, or 'what it is that makes a human being this or that particular person within a public-collective context' from 'the sense of personal identity, i.e., how people experience their unique selfhood' (p. 203). The former, he believes, may arise from biological properties of distinctiveness within the group, whereas a sense of personal identity requires the experience of a developing autobiography containing an agency centred in a unified self-consciousness. In these terms, the sense of identity is a sense of unity emerging from an experiencing self-reflective being, set in a collective where distinctiveness is a possibility.

Underwriting this is Harré's belief (developed more fully in Harré, 1979; 1984) that:

> not only are the acts we as individuals perform and the interpretations we create of the social and physical world prefigured in collective actions and social representations, but also the very structure of our minds (and perhaps the fact that we have minds at all) is drawn from those social representations.
> (Harré, 1983, p. 20)

Given these terms, to have an identity without a sense of identity would necessitate total objectification within the social field, and would involve either the loss of subjective self-reflexive consciousness (with its accompanying senses of agency and personal history), i.e., psychological death, or it would involve death itself. Ironically, a sense of identity requires that self-reflexive split which renders us inexorably alienated in a multitude of objectifications (pictures of ourselves), with only the illusion of continuity, as in the illusion of the motion picture. In consequence, this autobiography of objectifications, designed and shaped within groups of biographies, comes to stand, in its illusory (Imaginary) unity, in place of the immediately experiencing subject and that subject's prefiguration in 'collective actions and social representations' (cf. Sullivan's ideas of the illusory nature of individuality, and the role of 'mediate experience', 1950; 1953).

Harré, nonetheless, does not emphasize this illusory quality despite his originating the sense of identity in a split from subjectivity. His emphasis is more on its role in the aetiology of 'personal being' (which also includes the capacity for agency and initiating action), and on the presence of the person in a socio-historical location. He says:

> Neither self-consciousness nor self-activation and intervention is sufficient to establish personal being, since the structures of mind on which they depend and the forms they take are derived from the social structures and the linguistic practices of the communities within which people, to become people, must live. Personal being arises only by a transformation of the social inheritance of individuals. It is essentially a semantic transformation and arises through the use of cognitive processes typified by metaphor to transform the social inheritance. This capacity is itself a social inheritance and there may be societies whose members can never achieve personal being because the practice of individual transformation of social resources does not exist.
>
> (Harré, 1983, p. 23)

The similarity of this position to Lacan's is apparent despite emphases on different aspects. Like Lacan, Harré stresses the importance of symbolic systems (e.g., language) in the achievement of personhood or subjectivity. However, Harré stresses the positive nature of identity as a source of personal being. Entry into 'personhood' is acquired through the learning of theories of the self (i.e., creating a cognitive space for ideas of the self), these theories themselves having a socio-linguistic basis and being entrenched in the process of enculturation. Harré seems to regard the 'Imaginary Ego' in a more favourable light than does Lacan.

ERIKSON

Erikson begins his book on identity (1968) by referring to the perspectives of James and Freud respectively. He does this not by an exposition of their theories (although their main ideas are invoked implicitly), but by reference to their personal lives: a letter written by James to his wife (1920), and an address made by Freud in 1926 to the Society of B'nai B'rith in Vienna. As in many of his arguments, he ties their ideas to personal biography. Whatever the validity of such a method, it relates inevitably to his 'psycho-social' position. It leads to his posing a dual location for identity:

> for we deal with a process 'located' in the core of the individual and yet also in the core of his communal culture, a process which establishes, in fact, the identity of those two identities.
>
> (Erikson, 1968, p. 22)

In Erikson's writings, identity is of central concern to the individual but emerges also within the context of the social:

> At one time it [identity] seemed to refer to a conscious sense of individual uniqueness, at another to an unconscious striving for a continuity of experience, and at a third, as a solidarity with a group's ideals.
>
> (Erikson, 1968, p. 208)

The link between internal aspects of the person (particularly of the ego) and the specific social and cultural milieu within which the person lives provides the hallmark of Erikson's work, and is at the basis of his term 'psycho-social' (Erikson, 1950). His rewriting of libidinal progression in terms of ego development is well known. It would seem, then, that this perspective may provide the present thesis with a model of the individual as emergent from group life and as centrally located within the social dimension.

Consider firstly Erikson's descriptions of the process of identity formation:

> The process 'begins' somewhere in the first true 'meeting' of mother and baby as two persons who can touch and recognize each other, and it does not 'end' until a man's power of mutual affirmation wanes.
>
> (Erikson, 1968, p. 23)

Certainly this is a view of the formation of identity within an interpersonal context (a view shared by another translator of analytic theory, Sullivan, 1953). Erikson describes the process in some detail:

> In psychological terms, identity formation employs a process of simultaneous reflection and observation, a process taking place on all levels of mental functioning, by which the individual judges himself in the light of what he perceives to be the way in which others judge him in comparison to themselves and to a typology significant to them; while he judges their way of judging him in the light of how he perceives himself in comparison to them and to types that have become relevant to him.
>
> (Erikson, 1968, pp. 22–3)

A process of mutual reflection back and forth between actors occurs (cf. Cooley, 1964; Mead, 1934; Lacan, 1949). It is evident how easily Erikson may then posit his 'ego' in a developmental schema of interaction, mutuality and communality. The centre of the individual (here seen as the ego) is both the director of the personality and part of the interwoven fabric of a community of egos, all sustaining and reflecting one another. Always twofold, actor and interactor, the ego represents the fluidity of the psycho-social:

> One can only conclude that the functioning ego, while guarding individuality, is far from isolated, for a kind of communality links egos in a mutual activation. Something in the ego process, then, and something in the social process is – well, identical.
>
> (Erikson, 1968, p. 224)

And finally in discussing identity, as we now see, we cannot separate personal growth and communal change, nor can we separate the identity crisis in individual life and contemporary crises in historical development because the two help to define each other and are truly relative to each other.

(Erikson, 1968, p. 23)

However, what is lacking in Erikson's formulations is a view of the social field as greater than an infinite series of self-reflective mirrors. He lacks a view of the social as a system over and above the set of interactive players that it contains at any one time. His own writing hints at this lack, but quickly moves away from a full consideration. This is evident, for example, when he recognizes a social authority but does not extend it beyond the given here and now:

Man's need for a psychosocial identity is anchored in nothing less than his sociogenetic evolution. It has been said (by Waddington) that authority-accepting is what characterizes man's sociogenetic evolution. I would submit that identity formation is inseparable from this, for only within a defined group identity can true authority exist ... psychosocial identity is necessary as the anchoring of man's transient existence in the here and now. That it is transient does not make it expendable.

(Erikson, 1968, pp. 41–2)

To return to an earlier point, Erikson's ideas contain the central proposition that individual subjectivities are equated to biography, i.e., to personal history shaped in a community (hence the reference to the personal lives of James and Freud). In other terms, identity is equated with a transient intersubjectivity, and individual change proceeds invariably with historical change. He fails, however, to elucidate the proposition that socio-cultural evolution occurs within a symbolic system partially independent of the transient here and now of individual reflective egos. Such a symbolic system (e.g., a language, or system of rituals) supports the players of the moment both temporally and structurally. Erikson misses this point because although he stresses the social, the interpersonal and those momentary reflections of culture in present configurations, he fails to see a symbolic system independent of biography. Hence he has recourse only to a genetic/social structuring of history, and sees Freud's own writings as a biographical product, rather than an enunciation of a symbolic position.

LACAN

Lacan does not speak specifically of identity. It is safe to assume, however, that insofar as identity is conceptualized as a recognizable integrated whole across time and situations, it could be seen as pertaining to the ego. And, indeed, Lacan's discussions of the ego contain much that refers to identifications. It may well be that 'Lacan's concern for the larger philosophical questions allows him at times to subsume the results of some of the American empirical psychoanalytic enquirers, even while dismissing their techniques as reification' (Kurzweil, 1980, p. 144). And, in a sense, much that is said about the ego in American psychoanalysis by authors such as Sullivan (1953) (whose interpersonal approach was recognized by Lacan), and by Kohut (1971; 1977) and Kernberg (1976) (whose work on narcissism invokes a close examination of the Imaginary register) is not antithetical to a reading of Lacan's work. It is simply that, for Lacan, the place of the ego, and consequently our perspective of its nature and role within the psyche, is completely shifted. Instead of being the central aspect of the psyche (with its 'executive' tasks, e.g., of 'reality testing'and 'integrating'), the ego becomes the centre of the Imaginary, one of the three systemic registers of experience advocated by Lacan. The ego is relegated from the core of the psyche to become, once more, one of its agencies, as it was for Freud (1923).

Indeed this *is* the famous 'return to Freud' who asserted that the individual was multidetermined, overdetermined, split, divided and elusive within a field of interactive agencies. A single, central 'self' was never asserted.

The Lacanian ego is, nonetheless, a complex structure. In contrast to a derivation synonymous with individuality or 'self', it is fundamentally and genetically an agency arising not from a simple and central subjectivity, but from and through another. This ego is integrally tied to what Lacan described as 'the mirror stage' (Lacan, 1949). This stage occurs during infancy, some time between six and 18 months, and is indicated by the 'jouissance' shown by the infant at the apprehension of his or her own image in the mirror. Lacan reads this reaction of the infant as the recognition of a wholeness not readily and immediately felt in the everyday experience of the child, whose existence to this point has been, rather, one of unintegrated experiences, sensations, perceptions and movements:

> The fact is that the total form of the body by which the subject anticipates in a mirage the maturation of his power is given to him only as Gestalt, that is to say in an exteriority in which this form is certainly more constituent than constituted, but in which it appears to him above all in a contrasting size that fixes it and in a symmetry that inverts it, in contrast with the turbulent movements that the subject feels are animating him.
>
> (Lacan, 1949, p. 2)

The possibility of integrated wholeness is presented to the child in his own image. The spectral image is of a being biologically and spiritually akin to the other humans that the child observes. This image seems to *be* the other that is yet himself, that demonstrates his wholeness and power, yet has an alien 'otherness' about it. Narcissus, of course, recognized the otherness but failed fully to see the necessary difference between self and that other (Hamilton, 1979). The mirror stage infant, on the other hand, rejoices in having 'found himself', and introjects or identifies with the spectral image which will become the cornerstone of his developing ego, aiding the experience of integration. However, from that moment, integration can be bought only at the expense of a 'méconnaissance' with respect to that original alienation.

> Our view is that the essential function of the ego is very nearly that systemic refusal to acknowledge reality which French Analysis refers to in talking about the psychoses.
>
> (Lacan, 1953a, p. 12)

That mirror into which the infant gazes becomes the mirror leading into the realm of the Imaginary, which contains not only imagination, fantasy and dream imagery, but also the representations (in both conscious and unconscious thought) of all that we construct as our reality: our perceptions and our general way of apprehending our lives, attitudes and beliefs. Simultaneously gazing back at the child are those myriads of others that came to make up Erikson's (1968) community of egos. That is, those others meaningful throughout life, dominated by the (m)other who first confirmed the child in intersubjectivity, an intersubjectivity that can be maintained only by entry into the 'Symbolic'. If not, intersubjectivity is dissolved into a mystical union from which no escape is possible, where only one, and hence none, exists (as was the result for Narcissus, who merged with his image and drowned).

It becomes clear, then, that Lacan will accept the ego as built on an interrelatedness only and always at a remove from personal subjectivity. This view may seem superficially equivalent to Erikson's but is utterly different. Erikson's ego is set in the here and now of communal interplay, without reference to an overriding and historically located 'Law'. Lacan's ego emanates from a socio-cultural basis that has the dual qualities of (a) sychronicity: present interaction, mirroring and systemic interactivity; and (b) diachronicity: an historical-cultural structure, that underwrites any present emanation of its Law. Lacan's appreciation of social structure is in the tradition of the structuralism of Levi-Strauss, and of Jakobson and Saussure who stress the distinction and importance of synchronic and diachronic systems in language (see Chapter 3).

Such a substantial difference in the role and nature of the ego need not cause us to reject the findings of a psychology of personality based on the 'American' readings of Freud. However, on the whole it does turn that psychology about, and provides a superordinate theoretical container which will challenge specific interpretations of the evidence. Furthermore, as an interesting corollary, we can clearly see why a structuralist reading of literature and theory must be opposed to Erikson's biographical stance. For the former, the structural laws are of an importance over and above any one individual who is ultimately shaped within a tradition. The role of the individual author is to play an (Imaginary) variation upon a larger, given theme.

In returning to the theme of identity, we can acknowledge in Lacan's work an ego-identity built on identification with the spectral image and the 'other'. Accordingly, identification is not just one possible outcome of the oedipal conflict (establishing sexual identity), although this is one of its forms. It is a major process involved in establishing the ego itself. Further, Lacan does not force an absolute distinction between pre- and post-oedipal phenomena, except insofar as they form a part of the history of the subject. Both are ultimately structured by the oedipal configuration, present in the culture.

Kagan (1958) describes identification as having three major sources: (a) from a desire for resources held by others, (b) from love relations (i.e., 'anaclitic' identification) and (c) from a desire to master the environment. This latter idea is also found in Lacan's writings. It is the desire for mastery that invigorates the child's efforts:

> This illusion of unity, in which a human being is always looking forward to self-mastery, entails a constant danger of sliding back again into the chaos from which he started; it hangs over the abyss of a dizzy Assent in which one can perhaps see the very essence of Anxiety.
>
> (Lacan, 1953a, p. 15)

Self-mastery and the illusion of identity are, in Lacan, Imaginary possibilities which form the structural basis of man's separation from nature. They also form 'the site where his own milieu is grafted onto him' (Lacan, 1953a, p. 16). For it is in his subjective alienation (through his identifications with the images of others) that the body social operates. Identity is established clearly in the social network of identifications which, in the case of our own society at least, rests ultimately on its language, law and culture, and on the family with its oedipal configuration. That is, it rests on the foundation of the 'Symbolic'. It is ironic that our abilities to build and work within groups are founded on an unbridgeable distance from nature and from our own subjectivity. But such a view is neither more nor less than that which Freud put forward.

FREUD

Lacan's introduction of the Imaginary register, and its distinction from both the Symbolic and the Real, have helped overcome some of the problems found in Erikson's formulation of ego-identity. Whatever is said of the relationship between the writings of Freud and Lacan, a discussion of identity, set within the context of social phenomena, must also include direct reference to the writings of Freud himself.

To Freud, identifications play an important role in the development of the ego and in the theory of libidinal economy. The paper on narcissism (1914) is important in this connection. The paper begins with a question provoked by the observed psychotic phenomenon of withdrawal of libido from the external world. The question so raised concerns the fate of the withdrawn libido. Freud's answer is that:

The libido that has been withdrawn from the external world has been directed to the ego and thus gives rise to an attitude which may be called narcissism.

(Freud, 1914, p. 75)

After terming this 'secondary' narcissism ('superimposed upon a primary narcissism'), he raises an important distinction between ego- and object-libido. Libidinal economy is stressed and the libido is described as flowing out towards objects or being drawn towards the ego:

We see also, broadly speaking, an antithesis between ego-libido and object-libido. The more the one is employed, the more the other becomes depleted.

(Freud, 1914, p. 76)

Moreover the quality of ego-libido is distinct, not merely a displacement from object to object as in a sublimation. Freud makes it clear (in his critique of Jung's claims) that such a displacement would merely result in the psychology of an 'ascetic anchorite'. This distinctiveness is clear also in his description of neurotic and psychotic processes (Freud, 1924b). In short, Freud views the withdrawal of object-libido as bringing about a change in the subject's relation to reality.

Having traced his distinction between ego- and object-libido, the present purpose leads to some additional remarks made by Freud at the end of this paper. These remarks concern the establishment of the ego and, importantly, of the ego-ideal. He says:

The development of the ego consists in a departure from primary narcissism and gives rise to a vigorous attempt to recover that state. This departure is brought about by means of the displacement of libido on to an ego ideal imposed from without; and satisfaction is brought about from fulfilling this ideal. . . . To be their own ideal once more in regard to sexual no less than other trends, as they were in childhood – this is what people strive to attain as their happiness.

(Freud, 1914, p. 100)

Here the importance of the ego-ideal is established within the complex of libidinal vicissitudes. It is an incorporation of the *social* (that which is 'imposed from without'), and prompts a reading of secondary narcissism in trans-individual terms. Freud then continues by discussing some ideas of libidinal distribution in groups. This discussion is extended and developed in his later work (1921). This was presented briefly in Chapter 3, but requires elaboration now.

Freud on groups

Freud's formulations about groups were influenced by the writings of Le Bon (1920), Trotter (1916) and McDougall (1920), all of whom were keen observers of the changes that occurred in behaviour when people became part of large groups or mobs. However, their observations lacked a clarifying conceptual schema. Following Trotter's (1916) assertion 'that the tendency toward the formation of groups is biologically a continuation of the multicellular character of all the higher organisms' (Freud, 1921, p. 32), Freud develops a basis for a theory of group psychology via his understanding of the psychology of the individual. Nonetheless, Freud's theory of individual psychology in general, and his theory of secondary narcissism in particular, includes the operation of the *social* and necessitates a psychology of the individual located in a transindividual field.

Specifically, it should be recalled that the fate or aim of the libido is to move firstly towards that social scene of objects that cannot help but provide the disappointments that drive it back (transformed) in a reversal upon the ego. Yet, in that journey, the libido finds itself so altered by its object that, when turned inward, it has a 'higher', more social aim which heralds the emergence of the ego-ideal. Freud asserts in his later work (1921, p. 92) that individual and group psychologies are inextricably bound together.

The important point is that during the processes the child (and the adult) becomes libidinally bound to those in the groupings around him or her. Additionally, the idea of identification becomes important. Its importance lies in the 'mutual relations between the object and the ego' (Freud, 1921) which are extended and developed during the various identificatory processes. The 'identity' of the ego-ideal becomes formed because 'identification endeavours to mould a person's own ego after the fashion of the one that has been taken as a model' (Freud, 1921, p. 63). Furthermore, Freud clearly indicates that identification may occur with a loved or hated object, and is mostly limited and partial (in that it 'borrows only one or few aspects'), and may occur without a direct object-relation to the person so copied.

This latter point is illustrated by Freud's example of hysterical contagion whereby girls in a boarding school identify with one particular girl who reacts with hysterical jealousy after receiving a letter from one whom she secretly loves. Freud's point is that the girls wish to be in her place. One ego has seen a point of similarity ('a significant analogy') in another.

The theory is now ripe for an explanation of the formation of groups, although the presence of a leader is an additional requirement because it is the leader who provides the focus for the transformations yet to be described. Such seemingly diverse activities as being in love, hypnosis and group formation involve the substitution of the external object for the ego-ideal of the subject; those processes inherent in that agency are committed (for different periods of time and in differing quantities) to that object. As the lover may give over his judgement to his beloved, as the patient is commanded by the word of the hypnotist, so is the group member subject to the ideals personified in, and pronounced by, his leader.

The two processes are combined. Identification and the substitution of the ego-ideal, itself formed in the social, come together. Thus Freud is able to say:

we are quite in a position to give the formula for the libidinal constitution of groups, or at least of such groups as we have hitherto considered – namely, those that have a leader and have not been able by means of too much 'organization' to acquire secondarily the characteristics of an individual. A primary group of this kind is a number of individuals who have put one and the same object in the place of their ego-ideal and have consequently identified themselves with one another in their ego.

(Freud, 1921, pp. 79–80)

Although Freud first described the ego-ideal as an internalized watching agency, and later as playing an important role in secondary narcissism, he is now conceptualizing it as the agency linking the ego firmly to the social. The libidinal ties of the group have their origins in ego-libido; however, object-libido links the ego to objects in a qualitatively different manner. This is stressed in Freud's reference to the relations between sexual love and the group. Although common group activity (which involves the group bonding and identifications described) is present in many human activities, 'the one great exception is provided by the sexual act, in which a third person is at best superfluous and in the extreme case is condemned to a state of painful expectancy' (Freud, 1921, p. 92).

It is these two polarities, i.e., object-libido in relation to the object, and ego-libido in relation to narcissism, that Lacan emphasizes in his Schema R (a schematic representation of the relations between aspects of the psyche within the three registers of experience, Lacan, 1959, p. 197). Schema R represents these polarities as two lines stretching between the subject and object, and the subject and ego-ideal. Freud has shown us that it is the ego-libido/narcissism connection that lies at the basis of group life. His explanation may be distinguished from a theory of groups based on an interpersonal psychology of object-libido.

A full recognition of the place of 'identity' in the work of Freud may draw together many lines of argument. Identity is clearly seen as a social phenomenon, embedded in the agency of the ego-ideal which links the person to the social and the individual to the group. The links are mediated by a process of libidinal transformation which takes the path of reversed object-libido. Within its narcissistic adherence to the subject, object-libido carries with it the mark of the *social* (transformed object love) and forms the ego-ideal. A secondary incorporation of the *social*, via identifications, and the substitution of an object for ego-ideal, completes the libidinal circuit.

Identifications play a complex role in all of this. Some stand developmentally between primary narcissism and object relations, and constitute the 'first emotional tie' between subject and object (Freud, 1921, p. 60); others stand as the basic form of relatedness between subjects who may have no direct libidinal connections. Hence different forms of identification are involved in different social links. This is no simple social determinism. It reveals a layered complex of forces operating within an historical process, that is, the living history of a social being.

THE IDENTITY OF THE GROUP

The present argument has followed, thus far, the processes whereby an individual gains identity. Following Freud, we see that the infusion of the subject into the social arena brings about the development of the ego-ideal (understood as part of the superego in Freud's later formulations), a type of internal alter-ego attracting narcissistic impulses. Further, the relatedness of individual identities to other identities in group life is evidenced in the transindividual displacements effected by the leader (or leading idea). If we are to take Freud seriously, we must then regard the relatedness of individuals in groups with reference to four major dimensions.

1 Firstly, individuals may be tied to one another through both direct and aim-inhibited love. This is the dimension of object-libido, rarely expressed directly in group life, but common in its aim of inhibited or 'tender' form (e.g., friendship ties). This may be termed the socio-emotional dimension of the group, and may also include ties that involve the death instinct and its aggressive derivatives (e.g., relations of enmity). In the group object ties tend to be expressed through one-to-one interpersonal relations.

2 Secondly, group members are bound together through their narcissistic ego-libido which finds expression via the ego-ideal and its accompanying identifications. Freud specified identification as between those who share a common ego-ideal in the form of a leader. This model proposes identifications as (a) partial, (b) grounded on some perceived common characteristic, and (c) based on the other having a characteristic desired by the subject. The leader is leader because s/he commands identifications, for many, if not all group members. Moreover, we see that leadership functions may occur in a configuration which itself commands identifications and may not reside in any one particular individual. This configuration may be understood as the *symbolic leader*. It includes the common aim or primary task of the group, which is most often embodied in the leader. Thus this (perhaps unconscious) dimension relates to the group tasks.

3 Thirdly, group members may be bound by common affects (e.g., of jealousy, fear or anger, Freud, 1921, pp. 64–5). This bonding includes the identifications described by Anna Freud (1946) such as identification with the aggressor. Such an identification seems based on an aggressive identification against the ego, the unconscious line of reason being: (a) s/he persecutes/hates me; (b) I am despicable and I hate myself; and (c) we are, therefore, alike. Thus the identification is on the basis of self-loathing. In this sense, the subject lives in the identified ego-ideal and projects the loathed aspects of him or herself into those peers whom s/he now

persecutes. However, it is hard to describe the dynamics of such identifications without reference to libido theory; it seems that narcissistic ego-libido is involved in the service of self-preservation (the loathing is projected). Most likely, this form of identification involves both the libidinal and the aggressive instincts. Nonetheless, where fear and anger form a strong basis for identification, we can expect a dynamic that is distinct from one based more exclusively on libidinal identifications.

In such a case, leadership and devotion to the task are based on the viscissitudes of aggressive energy, directed either outward towards others or inward towards the ego. In some ways this third dimension parallels the former two, and is perhaps more properly designated as two (aggressive) aspects of those dimensions (i.e., aggression may be object- or ego-directed).

4 Finally, group members may be bound by their common resolution of the problems they face in expressing and structuring their libidinal and aggressive aims. A group resolution could arise from the nature of the group task and ideals, and may evolve into a long term group structure (see, for example, Freud's discussion of the church and the army, 1921). A group resolution may also emerge from the common defensive stance taken towards particular anxieties arising within the group. For a fuller description of these processes we need to turn to work such as that of Jaques (1955) and Menzies (1970) who describe how groups and organizations develop institutionalized defences in order to contain the anxieties inherent in their tasks and social structures. For example, Menzies' (1970) study of a large London hospital led her to conclude that the nursing staff employed several defences against anxieties that arose due to their intimate involvement with patients. Potential intimacy with the sick and dying, she argued, arouses deeply unconscious urges and phantasies involving libidinal strivings and fear of death. The consequent anxiety becomes difficult to manage for the nurse because her work world actually approximates such phantasies. Some of the defences employed to ameliorate the anxiety were professional distancing, devolvement of authority up the hierarchy, and division of labour on the basis of 'task' (rather than the nursing of 'whole' patients).

In proposing the abovementioned dimensions, it is not suggested that they operate separately in the group. Rather, they are the underlying dynamics of transindividual activity. Members may love or hate those with whom they identify in the various ways. In fact, it would be most improbable that they would have a neutral stance.

IDENTITY IN THE INTERGROUP CONTEXT

However, the identity of groups cannot be understood in these terms alone. As Breakwell (1983, p. 22) points out, 'the origins of the substantive identity of any group have to be examined at two levels: the social and the psychological.' On the one hand, a group develops its identity from its position in the matrix of intergroup relations; on the other, from the identities of its members and how they, in turn, view the group. It is the extent to which members are identified with one another, at the level of the ego-ideal, that influences the group's cohesion and identity from the inside, and that provides an emotional underpinning for the work of the group. This is also important for the group as reference group, i.e., in sustaining individual identity. To understand this basis for cohesion is to understand the observation that groups tied by sentience alone may neither constitute good working groups nor develop a long-term identity. This 'psychological' identity from the 'inside', as it were, lies in close relation to the work of the group: to its phenomenal primary task (Rice, 1963). Kellerman (1981) also relates group cohesion to the type of superego controls utilized collectively by the members.

Conversely, identity may be superimposed on the group from external sources. Aggregates, such as 'aborigines' or 'males', may be labelled with particular characteristics. This has an effect both on members of those aggregates and on those groups that share in their perceived characteristics via their membership. For example, any particular group of men will be influenced by prevailing societal attributions directed towards the aggregate 'men'. In addition to the labelling and stereotyping of aggregates, the more direct attribution of characteristics to particular groups by other particular groups often occurs more projectively than veridically. Also, it should be mentioned that the shaping of a group's identity from its surrounding social network is, in itself, bound and delimited by the general laws within the wider social system (e.g., the values of the larger social system).

Furthermore, it should be remembered that the identity of a group with respect to its environment is constructed by an observer (Maturana, 1970). The phenomenology of the group identity may be viewed as its structural ontogeny independent of its interactions with an observer. In this sense, its organizational identity is maintained via structures that compensate for outside disturbances. To the system itself, these changes are always intra-systemic and proceed from an already existent state. That is, the group members feel themselves to constitute the same group through a variety of changes. The environment is part of the domain of the observer's descriptions and, hence, has a causal role within that domain alone. It is the members as observers (of their own and other groups) that view group identity 'from the outside'.

In ending this section it may be said that a close analysis of the economics of libido theory in group life has led us directly to the familiar dimensions of socio-emotional relations, task relations and defensive structure, the three main dimensions fundamental to social psychology in its consideration of groups. Of these, it seems that it is the *task* dimension that is most closely linked to the role structure of the group, through the process of identification with the leader. The next section will examine leadership more closely.

LEADERSHIP AND AUTHORITY IN PSYCHOANALYTIC THEORY

In psychoanalytic theory, the father is normally viewed as the original authority figure, and later authorities are regarded as transference figures. Their authority rests on the original lessons learned from the child's relations with his or her father. However, these relations are influenced by more than the individual's own personal history. Implicit in Freud's thought is the distinction between *relations* (i.e., structural positions) and *relationships* (i.e., interactions). For Freud, the oedipal complex forms a set of universal structures within which specific relationships may occur. In this sense the oedipal *relation* places constraints on actual *relationships* with parents, and this results in a variety of outcomes (Freud, 1924a).

In Freudian theory, the structure of authority relations is basic to the organization of all groups. For example, Freud (1921) postulated that all leaders derive their authority from a similar source. He established his argument by way of myth or analogy. The mythical primal horde enacted the oedipal structure. A tyrannical father dominated the primitive group and monopolized the women. His power was based on coercion, rewards, threat, punishment and possibly charisma (cf. Schopler, 1965; French and Raven, 1959). These were his personal powers. The rebellion of the sons, their murder of the autocratic father, and their subsequent guilt, remorse and identification with him, established the particular group structure described by Freud (see p. 216 above). The authority of the father was most deeply established only after his death, because the identifications based on remorse *legitimated* his position at an unconscious level.

The form of leadership described by the myth might best be seen as *symbolic leadership*. According to Freud, modern humans do not enact the oedipal complex. For the most part it is retained as a set of unconscious and repressed thoughts. In Lacan's terms, oedipal relations form an integral part of the unconscious system of signifiers that structure us as subjects (Lacan, 1977). Lacan regards the original source of authority as the symbolic father, or as the signifier 'the name of the father'. This signifier is instituted as a symbolic organizer of culture, i.e., of that which distinguishes modern subjects from primitive members of the primal horde. Authority, then, is predominantly signified by the symbolic or dead father (Lacan, 1977). As with Freud, Lacan views relationships with actual fathers as constrained by unconscious oedipal relations. We can also expect that relationships with actual leaders are constrained by unconscious authority relations.

Freud, Lacan and Bion examine authority mainly in terms of the family and the small group. Rieff (1966) considers authority in the culture at large where, he argues, it takes three major forms: the interdictory, the remissive and the transgressive. Although he describes these mainly in the context of the psychoanalytic movement and religious authority, they may be used to describe authority in other contexts. The *interdictory* authority is that authority representing the major interdicts or values of the culture (or of the elite or powerful members of the culture). These are normally stated in terms of responsibilities and prohibitions. Moses presents a classic example of the interdictory authority, and the ten commandments a classic example of interdicts. Such authority is harsh and uncompromising because it tends to represent moral imperatives and absolute values.

In order for actual societies (or groups and organizations) to cohere through the inevitable deviations from the interdicts, a *remissive* aspect of authority is also normally present. Rieff argues that all religions have both interdictory and remissive elements. If sin is the consequence of transgression, then society must have means by which it is forgiven, or even acceptable. A culture tends, according to Rieff, to be predominantly interdictory or remissive and these two forms of authority tend to alternate or to balance each other.

The third form of authority is the *transgressive* (Rieff, 1982). This form tends to emerge when the former balance of interdictory and remissive authority is unable to satisfy most members' needs, wishes and values. The transgressive authority represents a new set of values that challenges the old order. Although a particular structuring of the society or group or a particular set of values may predominate for a long period of time, transgressive authorities may mobilize the energies of sub-groupings within the more dominant culture. The processes of more general legitimation may eventually render the transgressive into a new interdictory mode; however, many transgressive authorities exist without ever gaining widespread legitimation. They have influence outside legitimate structures.

The idea of legitimation (of authority) is central to many discussions of leadership in sociology and social psychology (Follett, 1941; Weber, 1947; Bierstedt, 1950; Hills, 1968; Gibb, 1968; and Scott 1981). However, the task of defining leadership, power and authority is complex and has been problematic in these disciplines. What follows presents some hypotheses about the nature of group identity, leadership and authority. These are derived from psychoanalytic theory and supported by research in social psychology (see Appendix A). These hypotheses are placed in the context of a working definition of a psychological group, derived from earlier chapters. The empirical work reported in Chapters 7–11 will attempt to explore their usefulness.

RELATIONS BETWEEN IDENTITY, LEADERSHIP AND AUTHORITY

Working definition of a group

Firstly, it is proposed that a psychological group be defined as *'a system whose elements are related by transindividual processes and whose present structure is directed toward, and motivated by, phenomenal and unconscious tasks'*. This definition includes the operation of transindividual processes (Chapters 2 and 3) but these are not defined, because their specific nature arises with the group system as it emerges (Wisdom, 1970). The definition also emphasizes 'structure' as task directed (Rice, 1965); that is, the elements (e.g., particular roles or positions) are related in the context of conscious and unconscious tasks (Freud, 1921; Bion, 1961). It is also implied that structures and elements change according to the nature of the particular group tasks, although the system, *qua* organization, may remain constant through a variety of structural transformations (Maturana and Varela, 1972; and Chapter 10).

Identification as a major transindividual group process

Secondly, it is proposed that identification is one major transindividual process involved in groups (Freud, 1914, 1921). It explains how group members are libidinally related to their (Symbolic) leaders and tasks, and it relates groups as systems to the biological and psychological aspects of individuals who are also group members.

Authority

Thirdly, it is proposed that *authority* is related to the tasks of the group in two different ways. One way is through conscious legitimation. Members and leaders may be given legitimate power and/or authority to fulfill certain roles and undertake certain tasks. The other way is through unconscious legitimation. This process refers to the attribution of symbolic leadership to particular roles in the group. This symbolic leadership may be regarded as a signifier within the Symbolic (Lacan, 1977), or a mythical role which members attribute to one person for defensive reasons (Gemmill, 1986). Consciously legitimated leaders (authorities) may or may not be attributed symbolic leadership. If a group has no consciously legitimated leader, or if it has many, the attribution of symbolic leadership may be problematic. However, leadership still remains an important signifier open to signification. In contrast, a particular member may be attributed symbolic leadership (consciously or unconsciously) but not be formally legitimated.

Identification with the symbolic leader

Fourthly, it is proposed that the processes of identification in groups are directed towards the symbolic authority (leader) more than to the formally or consciously legitimated leader. Normally, this distinction is not apparent because it is the consciously legitimated leader who is attributed with symbolic leadership. However, when this is not the case, the group structures will be directed by the tasks of, and identifications with, the symbolic leader, who may then become the transgressive leader (Rieff, 1966; 1982).

Significations of the symbolic leader

Finally, it is proposed that the signifier 'symbolic leader' has many significations (meanings). These become apparent only within the history of the group. As with all signifiers, the signification lies in the 'signifying chain' (Lacan, 1957), that is, in the actual *relations between* actual group members.

In the present work, it is argued that the study group consultant has legitimate power due to his or her leadership of the group-that-is-joined (Chapter 4). In this case the legitimation comes from several sources. Firstly, s/he is legitimized by the institution within which s/he works. This form of legitimation corresponds to Scott's (1981) 'authorization' and is consciously understood by the group members. Secondly, s/he is legitimated by the members' conscious acceptance of his or her authority and their (conscious and unconscious) wishes that s/he lead them. This corresponds to Scott's (1981) 'endorsement' and is a process probably understandable to members. Thirdly, s/he is legitmated by the myth of the group-that-is-joined. This legitimation occurs at a more unconscious level and involves transference processes on the part of the members. It engages those processes whereby s/he is instituted as the symbolic leader.

The longitudinal study presented in Part III will attempt to explore the usefulness of these proposals. Whilst keeping Breakwell's two aspects of group identity in mind, they will examine group identity 'from the inside' (Breakwell, 1983), i.e., the focus will be on the perceptions of group members about themselves and their groups. That these perceptions will be influenced by external attributions is inevitable. However, given the approach to groups outlined in Chapter 3, it is expected that the members themselves will contain elements of the externally attributing agencies, i.e., through their membership of other groups. Thus this allows at least some comment on the external attribution of identity. Before these empirical studies, however, methodological issues need to be considered more closely.

Chapter 6

Research methodology for group systems

This chapter will attempt to examine appropriate methodology for studying groups as systems and to argue for the use of particular methods of observation that allow for the application of transindividual concepts. Following the ideas presented in Chapter 2, it is once more noted that it is useful to see systems as defined from within, and explained from without. This implies that definitions may best emerge through a careful analysis of the internal *form* and, hence, meaning of the group's internal relations. Explanations may then emerge in an analysis that employs theoretical concepts that attempt to explain the structures so defined.

These arguments act as a methodological background to the empirical work to be reported. The entities and relations to be studied, the attributes to be examined, and the methods of observing and analysing the resultant data will then be presented. Because the present work attempts to explain the group data from two distinctly different theoretical perspectives (viz. those of psychoanalysis and social psychology), the research methods also reflect those differences. The former perspective predominates here, and the latter serves as a support and extension.

RESEARCH METHODS FOR GROUPS

THE PHILOSOPHICAL BASES

Following Von Bertalanffy's formulation of a 'general systems theory', Glaser (1984) proposes that all systems, whether in the social, biological or physical sciences, are subject to similar analyses. Indeed, the level of our knowledge of systems in this general sense is such that he feels present research is best concerned 'not with our powers to predict but with our powers to define and to define accurately', as Sommerhoff says in reference to theoretical biology (Sommerhoff, 1969). This process of definition seems to be most appropriate when the entities to be studied are seen to be complexly organized (Emery and

Trist, 1965), and when we wish to understand the form and structure of that organization (Katz and Kahn, 1978). Defining form and structure requires the use of structured descriptive methods. Such methods also form the basis of, e.g., many phenomenological research methods (Merleau-Ponty, 1962; Rogers, 1967; Misiak and Sexton, 1973).

These methods are based on *formal* (i.e., causes in terms of structural, synchronic patterning) and *final* (i.e., causes related to the anticipation of implicit outcomes of present predicates) models of causality (Rychlak, 1968; 1977) and may be regarded as basic to definition and formal analysis. Final causes may require some explanation here. The seeming 'teleology' of final causation does not invoke an actual future but one anticipated by the implications, inductions, deductions, etc., that stem dialectically from present 'precedent meanings' (Rychlak, 1977, p. 311). Implications which may direct future behaviour are regarded as synchronically present in structures.

This approach is similar to some explanations within structural linguistics (Saussure, 1959; Chomsky, 1965). For example, structural linguistics holds the view that the meaning of a sentence is not clear to the listener until the whole sentence has been constructed. In many ways the meaning of an utterance is retrospectively gained. For example, in the sentence, 'the dog was *chased by* the man', the verb participle and the preposition retrospectively provide the relation of *dog* to *chase*. Meanings are also anticipated both by the speaker and the listener. In the example given, the words 'the dog' predispose us to hear or utter other words that are syntactically and semantically plausible (Caramazza and Zurif, 1976; Linebarger et al., 1983). 'The dog was chased in the man' or 'the dog was married by the cup' are less likely constructions.

'Causes' in linguistics, then, seem to be 'softly determined', because linguistic productions are *constrained* by antecedent and by anticipated structures, at the phonological as well as the sentential level (Jakobson and Halle, 1956). This idea of 'constraint', involving both anticipatory and retrospective attribution of meaning, will be important during discussions of behaviour in groups.

With Rychlak, we may also constructively view all explanation as ultimately tautological, that is, as involved in the extension of meaning on either side of a relation. He invokes Whitehead and Russell's (1963) argument that mathematical proofs are tautological, and develops the idea that explanations involve varying degrees of description some of which are traditionally called 'descriptions', while others are traditionally called 'explanations'. Material causes may be seen as explanations, in terms of the extension of the meanings of substances; efficient causes, as the extension of meanings and relations through time; formal causes, as the extension of meaning in structure; and final causes, as the extension of meanings implicit in predicates (i.e., as an analysis of constraints). Rychlak's is a view, then, that gives a central position in modern psychological theory to what are essentially explanations in terms of linguistic phenomena.

The implications of this work for psychological methodology include the proposition that psychological explanations may legitimately include all four types of causal explanations (material, efficient, formal and final). The appropriateness of any one becomes the important question. Methods involving rigorous description seem appropriate for those research tasks that require an examination of structure and which look at structural changes in systems. This is because systemic change involves second order change ('Kierkegaardian leaps'), when the system is regarded as an entity, i.e., when the change is not of the parts within the system, but is change *of* the system.

METHODS AVAILABLE

There are a variety of strategies and methods available to the researcher studying small groups in a descriptive manner (Forgas, 1979; 1983; Friedrichs and Ludtke, 1975). Early work included methods of participant observation and interviewing (Whyte, 1943; Adorno et al., 1950) which, with refinements, are still popular (Harré and Secord, 1972; Argyle, 1976; Billig, 1978; Marsh et al., 1978). Interviews are particularly useful as an exploratory method (Gordon, 1975; Stewart and Cash, 1985), and as a method for clarifying and extending the understanding of processes observed in group sessions.

An extension of this kind of research is the 'action research' model (Clark, 1972; Bain, 1981). In this model the researcher systematically observes the functioning of a group or organization, and then uses the results of his observations to bring about carefully monitored changes in a collaborative manner with the client organization. The results of these systemic changes are then observed (Gilmore and Krantz, 1985; Bain, 1981; Trist and Bamforth, 1951; Cherns and Clark, 1976; Miller, 1979; Bowers and Seashore, 1971). This method allows the researcher to engage in the systematic manipulation of factors within the field, and to observe their effects. Extraneous factors are excluded or controlled where possible. Also their role in the formal structure may be examined.

Content or structural analysis of interactions in groups provides another method of research into group phenomena. This may be done through direct observation (e.g., Bales, 1950; 1970), or through the analysis of transcribed dialogue (Slater, 1966; Mills, 1967; Tuckman, 1965; Mann, 1966; Gibbard et al., 1974; Harré, 1979). Bales' (1950) interaction process analysis method, for example, categorizes interactions by a series of parameters such as 'asking questions', 'making statements', or 'showing anger'. These categories are applied either directly, during the observation process, or to an analysis of transcribed dialogue. Many such methods of processing interactions are available (Amidon and Hough, 1967).

The direct measurement of some aspects of the individual members is another method of studying groups. Bales, for example, derives role descriptions through questionnaires. His results by this method are comparable to the results that he gains from direct structured observations (Bales, 1950;

1970). Schutz (1958) has developed a set of scales that measure interpersonal 'traits' by questionnaire. Forgas (1982; 1983) measures cognitive representations of social interactions. Similarly, role construct repertory tests (Kelly, 1955) can provide a measure of the constructions used by individuals to view others. Grid methods may be adapted to measure the constructs used by members to evaluate a variety of elements, including other individuals and aspects of the total group. They produce data in a form that is readily amenable to analysis by correlation (Slater, 1977; Rathod, 1981; Yorke, 1985).

Although the measurement of traits and interpersonal interactions does not directly measure transindividual phenomena, it provides a descriptive basis from which the group level data may be derived, e.g., by conceptual or statistical methods.

THE PROBLEM OF MEASUREMENT

The ideas presented here are central to the immediate pragmatics of research in social and group psychology because this is an arena where subjects constantly interact with the results of their own observations and define the systems within which they are embedded.

The methods of research outlined above require the identification of entities (e.g., groups) and attributes (e.g., interactions between members). Although it may seem self-evident that 'things' or 'systems' (including human groups and organizations) exist and have measurable attributes, philosophers of science, researchers and psychometricians alike find this problematic (Bachelard, 1934; Katz and Kahn, 1978; Forgas, 1979; Young, 1984). For example, data may not be collected until the boundaries of the group or organization are clearly distinguished. Questions such as 'Which characteristics of this individual belong to his group membership and which to his extra-group activities or affiliations?' are examples of boundary issues to be addressed, even though they are not always easily answered. Appeals made directly to the individuals involved do not always help, because individuals' descriptions themselves are subject to stereotypes that inaccurately define a group.

It follows, then, that the raw data at the very basis of any research method are collected by the researcher in the form of measurable attributes of *already distinguished entities or systems*, even if that distinction is not made overt. 'Entities and relations (or the attributes distilled from relations) are the primary perceptions or proto-constructs out of which more refined constructs and scientific concepts are derived and elaborated' (Cattell, cited in Snyder, Law and Hattie, 1985). Consequently, before attempting to measure an attribute, the entities or systems to be studied should be defined.

However, the measurability of attributes is itself problematic. This is largely because 'data in themselves do not possess measurement characteristics.

Rather the measurement characteristics which appear to be possessed by a particular set of data are actually dependent on the interaction of the data with the model chosen to describe the data' (Young, 1984, p. 59). This implies that we never 'discover' attributes, but that we create them through our methods of observation, which themselves are measurements (i.e., insofar as they categorize or quantify). This problem has parallels to the above-mentioned problem of the observation of entities, which are also abstractions of the observer (Maturana and Varela, 1980). Observational methods define and create entities and their attributes. It is this circularity that leads Rychlak (1977) to the idea that, although important empirical facts may be established within a descriptive domain, all research is ultimately tautological. Further-more, the 'entities' of any scientific discourse, whose attributes may be identified and measured, were once the collection of unsystematized observations of former researchers.

Nonetheless, once the researcher has conceptually defined the entities, relations and attributes to be studied, there remain some further pragmatic problems. The study of groups, and of social phenomena in general, is subject to 'the data problem' in social science (Harré, 1979). This refers to the problem of the social construction of data. To Harré, the meanings of most social exchanges or actions are not self-evident but depend on context and the interpretations of the actors, including the social scientist observer. For example, studying suicide is especially difficult (Harré, 1979, p. 114). To become a suicide statistic, i.e., to qualify as a 'subject' for the study, requires only those who make account of the act (e.g., policemen, doctors, family members, witnesses), and their accounts are in themselves social acts. If we take a particular example of seeming suicide, we may find that some people prefer to account for the death as an accident, whilst others accept or even prefer the idea of suicide. These accounts may well be affected by religious beliefs or by personal or pecuniary motives. Essentially, the very datum of research into suicide – a suicide – is best defined by reference to motives that are part of the subject's total life history. Yet this may only be reached through the accounts of others. Although the study of suicide highlights the data problem (because the central actor cannot make his or her own account available), Harré believes that all social research is subject to this problem because there is no reason to believe that actors make the most valid accounts of their own actions even when these accounts are available.

Harré's attempts to overcome this problem have led him to employ methods that rest upon some important distinctions within (punctuations of) social life. To begin with, he distinguishes movements from actions, and actions from acts. This is imperative because in the process of social interpretation, movements are *interpreted* as actions, and actions are interpreted as acts. In Harré's words: 'Actions are the meanings of movements and utterances; acts are the meaning of actions' (Harré, 1979, p. 64). For example, the action of shaking hands may be interpreted as an act of friendship, a confirmation of a wager, a gesture of conciliation, or a dismissal, amongst other things, depending on the context.

From this primary distinction, Harré builds up, step by step, a hierarchy of categories of social interpretation. To understand the meaning of a social event or episode (which could end up as a statistic), each level of interpretation needs articulation within a total setting. Episodes are identified 'by reference to the acts performed within them', and acts are performed through 'conventionally grounded' sequences of actions, movements and utterances (Harré, 1979, p. 59). It is the 'conventional' meaning that is important here. Conventional meanings may only be surmised by the researcher, from the social history surrounding the events examined, and may change from group to group.

A second distinction drawn by Harré is between acts and accounts, the latter being 'the explanatory speech produced by social actors' (Harré, 1979, p. 127). The analysis of group dialogue involves the analysis of both acts and accounts.

It might be useful to view Harré's methods as a systematic organization of observations, which identifies social redundancies (in actions, acts and episodes) and consequently establishes meaning. This general approach could be applied to the study of groups. A group case study by this method, for example, would involve the segmenting of the history of the group into particular moments or states that may be seen to contain meaning. A pragmatic problem of great importance would then arise. It could be articulated by the following questions: Who segments the group history? Is it the researcher who observes the group text from the perspective of his or her theories? Is it the group member who, through his or her own actions (and as observer of these, through his or her accounts of her actions), helps shape the group processes that then seem 'naturally' punctuated?

Intuition, and the limits of a positivistic science, may prompt us to seek the organization of particular moments or states in the particular laws and regularities that occur across time. This is a respectable enough undertaking if we do not lose sight of the fact that nothing ever occurs twice and that history follows a one way path, even if part of a larger system. For, if repetition holds the key to knowledge, it is because our ability to recognize repeated events rests on our powers of symbolization (Freud, 1920). From this, it seems that the meaning of a moment in history rests not on a regularity in physical nature but on the *symbolic value* assigned to that moment. It is in this sense that a theory of trauma (e.g., Freud's), where meaning is assigned by the individual (or group) to events punctuated in highly memorable ways, is able to provide explanations not available to a theory of habit alone.

Group members, for example, punctuate the history of their groups and establish meanings. The researcher may examine the accounts of members for evidence of this. Moreover, this very process of segmenting the group's history, and hence endowing it with new meanings, leads members to act in new ways. The researcher is hard pressed to choose other than to examine the organization imposed on the group, by group members, through this process. The group's progress is anticipated, effected and retrospectively given meaning, through the accounts of members. As with the contrast between general psychological processes and linguistic phenomena (made in the discussion of Rychlak's work, above), a contrast may be made between social psychological and linguistic processes, as Harré (1979) and Forgas (1979) make clear.

Despite the problems outlined above, careful description requires an account of the 'punctuation' employed by the researcher. Glaser (1984), for example, offers some 'heuristics for systems mapping'. He states: 'In order to talk meaningfully about systems, it is necessary to define the nature of the outcome, its dimensional manifolds, the positional values of the elements within those manifolds, and the "system form" into which those elements are organized' (Glaser, 1984, p. 488).

Methods of segmenting group texts seem to follow Glaser's suggestions. For example, the 'nature of the outcome' may be represented by the topics raised in the group dialogue (or by any other outcome identified in the segmenting process). The 'dimensional manifolds' that may be used in the analysis may include, for example, the concepts of integration, identity and group realization as adapted from Winnicott (1945) and discussed in Chapter 4. The positional values of the elements in groups are complex and changing, but they may be indicated by such phenomena as the valencies of particular roles within particular group states (Bion, 1961), or the particular emotional polarities present at any one time. (This idea reflects Saussure's idea of linguistic value [1959] discussed in Chapter 3.) Finally the 'system form' of groups may consist of the series of structures and states identified as structuring the originally identified surface outcomes.

Such methods also bear some similarity to the application of phenomeno-logical methods of research in that they involve a rigorous description and definition from within the system (Merleau-Ponty, 1962). But whereas phenomenology in psychology describes human subjectivity as ideally whole and immediate (Misiak and Sexton, 1973), this is not necessary. For example, the view proposed by the present author is one where human subjectivity is seen as complex and split.

Furthermore, the place of human subjectivity in the group-as-a-system, as well as its existence-in-itself, is seen here as problematic. For example, we may, for purposes of study as scientific observers, examine 'roles' within the group system. This requires an objectification of aspects of subjective persons. However, we should not lose sight of its (the role's) connection in the person (i.e., within another system), lest we become entangled in semantic paradoxes. The researcher using the phenomenological approach, unless aware of such risks, may become misled. For if this approach involves a close examination of what *is there*, as Merleau-Ponty says, it should be stressed that what *is there* is not context free but is always structured, in science if not in philosophy, from without, by the symbolic system used in one's descriptions, i.e., by the meta-system. This is because what *is there* for the observer is first delimited by theory, as an entity with attributes. This holds for both substantive theory (Maturana, 1970), and data or measurement theory (Young, 1984). An application of this idea to the study of groups is presented in Smith (1982).

It seems, then, that the regularities observed 'naturally' in social life rest on the organization of historical moments in the symbolic register of experience. That is, they are predicated upon moments of symbolic significance (i.e., having symbolized meaning) to actors/observers in the living system observed. Because of this, all social science research (and perhaps all scientific research insofar as research is a social activity), may be seen as involving the attribution of symbolic qualities to its data (Knorr, 1981).

In concluding this section, it is emphasized that 'entities' and their 'attributes' are considered here as created by the methods of observation employed by the researcher/observer, remembering that in groups the members themselves act as observers constantly redefining the systems within which they act. Research conducted within a systems framework may usefully employ methods that best delineate those patterns that account for redundancies in the system, and that consequently rigorously describe it in an economic manner. In other words, the task is best regarded as 'to define and define accurately', as Sommerhoff (1969) would have it.

THE TASKS OF THE OBSERVER

Given these complexities, the researcher may be seen to have three main tasks to perform.

Firstly, it is his or her task to design a method for observing and defining attributes which aids the development of theory about the systems concerned.

Secondly, it is his or her task to observe and describe according to the method outlined. This will involve the use of meta-abstractions which serve economically to draw together many observations. Examples of such abstractions are scientific constructs, developed through semantic ordering and classification, and descriptive statistics of varying degrees of complexity, developed through mathematical ordering. Inferential statistics may also aid in the descriptive process insofar as they are able to provide information about the ability of the 'abstraction' adequately to represent more than the given sample. They provide an index of the economy of the statistical description provided by setting that description in an established sampling distribution (where this is available).

The third task of the researcher is to enable his or her colleagues to evaluate the import of the observations and constructions so that the methods of defining and measuring entities and attributes are congruent with the body of research in his or her disciplinary area. This may be done by a careful reporting of her methods and procedures, by comparisons with the findings of others, and by lodging findings within a meaningful theoretical context.

THE PRESENT RESEARCH

The intention embodied in Parts II and III of this book is to examine empirically some processes within the area of group psychology. Furthermore the paradigms of psychoanalytic theory and of social psychology, as outlined, will be employed; the former in a major, and the latter in a minor, capacity.

This section will outline how the reported research attempts to engage in some of the appropriate research tasks outlined previously. Firstly some background to the research will be presented. This will be followed by an examination of the aims of the research, the nature of the systems to be studied, the methods of observation employed and the manner in which the results are to be described, examined and quantified.

BACKGROUND

The research to be reported has evolved over a period of five years. During that time it moved from an exploratory method of observation towards a more systematized method, building on that which was learned in the early phases. For example, in the early stages of observation the author was able to quantify and organize her descriptions on the basis of segments of social action that seemed intuitively to form conceptual 'wholes'. The perception of these social 'wholes' was guided by the theories of Winnicott and Mahler in particular.

These early observations led to comparisons of individuals and groups with respect to the development of integration. Such comparisons, however, led to the formulation of questions that required the quantification of observations on a new basis. Consequently, later observations were organized around the questions of *identity* and *authority* in groups. The author came to recognize that key social events acted as central organizers of social action and reflection. Observations shifted from reflecting the segment-by-segment progression of the group's history (as recorded in transcripts of the ongoing group discussions) to a search for those events in the history of the group that organized the members' perceptions of each other, and which also organized their memories of the events which they themselves had shaped.

AIMS AND METHODS OF THE RESEARCH

The general aim of the research was to study groups and describe their major underlying structures with respect to certain specified processes. This approach bears some similarity to the approach taken by Levi-Strauss (1949;

1964) in his analysis of myth. In the present case, it is the group and organizational structures that were to be conceptualized and examined.

The methods chosen included a combination of those methods described earlier. A most fruitful approach to group research lies in a combination of approaches that both extend and validate each other. For example, the problems of research into subjects' accounts may include the possibility of an outcome of unsystematized collections of 'annotated quotes from social actors' (Forgas, 1979, p. 141). These problems may be overcome if accounts are combined with systematic statistical analyses of subjects' judgements (see Appendix B), and systematic observations of social 'units' derived through means other than subjects' accounts. The research (described in Parts II and III) attempted to combine a number of methods as suggested. It included a series of studies, each with different, although connected aims and methods.

Aims of the studies to be reported

The first study to be described is a cross-sectional study. This is reported in Part II. It compares the first session of each of three different groups by means of a detailed descriptive analysis. Similar descriptive analyses have been made by such authors as Bion (1961), Bennis and Shepard (1956), Slater (1966), Gibbard et al. (1974), Marsh et al. (1978), Boyd (1983; 1984).

This study had three major aims: (a) to describe the first sessions of three different groups in terms of *integrative* processes; (b) to identify those structures that 'organize' the early integrative processes in the groups examined; and (c) to identify a series of states or structural organizations that are able economically to describe the early integrative processes in the groups. Such states may be comparable to the 'positions' in Klein (1946), or the 'moments' of Lacan (1977).

A second study is described in Part III. This longitudinal study proceeded by an analysis of episodes (Marsh et al., 1978; Harré, 1979; Forgas, 1979; Geist and Chandler, 1984). The term 'episode' here refers to a unit of social interaction consensually identified by group members (the term is used somewhat differently by different authors).

This longitudinal study aimed first to construe the major group structures and processes underlying these episodes. This proceeded by: (a) an identification of the central or 'traumatic' events which acted to punctuate the history of the group; (b) a construction of the historical states, moments or structures so organized by this punctuation; and (c) inferring the underlying symbolic structures within the group.

The study aimed also to discuss the emerging identity of the group in terms of the states and structures identified. This examination of identity focussed on dimensions of political and socio-emotional identity (see Chapter 4).

The longitudinal study was augmented by data collected via repertory grids (Kelly, 1955). It was conducted in order to assist in the identification of group structures and processes by analysing the common constructs of group members with respect to each other. A series of interviews with the subjects was also carried out as part of this research. These were aimed at clarifying the meaning of the constructs employed by subjects in their descriptions, and, consequently, at clarifying the dimensions discerned in the multidimensional scaling analysis used to analyse the results. This additional study is reported in Appendix B.

'ENTITIES' OF THE RESEARCH

Before proceeding to describe the research it is necessary to outline the nature of the entities studied. The first step in defining a method of research involves defining that which is to be observed. It is no simple feat to locate the entities or systems to be examined in a study of group psychology. This may already be evident from the preceding discussions of (a) the 'paradox of reciprocal systemic relations' (Chapter 2) involved in observing human groups seemingly constituted of human individuals, and (b) the conceptual framework for a group psychology (Chapter 3), and the difficulties involved in knowing from what a group is constituted.

One of the major aims of the research to be reported was to define those structures that in themselves define the elements that constitute the group.

The entities selected for study in the present work are groups of adult students, constituted as groups through their participation in a common task. It is the group that is under focus, rather than the individual. The attributes and processes under consideration are contained within the dialogue during group sessions, in members' overt behaviours during sessions, and in members' constructions (Kelly, 1955) of each other and of staff members, as reported in rep tests and interviews. New entities seem to emerge during the process of the research.

The self-analytic learning group

The research drew upon a close analysis of the functioning of five groups of people. These groups were all formed for the purpose of learning about group dynamics and processes. They each took the form of a self-analytic learning group (Mann, 1966), and were conducted as part of a course of study at a tertiary education institution. It will be useful to describe the nature of these groups more fully.

The groups were conducted according to the 'Tavistock' style of group (Rice, 1965; McLeish et al., 1973; De Board, 1978). In these groups, the participants are given the task of learning about group structures and processes by examining the ongoing dynamics of their own group as they occur. The staff member present has the role of aiding the participants or members in their task. S/he does this by means of interpretations about group process. These interpretations are developed from his or her own experience within the group.

The theoretical bases for these groups are largely psychoanalytic and have been strongly influenced by the work of Bion (1961). For example, unconscious processes are examined, and the relations of member to consultant and of member to member are seen to include transference phenomena. However, a variety of theoretical influences are present, including Redl (1942); Foulkes (1964); Rice (1969); Cooper and Gustafason (1981).

Basically, the group members are free to conduct the group as they wish, given their primary task of learning. The consultant aids them in the task and interprets resistances to the task. The members usually discuss a great many themes, e.g., personalisms, relationships, ways of approaching the task, the consultant's role, the members' roles, leadership, individual emotions, the group mind, evaluation of progress, etc.

The performance of students in their groups was not evaluated academically, although all students were required to write an academically assessed essay at the end of their group experience.

THE ANALYSIS OF THE DATA

Part of the second major task of the researcher, as outlined earlier, is an economic description of the data. In the research to be reported this was primarily achieved by a qualitative analysis. (A quantitative or statistical analysis of data was also employed in a supportive multidimensional scaling study, reported in Appendix B.)

A qualitative analysis

The observations in each qualitative study substantially involved an analysis of the text of group meetings. To allow for this, all group sessions were taped and the tapes transcribed. The textual analysis allows for the detection of phenomena capable of explaining systematically the behaviour of the group members. It involves segmenting the text into meaningful units, which are then interpreted and related to the text as a whole.

The basis for segmenting the text of a group evolved as the reseach progressed. In the cross-sectional study, the theories of Lacan, Winnicott and others served as a guide to the process. They provided the conceptual basis for distinguishing meaningful units in the group text. So too did the meanings that emerged in the course of the analysis of each group. The work of Harré (1979; 1982) was used as a guide during the longitudinal study where segmenting the text was based on consensual agreement by group members.

In the present studies, a descriptive process began, firstly, by an examination of some theories established within the fields of psychoanalysis and social psychology, in order to define those concepts, attributes and processes that might profitably be applied to the observation of group dialogue, and of behaviours in groups. This then led to specific methods of categorizing observations. These were applied to the transcriptions of group dialogue. The methods employed substantially included those introduced by Freud (1921), Bion (1961), Winnicott (1945), Mahler et al. (1975), Slater (1966), Harré (1979; 1983), Marsh et al. (1978) and Billig (1978). They are the traditional methods of case history, whether of individuals, groups or organizations. Additionally, these methods locate the subject longitudinally, in an historical context (Lacan, 1977). Specifically, the procedure involves three steps:

1 Certain identifiable group outcomes, e.g., segments of group dialogue differentiated on the basis of overt topic areas, or selected episodes in the life of the group, were examined in order to discern an underlying structure. Selection of segments was guided by theory and by the methods of Harré (1979).
2 The dynamics underlying the outcomes were examined (e.g., processes of integration, projective identification).
3 Finally a series of structural organizations (states) which link the above-mentioned outcomes through the dynamics were discerned. The structural models of Freud (1921), Winnicott (1958), Mahler (1968), Bion (1961) and Lacan (1977) guided this process.

These steps are consistent with those proposed by Glaser (1984).

QUANTITATIVE ANALYSIS (see Appendix B)

A quantitative analysis, used in a study of group member perceptions of each other, involved those statistical methods that operate on quantifying relationships of co-variance and extracting the underlying factors (factor analysis, Cattell, 1978) or dimensions (multidimensional scaling, Torgerson, 1952; Shepard, 1962, 1974; Kruskal and Wish, 1978; Schiffman, Reynolds and Young, 1982) that economically describe those relationships (Snyder, Law and Hattie, 1985). Modern methods of analysing repertory grid data (Kelly, 1955; Bannister and Mair, 1968; Bell, 1984; Slater, 1977; Rathod, 1981 and Yorke, 1985) are grounded in such methods. Forgas (1979) recommends MDS methods for the analysis of social perceptions.

Part II

The cross-sectional study

Part II comprises Chapters 7–10, and reports a cross-sectional study of each of the first sessions of three 'study groups'. Chapter 10 attempts to compare, summarize and draw some conclusions from the study.

Part II

The cross-sectional study

Chapter 7

Group 1, session 1

THE GROUP

The group consisted of 12 student members (seven women and five men) and a female consultant. All student members were taking part in a 'study group' as part of a course entitled 'Group behaviour' conducted in Melbourne, Australia. Students were informed about the task of the group by their tutor prior to its commencement. The course that they were taking also involved a series of seminars where theories of group processes were discussed.

The task of the group was to 'study the processes of the group as they occurred'. The consultant's role was to work towards this task with the group. She used her own experience of the group to enable her to formulate interventions that would aid members in their understanding of group processes, structures and dynamics. The present author acted as consultant to this group.

THE METHOD OF STUDY

The group met for 14 two-hour sessions over a period of 16 weeks. Sessions were taped to enable members to review the ongoing work of the group. Transcriptions of these tapes, together with the author's own experience and observations in the group, form the data basis for the analysis to come.

The first session of the group is analysed by dividing the discussion into several segments (regarded as 'group outcomes', see Chapter 6) that centre on different themes. These segments were selected on an intuitive basis informed by the theoretical material presented in the previous chapters. That is, the segments seem to form natural 'wholes' or topic areas within the ongoing flow of the group and each seems to be interpretable in terms of the theory presented. The analysis proceeds by a summary of each segment, including transcript passages where relevant, and may be seen to proceed through the three steps suggested by Glaser (1984) and outlined in Chapter 6:

1   Certain group outcomes, (i.e., *segments of dialogue differentiated on the basis of overt topic areas*), are examined in order to discover an underlying structure.
2   A series of *structural organizations (states)* are to be identified. These serve to link logically the outcomes discerned in step 1 (the structural models of Winnicott, 1958; Lacan, 1949; and Bion, 1961 inform their identification).
3   During the process involved in step 2, reference will be made to some of the *dynamics* which form the structures.

Groups are systems of great intricacy. As with Sommerhoff's research (1969), the present analysis attempts to understand the structural relations present within time segments, in order better to understand the complex dependencies operating in the groups being examined. These complex dependencies are like those found in language (see Chapters 3 and 4). Meaning arises through an appreciation of the constraints that prior segments place on later ones and the retrospective meaning that accrues as the group proceeds. Consequently, the segments will be described and discussed separately because the analysis of each builds on an understanding of preceding segments, and the meaning of each segment becomes clearer in retrospect. For these reasons, comparisons between segments will be presented during the discussion.

ANALYSIS OF GROUP 1

Segment 1   Introductions

After the consultant restated the task of the group, members introduced themselves by name and one member demonstrated her ability to remember all the names. This brought her some admiration and some very mild mocking.

Introductions in this case allowed for a stabilizing point, a centre for the group, which placed all members on a theoretically equal basis. This equality was broken by the demonstration of remembering names. The member responsible then became the centring focus herself. However, she also provided a reinforcement of the integration established by introductions. Interestingly, this member later referred to herself as the 'earthmother' figure of the group, while claiming that she wished to rid herself of this image. Others came to see her as the early socio-emotional leader (McLeish et al., 1973) as well as alternately being either helpful and friendly or dominating and overwhelming. By being the first member to establish a 'difference' from others she may have been seen as taking a role that students normally feel belongs to the teacher, who in this case was not taking the lead.

Here we can see the group beginning to find a point about which to integrate. Another such point is found in the next segment.

Segment 2   Discussion about another group

A group member raised the topic of a video film that psychology students saw in the first year of their course of studies. This film series was produced to illustrate features of a typical discussion group. In the film the discussion is stopped at several points in order to allow comment on the dynamics involved. In discussing the film, the group members compared themselves with the film group:

Ju   Well that's right because the group was put together, it was just a discussion group, wasn't it?
Mi   Yeah. Yeah.
Ju   They decided they had to talk about something.
Mi   Yeah, just like we are now.
Ju   Like we should do too. . . .
Mi   Like what are we going to talk about now? You know, suddenly there are a million things we could talk about. . . .
Ju   Yeah.
Mi   Suddenly we don't know what to talk about.
Ju   Oh that's right, they had a discussion about a discussion.
Mi   Yeah, and that's perhaps what we're doing at the moment.
Ju   I think we should do it now.

In this segment the group members are attempting to integrate by contrasting and comparing themselves to another group perceived to be doing what they are supposed to be doing. The two members, quoted above, illustrate the double attitude of (a) 'We are doing what they did' (Mi), and (b) 'We should do what they did' (Ju). Implicit in this attitude is the forming of an entity, the centre of which fluctuates between (a) the group that they are becoming, (b) the group on the film, and (c) the group that they should be. These fluctuations are reminiscent of Lacan's mirror stage (Lacan, 1949), where the infant ego is seen as developing from a process of shaping in response to the other, the ego first being a reflection of the other yet sensing a wholeness in that reflection, a wholeness that is recognized predominantly in the mirror. The mirroring of the other (mother) produces an ego from the desire of the other. That is, the child tends to become what the mother desires. In the case of the group, 'that which desires' is viewed as being the desire of the figure, leader or group behind the 'should'. This is implicit because 'should' is an imperative. Hence the group is developing its fragile identity (better termed its 'entity' at this point) from a point of comparison not only with the overtly discussed video group, but also from the covertly present group that is fantasied to desire them to exist in a particular manner.

In Winnicott's terms, the centre of the integrative process at this stage is fluctuating between the inside and the outside of the group, remembering that the boundary that fixes such locations is still embryonic.

Segment 3 Expectations

The discussion about the video group was closed by the same woman who had remembered the names earlier in the session:

Mi   This sort of situation just reminds me of that film and that they did appear to have some sort of goal to talk about each time they met, and I think that's the whole issue.

T   Perhaps we need to know what each person hopes to get out of it before we can establish a goal.

In this latter statement, T moves the group clearly to within its own boundaries. The task she proposes is a variant of the introductions made earlier. By taking up her task the group re-establishes its own integration and recognition of a boundary between inside and outside.

The discussion then centred on the expectations of various group members. During this discussion, the first disagreements arose between members. They explored the reasons for each of them being in the group and they discovered differences. There was, however, a particularly aggressive questioning of each other together with a marked suspiciousness.

R   I said what do you expect to get out of the group! You're blithely making comments. . . .

A   To live, to live better in groups. (Ju laughs) I think I'll fall in with what M said. She said she's coming here because she's very interested in the subject.

R   Mmmm.

A   To be interested in the subject; you're not interested in the subject for nothing I think. Even if you can't admit it to yourself there are certain purposes.

And later. . . .

R   Well what do you hope to get out of the group?

Mi   Me?

R   Mmmm.

Mi   Well I'd like to learn more about people in here, in the room, uh. I'd like to form a closer association with people in the room, uh, a working/class relationship, and socially, um, and I'd like to . . . and undoubtedly I think we'll all learn bits and pieces about our makeup that, er, irk other people that we could probably all rectify in time.

B   What happens if you don't reach those expectations though? That's what I was getting at before about expectations. You might expect all of these things and if they don't come to fruition, by definition the whole thing's a waste of time.

R   But you're implying that you don't come to the group with
    expectations.

B   No, I haven't got any preconceived expectations.

R   That's a load of bull! (laughter from others) It is! I mean you come,
    you enter anything with expectations.

The suspicions, voiced by A, that others are in the group for their own
purposes leads to further questioning by R. On the voicing of doubt by B –
'What happens if you don't reach those expectations though?' – some of the
suspicions are able to be translated into direct attacks on others, e.g., 'That's
a load of bull!' An angry yet lively argument then ensued in the group around
the question of whether or not people have expectations when entering a new
social situation.

There is, then, even at this stage, a vague background awareness of the
group-that-is-joined, in the form of a group that things come out of: 'What do
you expect to get out of the group?' Additionally we can say that, in Kleinian
terms, the incidents described above may be a demonstration of the projection
of persecutory anxiety onto specific others in the group. Members feel
criticized by their motives being called into question, and a direct attack on
others helps to focus the anxiety in a source outside the self (Jaques, 1955;
Menzies, 1970).

In Winnicott's terms, we can see these behaviours as serving a dual
defensive purpose. Firstly, individual members are able to deal with their own
anxieties and hostilities by means of projection. This is evidenced in the
'bickering' arguments which tend to attack the positions of others at the
expense of carefully clarifying one's own position. Further evidence is
provided from discussion during the next segment, when it became apparent
that the major source of anxiety for members derived from what they thought
others might do to them in the group. Some of these fears derived from stories
told by students from previous years because there is, as with many ongoing
courses, a generalized mythology about the course.

Secondly, the group as a whole is able to integrate around the emotional
expressiveness inherent in the fight. In Bion's (1961) terms this is an example
of basic assumption fight. It is R who leads the 'attacks' on members at this
stage. He is later seen as a task leader.

It is interesting to contrast this segment of the group's first session with the
previous segment. Analysis shows that both segments demonstrate an attempt
by the group to integrate. In the former segment this integration places the
group identity in a mirror relation to an external group. Then the group
became cohesive by members acting as if they were in an entity comparable to
other groups (i.e., the idea of an 'other' presupposes the idea of a comparable
present group). In this segment, integration is achieved through a corresponding internal division. Here identity is found in dissension. The centre of
this identity is within the group evidenced in the acceptance by members of

claims that they are in a group that may provide them with satisfactions. However, through the processes of projection and splitting, this identity is not felt by the individuals to be in *them*. Another way of stating this is to say that although members feel themselves to be in a group, they speak as if it has a presence outside of their personal abilities to interact. This position of member with respect to the group, indicates the operation of projection. In Mahler's terms we could say that the group members are in symbiotic union, where the group boundary is becoming clearer but internal boundaries are fluid and diffuse. Symbiotic union with the consultant is not clear here, but is demonstrated by members responding to interpretations as if they are statements of permission or prohibition to act. For example, the consultant pointed out that the group was forming around the fight over expectations. The group members responded by pursuing their debate extensively in a less hesitant manner, as if they had been encouraged or given permission to do so. This aspect of the symbiotic fusion will become clearer in the next segment.

The gradual defining of the group/environment boundary is also evident in this segment. As identity begins to form around internal issues, members were able to speak more clearly about this group as a particular unit in their psychology studies. They began to delineate its specificity.

Before leaving this segment, it is important to note its central content of expectations. The often stated 'What do you expect to get out of this group?' gives evidence of an overt imagery of extracting information *from* the group. There is no talk of what members might give one another. A more covert image of feeding and extracting nourishment may underlie this, evidenced by, e.g., the idea that one's expectations may 'bear fruit'. An unconscious process may be taking place, with one implication being that the group already exists as an entity that is able to nourish. The conscious expectations of members overlie the unconscious expectations that relate to the group that already exists. The doubts about meeting these expectations may well have been the catalyst for the open expression of anger.

Segment 4   The symbiosis

The previous segment ended with R, who had previously questioned the others as to their expectations. He put forward his own expectations hesitantly, including: 'I expect there will be conflicts.' After a brief discussion about whether or not conflict was wanted, the consultant commented: 'One of the patterns I'm picking up is that the men are taking on the role of putting forward arguments, and the women are taking on the roles of translators and modifiers and questioners.' This led to the re-emergence of T, the female mentioned earlier. After agreeing with the consultant, T made a long statement about her own expectations and in doing so she shifted the discussion from a 'fight' to a 'confessional' mode.

T   OK, I'll go for my life. I've got expectations of the group and I – R
     was just talking about conflict – I expect that there probably will be
     conflict and a whole lot of other interactions. I hope to use the
     group in order to examine how I relate to people and how people
     react to me, in the hope that I can use it in my personal life, and
     that I can experiment with behaviour in here and feel that it's a
     fairly safe environment because you know why I'm doing it, and it's
     really not safe to try these sort of things with people that you are
     very close to. So I hope to learn from the group and apply that to
     my life. And that's what I hope to gain. I can't be sure that I will
     gain it. That's what my aim is. Does anybody else have similar
     aims? (looking around)

She immediately got a response from another female, and she continued to
inquire quietly about the feelings of others.

A   I don't understand what you're trying to achieve.
T   I'm trying to see how people are feeling about things. I'm trying to
     get a more personal feeling of how people feel about the group.

T is central to this segment as she openly expresses some of the anxieties that
have been present, yet unexpressed, from the start.

T   It seemed to me that, talking to people before they came into the
     group, a lot of people said they were afraid, and that everybody
     seemed to be sitting around saying, well: 'I'm afraid. What if people
     don't like me? What if people attack me?' And nobody seemed to
     be sitting around saying, 'Well, when I get in there I'm going to
     attack people.' So I wonder who everyone was afraid of. I mean if
     everyone has these feelings – being afraid – that I had too, you're
     assuming that somebody is not sharing that feeling.
Ju   Yeah, but that kind of feeling is not specific. You know something's
     going to happen . . . it's never. . . .
T   Yeah, but there is an assumption that the other people are not
     sharing your feelings if you think people are going to attack you,
     there must be some people who are different from you, who aren't
     afraid themselves, or just going in there to tear people to pieces.
Ju   No. You can attack other people too.
T   But is the attacking a form of defence?
Ju   Yeah, for sure!

In this segment some of the previously preconscious material emerges in the
group discussion. The fears of attack and the defensiveness of counter-attack
are discussed. Thus, while the anxiety felt earlier begins to surface and be
understood, the group begins to integrate around the members' feelings.

Some further discussion of feelings, and more conflict, ensued about whether or not the males were expressing feelings as much as the females.

The symbiotic union with the consultant is quite strong at this stage. Additionally, we cannot disregard the consultant as perhaps one of those who is seen as unafraid and likely to tear members to pieces (i.e., she may be, in the eyes of members, the source of some of the persecutory anxieties). T, the female who first presented a point around which they could form an identity, re-emerges as a central figure. She agrees with and develops the points made by the consultant. However she does move the emphasis from observation of style (arguer vs. mediator) to one of content (superficial expression vs. expression of deeper feelings), as the following quote from the transcript shows:

Mi   I wonder if a male is . . . I'm doing it again . . . I wonder if a male is more prepared to discuss those sort of internal feelings than perhaps a woman is?
(Lots of voices come in to protest)

T   What's been happening here seems to me to argue the opposite.

Mi   Yeah?

T   That the males are intent on keeping things on the surface. The females are much more. . . . (drowned out by female voices agreeing)

B   What a sexist comment!

R   But if you think right back to actually what was going on before, I would agree very much with that comment in that a lot of stuff we were arguing about really had nothing to do with anything. . . .

At this stage the group has begun to act out more extensively a division (male/female) pointed to by the consultant. This polarity may be a comfortable focus to represent the internal disagreements discovered in the earlier segment. It is as if the recognition of many possible differences and potential conflicts leads members to focus on one or two main divisions in order not to feel lost in the many fragments (Turquet, 1975). At least it may provide a temporary focus for members' thoughts about the group. If we take Mahler's view of the symbiotic union, we may review this segment in the following manner:

1 In turning from its earlier mirror phase, the group discovered its identity to be in internal confusion. The wholeness felt in the presence of the external group no longer seems present.

2 Persecutory anxiety is experienced, and members begin to suspect each other of hidden motives.

3 Retaliatory aggressive questioning appears.

4 The consultant intervenes by commenting on one of the internal splits. In this way she is seen to provide a focus for integration. Her comments

provide an opportunity for the group to use her as a containing ego (cf. Winnicott's idea of the good-enough mother and the development of an area of illusion, Winnicott, 1971).

5 This new focus for integration is within the symbiotic union of members and consultant. This symbiosis is evidenced in the members acting as if the consultant's *observations* should *direct* the behaviour of the group (more so than any other member's observations). It has two major effects: (a) the group seems more able to explore overtly the members' anxieties of being attacked (the containment is good-enough to allow this); and (b) the group is able to develop a greater sense of integration, identity, and reality, by pursuing the observations of the consultant and, in a sense, actualizing or reifying them. If an underlying fantasy involves the group becoming what the consultant desires it to become, then members may well perceive her observations as directions.

The next segment will illustrate how this new basis for identity, discovered in the symbiotic phase of the group, does lead to a new development: that of the first moves towards the anticipation of independence.

Segment 5   Symbiosis continued

This segment appears to contain the precursors of a group rebellion (Bennis and Shepard, 1956; Slater, 1966). Ju appears hostile towards, and critical of the consultant (three sessions later, on behalf of the group, she asks the consultant if she would leave the room were the group to ask her).

It seems useful now to indicate some clear differences between the hostility expressed here and a rebellion proper, because such a distinction is necessary to explore the nature of hostility during the symbiotic stage. Firstly, the data:

Ju   That's the unnatural thing about this group, that you (the consult-
        ant) are sitting back and watching, giving your interpretations
        which are immediately more important than any we might be
        having.

B   Oh, it's a good point I thought actually.

Ju   Yeah, but if S (the consultant) hadn't said that, nothing would've
        happened, so it's kind of an unnatural thing.

B   We mightn't have picked it up.

Consultant
        So in some ways instead of this group forming itself around what
        seemed to be its overt task of exploring difference, it's forming
        itself around its expectations of what I want.

Ju   Possibly. Yeah I think so. Everybody picked up on that one, and
        they've picked up on everything you've said.

M   But I think it's very beneficial if you can point out to us ... OK we
        were going along a certain line, and for someone to point that out

and say OK this is what happened, well it gives you something to work on and it lets you know what you're actually doing as a group.

J   I'm glad S pointed out that we could be making a split between male and female because I find that far more frightening than revealing myself.

Ju   Yeah, but originally S pointed out that difference between male and female, and we sort of trucked on for a while, and then she came back and said: 'Hang on now, look what you've done. I said this and you've blown it up out of all proportion.' So if she hadn't said that in the first place possibly we wouldn't've been where we were that she had to correct us from, uh, to.

Mi   But we might not have had the other input from the other girls.

B   We were starting to talk about that ourselves. It's not something S raised as an issue. The thing was working towards that way.

Ju   I don't think so.

B   S just pointed it out. That's the way I saw it.

R   But I don't think it was myself.

Ju   I think S raised that.

B   Yeah, but what I'm saying, it was raised out of something that was really happening.

T   Yeah.

B   It wasn't an artificial observation.

Ju   Oh yeah.

R   No. No.

Ju   But it became overt then.

R   Well yeah.

Several points can be made about the above. Firstly, the dialogue constitutes an argument about whether or not the consultant created the difference being discussed (i.e., between males and females), the alternative being that she simply observed and commented. Ju, supported somewhat by R, is challenging the role and behaviour of the consultant; whereas B, M, Mi and T are attempting to justify this role in support of the consultant.

The argument is not clearcut, though. Ju herself is unclear as to whether or not discussion of the male/female issue was solely created by the consultant. 'So if she hadn't said that in the first place *possibly* we wouldn't've been where we were.' The group members seem to be very confused over this issue and are unable, at first, to decide whether the split was created by the group or by the consultant. They eventually decide that the observation was not artificial, but did create the issue in their consciousness, i.e., the observation made the split overt and gave it meaning.

Further, the consultant's comment that the group was forming itself around her expectations was accepted and wrestled with in this argument. This comment recognizes the symbiotic unit of consultant/group at a time when members have formed their identity within this containing unit (see segment 4). The integration started in segment 4 becomes overt. The difficulty experienced in deciding who creates action in the group marks a difficulty with the identification of internal boundaries between members. It seems similar to the infant's difficulty in seeing itself as separate from the mother during the symbiotic fantasy. It is a problem of developing identity, at the level of integration, and of construing the self and nonself.

Importantly, it seems that it is only when the symbiotic unit is at its height, i.e., when the group integrates in, and centres on, a duality, that the group can begin to separate and 'hatch' (Mahler, 1968) from the symbiosis. Ju's recognition that the group is formed within the symbiosis (in Lacan's [1977] terms, born into the desire of the mother) allows her to act as group catalyst for the hatching process. In this sense, her action is not one of 'leader of the rebellion', although hatching may be seen as a precursor of later forms of rebellious autonomy, both in the group and in the child.

At this stage, the group under consideration is not ready to hatch in the full sense of developing its own autonomy of direction. Members are willing, however, to agree to the idea of being created in the desire of the consultant, whose role they see as guiding their development and bringing this to consciousness. They begin to recognize the symbiotic unity of the group/consultant. Additionally, they experience the consultant's interpretations as realizations of their own unconscious formulations. This provides further experience of the area of illusion (Winnicott, 1971), and the possibility of testing reality.

Segment 6   Understanding the symbiosis

In this segment we can see the manner by which this group began to work on understanding the symbiotic consultant/group duality. This process allowed group members to prepare themselves for 'hatching' proper, or for forming a tentative independent group identity with autonomous motives or desires.

There are three main issues that are raised and discussed by the group at this stage.

1 What is our task?
2 What are our roles?
3 What is our major emotional concern?

Each of these issues is dealt with at various levels of consciousness, and the consultant's observations are more readily accepted and acted on than previously.

During this segment T again takes on a central role. In contrast to Ju, who acts as a catalyst for hatching, and perhaps represents the pole driving for autonomy by rejection of the old order, T seems to represent aspects of the consultant that act as a central integrating point for the group. Consider the following examples:

Ju   We're all saying things, hoping people will agree. If they don't agree
      then we've found another difference, more than we're looking for
      difference. I mean, is anybody really saying inflammatory things
      just for the hell of it? (laughs)
A   I was thinking before about T. What she said before, did she really
      mean? I thought she was trying, sort of, to influence things.
Ju   When was that?
A   I don't remember, but about ten minutes ago.
Ju   What did she say?
A   Whatever she said she looked like she was trying to sort of. . . .
Ju   Get things moving?
A   Yes, rather than express her real feelings at the time.

This accusation against T is very similar to that made earlier against the
consultant by Ju, i.e., with regard to raising the male/female issue herself. It is
seen as an overt attempt to influence. Additionally, it comes shortly after T
has continued to talk of possible gender differences, against the wishes of
other group members. Also, note the following which came shortly after:

Th   That's right. So we're doing what we're meant to be doing.
Consultant
      I wonder who's meaning you to do these things? Who's the person
      that wants you to do things so that you can say you might be doing
      what you're meant to be doing?
T   Yeah.
Ju   Well we're still here in a course and we're. . . . I suppose we know a
      little bit about how groups work and that sort of thing, so I'm sort
      of sitting here nattering away, trying to work out if people are
      fitting into different roles, just in my head.
T   Yeah but who's meaning us to do it? We haven't said: 'Look, this is
      our goal which we all agree on, so we're following our goal and doing
      this.' We're saying: 'Are we doing what we're meant to be doing?'
Ju   I think it's a bit of an unstated thing. I mean you're doing that a
      lot. . . .
T   As if there is a goal. . . .
Ju   You're sort of pulling it back a lot to the traditional sort of, well
      not traditional, uh. . . .
A   It is traditional. . . .
M   Self-examination.
Ju   Yeah. Sort of textbook-type self-examination, and saying: 'Look
      what's going on here', and that sort of thing, in a really
      psychology-minded sort of way.
T   Mmmm.
Ju   And we're all feeding into that and saying: 'Oh yeah, T's got a point
      there, this is what we should be doing.'

Here **T** has closely identified herself with the consultant by taking up the latter's question of 'who's meaning you to do this?' She is criticized for being 'psychology-minded', textbook-like, and for preventing the group from developing its own direction and identity.

It may be that the group is splitting the consultant into a good/bad duality, with different members representing the good and bad parts. This mechanism (described by the object relations school, e.g., Bion, 1970; Klein, 1946; Ogden, 1979) may be more strongly evidenced once the group has achieved enough integration to 'hold', as separate (although together), the good and bad as entities without total loss of the symbiotic union described earlier, that is, without excessive anxiety about the members' own destructive capacities towards the consultant.

When the group is able to differentiate and expel the 'bad' from its inner orbit, the possibility of greater personalization occurs. Such personalization, and centring on the 'good', enables members to identify more closely with each other, and, hence, to explore inner experiences with greater confidence. The split developed here is more organized than the splits experienced earlier in the group. These were experienced in bickering and confusion. Now, however, splitting the consultant, and attacking part of her in T, indicate that she is beginning to be seen as a possible identity separate from *their* group (i.e., the group that is experienced now). Members are able to integrate their group, and to explore the symbiotic unity while projecting the 'bad' into one member, and then outside the group altogether, as may be seen in the next quote:

> T defended herself, and the group began a discussion on the difficulty of getting out of a role once having taken it up.
>
> R   I think that it's a case of the role not only being placed on you but you assuming the role. I mean, no one can put a role on you unless you want it there. So what you've got to then think about is: 'Why do I want this role?' or 'Do I want this role?'
>
> T   I'm not sure if that's correct, that no one can put a role on you unless you want it there. I think that they can.
>
> Th   That they do!
>
> R   That someone can make you act in a certain way without you wanting it?
>
> T   Yeah, if there are enough people saying that this is your role and this is what we expect, and refusing to respond to anything that doesn't fit in with that role. You can be forced.
>
> Al   Doesn't that depend on how hard you're prepared to fight back? Because I know what you're talking about. People will try to push you into a role, but there's times when you can say: 'there's no way I will do that. I will do the opposite!'

T   Yeah but all the fighting in the world won't stop it, sometimes, I think.

Al   I'm thinking of instances when it would happen. . . . I'm trying to think of an instance.

B   Well what about the role of a mother? I mean it's pretty hard to fight that. Society expects certain things of a mother and you know it's pretty hard to turn your back and say, 'yes society expects this of me, but I'm not going to follow that role'.

The above segment of the transcript is rife with many meanings and innuendos. Members are discussing the ability of the group or consultant to coerce and force them to behave in particular ways. They are discussing the struggle for independence that may first be expressed in counterdependence: 'There's no way I will do that. I will do the opposite'. They attempt consciously to put the 'bad' into mothers and society outside the group. However, B (who is male) clearly expresses the fear of the group/child who begins to anticipate independent existence, that is, the fear of a desertion that seems imminent for the child of a mother who says: 'Yes, society (the group?) expects this of me but I'm not going to follow that role.'

This issue is explored further by the group after the consultant made an interpretation linking the fears of exposure, expressed earlier, with the fears of being coerced and forced. The point to stress at this stage is that the ability to split the consultant/group into good and bad (Klein's paranoid/schizoid defence) allows the group to accept and follow the interpretations made by the 'good' consultant and hence to explore more fully the fears of desertion and independence that naturally arise as 'hatching' is apprehended. This acceptance contrasts with the earlier 'acceptance' that involved acting as if the consultant's comments were instructions. Now, members begin to explore and work with her comments. By dealing with their fears, instead of repressing or failing to symbolize them, the group is able to emerge from the symbiotic union and discover independent identity. To do this the projections are reintrojected:

M   I think what you said before about taking on roles in here, something clicked in my mind as well as what I said before. I suppose there always is the fear that you'll always be the one sitting back and not getting a word in; or people will expect too much of you, and I think for me, that sort of scares me somewhat.

and,

Th   I think at the back of my mind was, what does the group expect of me? That sort of makes it a bit clearer now. Coming here it's not so much, 'What do I expect from the group', but 'What does the group expect from me?' and that frightens me.

and,

Ju   I think the whole thing of ending up with roles in the group is pretty frightening to me.

At this stage the group had begun to explore the possibilities of developing an identity of its own. This would be integrated around the developing structure with its associated roles, and would be centred in group members and their feelings. With this tentative, if somewhat anxiety-provoking integration, they were able to arrive at a point where they could begin to differentiate themselves from the group-that-was-joined. Note the following:

T   Yeah, I think maybe everyone would like to sit back and see how the group's going before they become involved in it; until they . . . it's all unknown . . . and if they could see how it's all evolving and plan their entry into the group they would feel more comfortable. But if everyone did that nothing would happen, so we all feel sort of a compulsion to start things going.
Consultant
     Well there is a myth that there is a group to join rather than a group to create.
T   Yeah.
Consultant
     And it's my group to join because I created the time to meet and so on.
T   Yeah, the willingness with which we accept how you interpret what's going on because it is your group. When you say things we think: 'That's what S thinks. That must be right. I must agree with that.'
A   We can assume that we are all going to stay here for the next 12 weeks and come to function as a group. No one has voiced an objection to these things. Maybe we can proceed by forming some rules or guidelines as to how we are going to operate.

The question 'Whose group is this?' was a question that took up much time in later sessions. It became a possible question to be explored and acted upon, possible only since the group had developed an initial tentative identity.

As with the mother/child bond, the consultant/group bond continued throughout the life of the group. However, the 'hatching' from the initial symbiotic union was achieved after the first few sessions. The interpretation about 'the group to join rather than the group to create' shaped a lot of what was to follow. It was accepted by the group as a transitional phenomenon (Winnicott, 1971) in the sense that it acted to symbolize the link between 'me' and 'not-me', or between the group and the consultant, or what *they might create* and what *was given*.

SOME CONCLUDING COMMENTS

This chapter has used the concepts outlined in Chapter 4 to make the early events of a self-study group more comprehensible. Parallels with the early psychological integration of infants have been drawn. The following discussion makes some tentative comments that may be of value during the examination of the groups discussed in Chapters 8 and 9.

It seems that the ability to integrate, or to become a unique unity, may be necessary in order to effect cohesion and the possibility of realistic work in a given environment. From what has been said, it also seems that integration is likely to be achieved within a context of previous organization. In the case of the infant, this context is the general containing and supportive figure of a mother. However the mother's work with her infant consists of her ability to both contain or 'hold' her infant, and to act as a partner in his or her development. Similarly, the new group integrates in the context of supportive and containing leadership. In the case of the group described, the formal leader or authority was a group consultant. Leadership functions may or may not remain within the role of a single individual. More often they shift between group members and it is the functions, more than an individual person, that act as partner and container for the developing group, although these functions may seem to belong to one person who is the 'mythical' leader or who may act to signify the 'symbolic leader' (Lacan, 1977; and Chapter 5).

Beyond the particular leader or functions lies the general context of the 'social'. It is the social experience of members that allows for the myth of the group-that-was-joined, although the particulars of the myth belong to the reality of the origins of the particular group concerned. Or perhaps, rather than to the 'social', we should refer to the underlying unconscious cultural/linguistic source of this myth, for it is in the process of cultural symbolization that specific societal forms themselves are realized (Levi-Strauss, 1964; Lacan, 1953b).

Chapter 8

Group 2, session 1

Like the previous chapter, this chapter will proceed with an analysis of a group's first session. Segments of transcript will be examined, the segments being selected on an intuitive basis and refined according to the theories of Freud (1921), Winnicott (1958), Mahler (1968; 1975) and others (see Chapter 3). Comparisons with group 1 will be discussed in the text as appropriate.

THE GROUP

This group consisted of 10 student members (women and men) and a male consultant. All members were university, final honours, psychology undergraduates, enrolled in a unit called 'Interaction in groups'.

Segment 1 Introductions

The consultant opened the session by briefly stating the task of the group. That is, 'to actually participate in the group process and at the same time to observe ourselves as we form.' After a couple of questions directed to the consultant, members introduced themselves at the instigation of member L. During these introductions, another member, Q, described himself as the 'old man' of the group. When all members had stated their names and given some brief personal details, a female member hesitantly asked the consultant:

Member
    Are you going to. . .?
Consultant
    Yeah, I'm C. (general laughter) Instructor in charge of unit 363.
E   Are you 'old man'. . . ? Do you claim to be 'old man' of the group or
    would you let that lie . . . lay?
Consultant
    I'll let it lie.
Q   Thank you very much.

As with group 1, the introductions may provide a stabilizing, theoretically 'equal' basis for members. However during the introductions Q claimed a special role in the group. Others simply reported some external personal details. The import of claiming a special role so obviously and so early is seen in the joking banter with the consultant. It is as if group members are hesitantly testing him with regard to the possibility of his accepting challenges to his role, which may be challenged by other members simply having a role in the group.

Segment 2   Comparisons with other groups

After sporadic conversation about the difficulty and discomfort involved in self-disclosure, a comparison of the present situation with another group is raised.

Ka   ... we did that last year when we went to X in at R. We sat around on the floor and it made a difference. People divulged a lot more about themselves.

F   What? How were they sitting?

Ka   Against the wall, but on cushions, and it was the same kind of thing, face to face, more personal.

Y   Sitting in a chair. . . . (inaudible)

O   It was just as uneasy at X as it is in here.

Ka   Oh, I thought it was easier.
   (Undistinguishable female voices: It's uncomfortable. . . . It's uneasy.)

O   There was an agenda out there: we followed that too. There was something to explore, which is not reflexive. Something to, that is the appearance of being in a place like that and um, of having lived there, and it's comforting the idea that we're not so different after all. That provided some sort of nucleus around which we could discuss something.

Again the similarity to group 1 is apparent. The lack of a 'nucleus' or a centre around which to integrate is apparent, and members are drawn to discuss another group which in retrospect appears whole and formed, and perhaps contained some of the qualities that some members desire. The external group, however, is not identical to the present group. Some of the present members had not been to X, and were excluded from the memory that had provided a point of integration for others. The discussion of this group ends in the following manner:

Ty   The lecturer was hysterical. Such an amazing man. He just sits there and (inaudible) the whole time. . . . It's something that you do voluntarily – but everyone turned up religiously voluntarily, every week.

Ka   You had to be there or you felt bad about it.

Ty   Yeah.

      (long pause)

The description of the 'lecturer' could well fit the present consultant and may remind group members of their duty to him as students. An initial attempt to integrate in a memory of the past which excluded some members, and particularly excluded the present consultant, is abandoned with some associated guilt feelings.

It is important to stress at this stage that the guilt feelings expressed here by Ty and Ka are best understood if we consider them as overdetermined. Two determinants, perhaps, are (a) guilt recalled from their experience of the previous group, and (b) their feelings are aroused in the present at an unconscious group level. The argument for these hypotheses is by way of analogy with the process of condensation in dreams.

> A dream is constructed by the whole mass of dream thoughts being submitted to a sort of manipulation process in which those elements which have the most numerous and strongest supports acquire the right of entry into the dream content ... each one of those elements is shown to have been determined many times over in relation to the dream thoughts.
>
> (Freud, 1900, p. 389)

If into Freud's text we substituted 'manifest group' for 'dream', and 'membership thoughts' for 'dream thoughts', the meaning becomes apparent. Freud's descriptions of the processes of the unconscious (condensation and displacement), and their determining effect (in the manifest content of dreams, slips of the tongue and pen, jokes and neurotic symptoms), become relevant to the discussion of the problem of group content. Not all group content would be determined by unconscious processes, nonetheless the link between the content of the group and the members' thoughts is a complex one. Consider the puzzlement expressed as the group member, responding to a consultant's interpretation directed at the group as a whole system: 'I was not aware of feeling *that* at the time.' This need not be a denial on the part of the member. The group experience, however, records the consultant's view that, at that time, some elements in the system seemed to be directing the content. The specific content elaborated in the text of the group-as-a-whole may be due to its overdetermination amongst the membership. That is, it may be the content most acceptable to most of the members, even if at an unconscious level. This then accounts for the tacit acceptance by the group of those contents which proceed in a continuing and recurring fashion, e.g., recurrent themes in the group discourse. In this manner, the content may be said to be relevant to the group-as-a-whole, not just to the members actively engaged in expressing that content (Foulkes, 1964).

In the present group, it is reasonable to suspect that Ty's discourse about the lecturer at X, and the paradox of voluntary, yet emotionally compulsive attendance, acted as a nodal point (or condensation, Freud, 1900) to gather members' feelings towards the present lecturer and the present group. The long silence could be interpreted as an experience of shared guilt or discomfort, and a return to the search for a beginning that might be said to be their own. The fact that an external group was overtly discussed also points to the simultaneous occurrence of displacement phenomena, and, perhaps, the silence is a recognition of displacement.

What ensued in the group next was a long discussion about groups of delinquent children. Q had mentioned working in a programme with these children and the conversation centred largely on questioning him. Sub-topics during this time may be summarized:

1 Q described taking the children/adolescents away in a bus, 'the idea being to learn social skills and to learn a bit of pride, both in themselves and to learn a bit about the impact of their behaviour on others.'

2 Discussion also centred on an American experiment where delinquent adolescents were taken into the 'wilds' to learn similar social skills as well as survival skills.

Q   It teaches them team spirit. They have to think about others because they become reliant on others ... they're forced ... oh it doesn't start like that, but ultimately they're forced into some sort of group cohesion to survive. They have no choice. They're in a harsh part of the outback.

3 A discussion then took place about the aggressive nature of some of these adolescents, and the fear that such aggression generates.

Q   This guy and another guy had both physically threatened to punch the shit out of me, and I'm not physically very strong and that scared the hell out of me 'cos these guys don't feel a lot of pain and on both occasions I didn't know how to respond except I was shaking and I was afraid. As soon after the event as I could, I told them both (they were separate events), I told them how much they frightened me and how scared I was and neither of them from that day on ever lifted a finger towards me again and I could say anything that other people couldn't.

After this vignette various group members discussed why this tactic of Q's had worked. The general conclusion, encouraged by Ty and Ka, was reached as follows:

Ty   Maybe you were just a bit more human to them.
Q   I don't know ... sometimes a tendency to hide part of yourself away from them. . . .

Ka That's what I was getting at. Perhaps you exposed yourself.
Q   And I just decided not to. . . . I couldn't deal with it in any other way so I said this is how I will deal with it.
Female
    Mmmm.
Q   You see, they're very egocentric. They say: 'Where were you? You're never around!' My style now is to say 'You're never bloody around when I need you', and I trade it off.
Female
    Mmmm.
Q   They were good lessons there.
    (long pause)

4 The final aspects raised in this context were those of drugs and sex. In this case, members felt that rules should be rather strictly applied in order to control the adolescents. The conversation ended in another pause.

During the discussion about the delinquent adolescents, group members appear to be engaging each other in the formation of values; individual values about how to deal with aggression and fear are revealed, but the group as a whole also comes to some conclusions. Honesty and openness are posited as effective values in order to handle aggression; strict rules are tentatively accepted as effective in dealing with drugs and sex. There may be an implicit message between members and to the consultant, to the effect that: *if we are honest and open then you shouldn't attack us. Also we expect our libidinal strivings to be contained in this group*.

Interpreting this discussion as a reflection of membership concerns about their own emotions is supported by reference to an exchange earlier in the session:

Q   Why is it that it's so hard to divulge bits and pieces about ourselves to strangers?
F   It's not very difficult.
Q   The rest of us seem more concerned.
    (F goes on to claim that the impersonality of the group helps)

The concern then, as now, was with self-disclosure. The implication here is that if, in order to form a group, members must divulge personal information, hence becoming more attached to one another, and perhaps more emotionally regressed (or adolescent), then the possibilities of aggression, sexuality and self-indulgence are anticipated.

In short, the voicing of values might be seen as a tentative attempt to anticipate emotional relations and to build a group structure to contain these. All this is managed, however, through a discussion of outside groups of adolescents. This process is comparable to displacement and seems overdetermined. Notwithstanding members' genuine interest in the 'open family programme' which is overtly discussed, this discussion also served economically to anticipate or constrain internal group cohesion, identity and integration by a comparison with external groups. Comparisons, of learning social skills and of being forced to become cohesive, are readily available at the commencement of the discussion.

Interestingly, one member, G, comments on this very process near the end of this segment: 'That's much the same as everyone that's spoken in the group so far. Maybe that's been disguised in order to find some sort of rules or purpose to extend to this group.' G is ignored by the others and appears in this session to be a member who rarely speaks.

As with group 1, this group has begun to integrate by means of a mirror mechanism. The time taken is greater than in group 1. However, as Cissna (1984) indicates, an expectation that groups will go through similar phases at the same speed is unrealistic. It is enough to demonstrate that similar phases are experienced in a similar order, to support a thesis of general development. To support ideas of the effects of group histories, perhaps it is merely enough that similar phenomena occur and give rise to similar structures.

In the last chapter it was suggested that, during the 'mirror phase', the group's centre of integration fluctuated between an outside group, the existent group, and the covertly present group-that-was-joined. The present group continued in the following fashion.

A member noted that the group had become less 'egocentric and self-conscious' by discussing the adolescents (egocentricity was also mentioned several times as descriptive of the adolescents themselves).
The consultant made an interpretation linking the discussion with the present group. Members then discussed whether or not the lack of rules in the group was discomforting or frightening. The need for guidelines was raised, then the following occurred:

Co   ... and then we sort of got into this pattern and so we needed sort of some guidance of what to ... and where we were going ... what was the group doing. ... I mean are we here just for conversation? And I agree that the conversation was a bit metaphorical, us all sitting here in this room and I sort of felt like, oh, one of the kids on the bus.

Q   You felt discomfort for you or for the rest of the group?

Co   Mainly me.

D   (laughs)

L   Can I ask you about that because that surprises me? I mean, um, I sort of heard what (the consultant) said and I wonder if that's possible. Sorry, are you saying that you really did do that. That you were, sort of had a personal investment. Well...?

In this group the mirror relation is not apprehended explicitly. A conscious acceptance of comparison with 'the kids' is resisted, perhaps because the discussion was successful in reducing discomfort (in its disguised or displaced form) and members were more readily able to move into a discussion of their expectations and anticipations. Moreover, the fluctuations between discussing the present and outside groups continues in the context of perceived prescriptions for behaviour.

Ty   I mean. . . . I don't know. . . . Like, I've been at Lifeline for two and a half years and we are in groups quite a lot and we generally have an issue which we focus around . . . and I guess the groups are structured in such a way that you sort of build up a lot of trust in each other.

F   But the Lifeline thing's different because you're in a sort of helping mode whereas. . . .

Co   There is some learning.

Ty   You're there for yourself as well.

Co   And I hope we're in a learning mode now.

Members then discussed other university groups and the presence or absence of structure in them.

It seems that, as with group 1, this group has its integrative centre fluctuating between outside groups, the present group and the covert group-that-was-joined and which exists in order for them to learn. Groups mentioned last by the present group (Lifeline and the other university groups) are consciously compared with the present group and the mirror function becomes more explicit. It is more acceptable for members to see themselves as Lifeline helpers or as similar to other students than it was to see themselves as delinquent adolescents.

Finally, statements are made (and heard) that clearly integrate the present group within its own boundaries and aid in the formation of internal identity. F says: 'We don't want to become like . . . well another Special Studies group or whatever.'

Segment 3   Internal focus

This segment of the transcript clearly sees the group dealing with its own internal issues. The discussion begins with a consideration of group structures during which internal disputes become apparent. For example:

Q   You can always put structure onto it. I think I'd quite like to do – I don't know whether it's appropriate – at the end of each session to have . . . go around and see what we each seem to have learned on the day.

Co   I tend to find that very trivializing. I mean only for me. It comes round to me and I think: 'Oh what did I learn today?' and I have to

> sort of perhaps make something up. Or . . . 'cos what I have learned
> is so complicated. . . .

Q   Then say nothing.

Co   I'd take days to reflect over it.

Then a few interchanges later:

Q   One thing I wanted to ask you is, you said you were uncomfortable
before.

Co   Yeah.

Q   You're not sitting like someone who's uncomfortable.

Ty   (interrupting) Well yes.

Q   Your voice has been fairly strong. . . .

Co has 'put down' Q's idea and Q returns with a personal challenge. This is a
fate typical of suggestions made by members when internal relations are in
flux. However, at this early stage, internal disputes are not simply about
power. Consider the sequel to the above exchange:

O   Wouldn't it be best to have some sort of a raw ending left over from
each week anyway, so we can start off the next. I think if we, ah, if
we make some sort of precise psychological abstract at the end of
each session we'd have more trouble starting off the next. It's best
to, um, dwell on the others for a week. . . . What's been left over.

Ka   You can always bring it up at the next session.

Ty   We should attack someone at the end of each session so they're still
angry next week.
(general laughter)

Co   Would you volunteer to be attacked?

Ty seems to have seen the attacks dealt out by Co and Q. Her joke acts to
present this consciously to the group. The material that was earlier projected
outward during the discussion about the adolescents becomes discussed in the
group. As with group 1, the process of internalizing group projections results
in internal dispute. A clarification of external boundaries allows for the
identification of internal boundaries. The aggression previously located in the
adolescents is now within the group and members struggle with its containment. The earlier discussion on honesty and sensitivity has already provided
a framework.

Ty   Maybe if people feel ripped off they should say something when it
happens. If they're feeling angry, like if they're feeling angry about
being jumped on . . . they deal with it right then and there . . . they
don't get carried over. These sort of things can . . . can steamroll,
basically. You know, you start to feel a little bit aggro this time,
and you're a bit more sensitive next time it happens, and you get
more and more sensitive and then you start to feel persecuted, and

> then you start getting angry and the group falls to pieces in a great
> big heap.

Ty is referring specifically to Q, but she is also voicing the general fears of
group members with regard to aggression. The heightened feelings of persecution that accompany a reinternalization of projections are well described.
Ty plays a role parallel to that of T in group 1.

> Group members continue their discussion by considering the dichotomy of
> 'feelings' vs. 'intellect'. Feeling deserted by the formal authority figure, they
> refer back to what is expected of them.

O   One guideline which we have is to ... we're supposed to be reflecting
     on the group's behaviour which is to some extent reflecting on our
     own, which means a third eye ... which is what the intellectuality is
     all about, rather than the idea of just, um, well a lack of self-awareness
     ... developing material and getting this all reflected back to you ...
     nice and warmly, without getting a topic to shake the foundations.

Yet this task has already been identified as somehow malevolent:

L   I have definite disc uiet at present and it's probably just me reflecting
     on me. That's, I'm listening to the group and I think: 'Oh, yes
     somebody's saying that.'. . . Um, I think, I guess, I look at myself
     and I think of the time I used to play the role of the you know, sort
     of smart bastard. That is, working out what people were doing, and
     I remember I was in a group in Sydney once and some lady said some-
     thing and I said: 'Oh yeah.'. . . Sort of sit there. And this lady broke
     into tears and I thought: 'You bastard. You're just playing games.
     You're just working out what's going on and picking it out, playing
     with it. And I guess I have a disquiet, for me at least, that ... am I
     learning to play smart games and lose some compassion for people?
Y   It seems always to be a problem in psychology though. Because
     that's what you're studying ... it's people and you're one yourself.
Co   And you've got to write 2,500 words being a 'smart bastard' later on.

In the case of this group, the group-that-was-joined, being the consultant's/
psychologist's group appears to have persecutory and malevolent intent. At
least it is this aspect that is focussed on here. Freud notes the evolution of the
'internal watching agency' in the ego and its relationship to paranoid
persecutory feelings.

> It would not surprise us if we were to find a special psychical agency which
> performs the task of seeing that narcissistic satisfaction from the ego-ideal
> is ensured and which, with this end in view, constantly watches the actual
> ego and measures it by that ideal. . . . Recognition of this agency enables us
> to understand the so-called 'delusions of being noticed' or more correctly

of being watched. . . . A power of this kind, watching, discovering and criticizing all our intentions, does really exist.

(Freud, 1914, p. 95)

The malevolent group-that-was-joined, with its consultant/psychologist, forms the basis of an identification, although the students feel uncomfortable about such an identification. Also, it seems that the group members are enacting aspects of the watching agency, feeling it sometimes in themselves and at other times in the consultant/psychologist, or in the implicit group-that-was-joined with its demands that they 'analyse' others without compassion.

What can be said about the group at this point? On the one hand members have begun to integrate within a boundary that distinguishes them from other groups past and present. They are clearly concerned about aggression and attack, which may be fear of retaliation for their own anger at being abandoned by the consultant, or may be a general social reaction to close proximity with a group of relative strangers in a new and strange situation, though it is brought clearly into the group. The theme of aggression manifests itself in some initial bickering which is consciously noted, as well as in a growing fear that the group-that-was-joined (with which the present group stands in a symbiotic relation) is malevolent.

Schoeck (1966) and Klein (1975) note the relationship between envy and persecution. Schoeck, especially, demonstrates the function of the 'third eye' in cultural myths as the projected eye of envy (cf. O's statement above). The group-that-was-joined by these members contains not only the watching agency, but also their desires (to become psychologists), their envy (they are still only students) and their agency of judgement (embodied in the consultant who marks their essays).

Segment 4 The symbiosis

The discussion moves to the problematic of group phenomena. W and Ka question the idea of the group as 'over and above' the individual. Ty and D attempt to convince them that group phenomena do exist.

Some criticism of note taking ensues. One member states accusingly: 'I thought this was an experiential thing!' The consultant then makes a lengthy interjection:

Consultant
    What I've been hearing a lot of is, bouncing around between various polarities. Is it intellectual? Is it emotional? Do you observe or do you participate? Other people are saying are they necessarily dichotomous? It seems to me that dichotomies are useful, if only to allow you to take a stand. But there's a lot of what I'd call ambivalence as well. Once you take a stand out here you've lost the other one if you

can't also keep it in perspective. Likewise when you're over this side you've lost what O wants this group not to be – purely emotional, subjective. He wants an intellectual comment. I, as course instructor, would certainly agree with that and I can't justify it on any other grounds. On the other hand most of your courses are taught from an intellectual viewpoint, so that the other ways . . . are also important.

Much of the latter part of this session, after the above comments, deals with the members' relations to the consultant. The 'good' aspects of the consultant become points of identification. For example, at the level of conscious content, the members attempt to discover what it means to become a group, a task set by the consultant. They take up the question of integrating intellectual and emotional aspects of their functioning. They use the consultant's term 'polarities' in the debate which follows.

Similarly, at a less conscious level, the development of roles seems to reflect aspects of the consultant. O appears to have the role of 'intellectual' at least insofar as he pushes for intellectual rigour (something that a course instructor would certainly agree with). Such a role puts him in close relation to the consultant and, during an extended debate over 'intellectualizing', other members attempt to convince O of a need for emotional expression, which is the other aspect referred to by the consultant. This long debate seems to represent dual aspects of the good benevolent consultant/psychologist's group-that-was-joined. J enters this debate somewhat abruptly:

J   Look, I find you're talking above us, to put it bluntly.
O   Oh well I've been told that before, yeah.
J   I find you're talking above. . . .
O   Am I making sense to anyone?
General
        Yes, yes. (to J) Why do you think he's talking above us?
J   I don't know half the words. I can't understand. Maybe I'm . . . I
        don't know . . . alone.
O   Can you give me some examples because at the moment you're
        above me.
        (laughter)

and later:

J   I don't know. I find we're talking about what a group should be
        doing rather than being a group, and that's where O's intellect
        came in, so we are kind of theorizing about what a group should be.

J does challenge, in a rather confused and tentative way, the whole question of authority through intellect. He emphasizes a dismissal of the 'should', the interdict of authority (Rieff, 1966). As with Ju in group 1, this is not so much part of a rebellion as an early attempt to question the genesis of action in the group. J is a problem to the other members because he seems to stand totally against the identification with the 'good' consultant. From their point of view, his critical attitude is difficult to assimilate and stands not for the 'malevolent bad' aspect identified earlier, but for an alienated part that is not included in the symbiosis and somehow acts alone.

Ty   Do you feel that you're satisfied with the answer you got? Do you feel like you asked a question? You probably put forward a protest. Do you feel like that's been attended to? Or do you feel like you were stomped on?

J   I don't really know. I don't feel in the right mood to really go deep into it.

Unidentified voice
      Well what would you like to do then?

J   At the moment have a drink.

Ty   Right, off to the – (hotel)

J   Yeah, because it was very tough getting here. I had to break through the Moomba (festival) crowd. (laughter) And they're all going the wrong way. (laughter)

Voice
      What, towards Moomba?

J   Like when you're trying to get down to C– and they're all going the other way.

Co   Do you feel the group is going the wrong way compared with you, as well?

Both Co and Ty attempt to reintegrate J by attempting to 'understand' him. The session ends with some hope. Members seem to have found enough good in their enterprise to overcome the malevolence experienced earlier. A close identification with the good consultant/teacher sustains them.

More importantly, the symbiosis with the group-that-was-joined is centred around the benevolent aspects of being in the group. Evidence for this can be seen in the belief of some dominant members that becoming part of the group means feeling emotionally close to the centre of the group. Take Ty's earlier comments:

Ty   I sort of see it as me standing back and watching like I sort of really feel I'm intellectualizing. I feel like I am standing back. And when I'm feeling, I'm really sort of right in there. There's a difference. I'm standing back and looking at the whole group and what's happening, the sort of overall patterns and it's playing the intellectual games. Or you're right in there and feeling something, and your primary concern is sort of dealing with what you're feeling . . . how close you are to what's going on.

This belief extends to anger expressed at those who take notes:

W   I figure we've got the cassette and we can chase it up afterwards.

Ka   Yes I agree. I'm surprised. . . .

D   What about the things that don't get conveyed on the cassette?

Ty   Yes, but you've got a memory.

W   You've got a memory. You can write it out afterwards.

Ty   If you're gonna. . . .

Voices

    But how? That's ridiculous after an hour and a half.

Ty   If you don't see it . . . sort of intense interaction.

The argument posed by W and Ty implies that those taking notes are not being part of the group, 'right in there'. Underlying this is the division between those who live and hold the group memory, and those who are outside and have a memory only through notes or tapes. One is either intensely part of the group, or is outside, observing. In this sense, the group is living the two positions (of participation and observation) stated at the very outset by the consultant. Insofar as the consultant represents the group-that-is-joined, these members may be seen, at this stage, to be living the symbiosis.

CONCLUDING REMARKS

The relationship of the consultant to the group-that-was-joined is an important one. Clearly, in the present case, the consultant, as instructor and psychologist, represents that group and holds authority within it. Most importantly he provides the major structural bases for the group's symbiotic relationship in that the consultant/group-that-was-joined entity acts as the container for the growing tentative identity that will become a group. The potential group is protectively contained.

The major structural bases are:

1 Provision of a primary task for the group (Rice, 1965);
2 Provision of a structure that allows for organizational defences against anxiety (Jaques, 1955; Menzies, 1970).

In the present case the primary task is given at the beginning of the session as a divided task: 'to actually participate in the group process and at the same time to observe ourselves as we form'. Much of the first session may be seen as an attempt by group members to integrate around this dual task: out there watching, or, in here feeling. The dual task provides a ready made mechanism for discriminating good from bad in terms of the group. It seems that it was easy for some members to experience the split as the malevolent 'bad' watcher and the good engaged 'feeler'. In this way, attacks can safely be made on those who merely observe or write notes, or on those aspects of oneself that are not engaged in the group. Both of these aspects are seen as relevant to psychologists, and in a broader sense are reflected in the field as a whole, i.e., the objective observers and researchers, and the empathic helpers.

Chapter 9

Group 3, session 1

Group 3 consisted of 10 student members (seven females and three males) and a female consultant. A male observer (member of staff) was present and sat outside the group circle. All group members were students enrolled in a Bachelor of Arts degree at a Melbourne college. The group session to be discussed was the first in a series of 14 sessions that were part of a course on group dynamics.

Once more, this session will be analysed by an examination of segments of the transcript. Before this session began, the students had already met together once with their tutor (who also acted as observer during this session) to discuss general course content. During this time, initial name giving introductions occurred. A 30-minute coffee break then ensued before the study group session began.

Segment 1 Initial anxieties

The session begins with some members requiring clarification of the task with the consultant and amongst themselves, the very first comment being: 'Are we doing what we're supposed to be doing in the second part now?' A comparison with past seminar groups then occurs:

Ha   I was just thinking back to first year when we were first having to, um, say a seminar group, when the first few sessions, you know, we'd always direct a comment to the tutor and then after that we'd start to direct them around the group . . . just mentioned that in case we wanted to short circuit the first part of that and go. . . .

Consultant

In fact the first part wasn't short circuited because the first questions were to me.

Ha   Yeah I realize that. I realized that once I had directed to you.

Er   Which sort of answers the question you directed at (the tutor) earlier, that even though we know what's gonna happen, are we going to avoid it by knowing what's happened? We knew what's gonna happen but it wasn't avoided.

Ha   Yeah, that's a good point.

Implicit in this discussion is the paradox of both desiring to please the consultant ('doing what we're supposed to be doing'), and of resisting the consequent dependence ('short circuiting the first part'). Members believe this resistance is what the consultant seems to want. Hence the group begins by entering the paradox of desire: in this case, that the group be special in fulfilling the desire of the consultant for a group that learns. This is comparable to the mirrored desire of the infant/mother dyad (Lacan, 1949). Additionally, there is a fear that by making desire conscious, that which is desired will be spoilt. This thinking is not only verbalized but enacted at the outset of this group, i.e., the behaviour to be avoided is enacted. Ha enacts this paradox of desire by demonstration. He shows the others that knowledge of groups does not prevent typical behaviours. The wish to be special is not spoiled but is untested and put aside.

This group phenomenon is similar to the magical thinking of the child who makes a wish but will not divulge it lest it be negated; or to the unconscious processes which protect 'good' part-objects from 'bad' internal part-objects, according to Kleinian (1946) formulations.

The wish here is to be different from other groups; to be special. The fear is that the task, embodied in the consultant and present in the group-that-was-joined, will spoil the group-to-be-created by the members. The task is to make conscious the processes of the group. The fear is that knowledge is destructive. The demonstration is able to alleviate the fear by showing that (a) knowledge does not necessarily change anything and need not, therefore, be destructive; and (b) the wish to be special is protected by not really testing its validity in reality.

We will return to a discussion of these processes at a later stage, when the group itself re-examines the issues. It is sufficient to say now that they are mentioned by Bion (1961) as part of the Dependency Group, and may be considered part of the broader domain of the Imaginary (Lacan, 1977).

The group discussion continues with members discussing their anxieties about being observed and recorded:

Fr   You can see the observer, observing. We are the guinea pig. (laughs)
Ha   It's very hard to, yeah, even start a conversation when you're just, well, when you're with people you hardly know. And also it's very difficult to talk when you know you're being recorded.
Er   I don't know about that. . . .
Al   We'll probably all get to a stage where later on we all just forget that they are there.
Ha   Once we forget what are there?
Ge   I was thinking that. That eventually they won't be as important as they are.

The anxiety about being observed is strongly evidenced not only in the overt comments, but also in the ambiguity about the microphones. (Ha asks 'forget what are there?', referring to both the microphones and the staff members.)

An attempt is made to avoid the anxiety by focussing on individuals:

Ca   Do you think we could, um, focus in on something else. We could perhaps look at how we could get to know each other.
Er   OK fire away!
Ca   Me? Alright. What do you want to know?

In summary, the initial anxieties of members centre on their desires to do well and to be special. Yet to do well in the eyes of the consultant is to demonstrate knowledge of groups from a study of the group itself. That is her given task. Hence to fulfill the perceived desire of the consultant, a demonstration of knowledge is required.

Anxieties about performing this task whilst being observed are then discussed. In Freud's (1921) terms, we can say that the consultant at this stage provides the ego-ideal; this is a point of integration for the group. The 'watching agency' (Freud, 1914), structurally linked to the ego-ideal, reveals its presence in the fear of being observed, which is prominent but remains unexplored. Group members move defensively to an examination of individual members, although the focus is on the individual outside the group, as shall be seen in the next segment.

Segment 2 Two members

The second segment of the group transcript centres around two members who give details of their lives and are questioned by others. Questioning leads to an emphasis upon the work life of the two people concerned. Both describe themselves in a helping role with the public, however the first describes herself as a consultant and is questioned extensively on this role. The second member is questioned on his contacts with unemployed people, whom the members basically perceive as angry. One member says, for example: 'The anxiety of unemployment would make them angry.'

As in groups 1 and 2, this discussion is about groups external to the present group. The groups under discussion are people with marriage breakdown problems and the unemployed. Given the previous comments about overdetermination of group content (Chapter 8), these two problems seem relevant to a group that is experiencing difficulty in relationships, and whose members feel that they don't have a concrete task or employment.

The following comments by members are relevant:

Ca   I was under the impression that we were going to be set a specific task. When we discussed that I was outvoted three to one.

Ge   It was strange. I said before, when we were talking in the coffee
      break that I thought it'll all become fairly clear in the first half hour
      how people will handle their anxiety.

It seems that 'handling their anxiety' is partially achieved by a discussion of
the group's problems in the context of external groups. Once more the mirror
function must be stressed. It is as if members both reassure themselves that
their problems are not unique and insurmountable, and they attempt to
examine those problems 'at a distance'.

Interestingly, this group centres its discussion of outside groups on the
leadership or consultant role in those groups. The questions directed to the
'consultants' are largely about how they handle difficult situations with the
people they encounter, itself reminiscent of the group 2 discussion about
handling difficult adolescents. For example:

Ty   Do you carry out the role of trying to patch up marriages that seem
      to be, uh. . . .
and,

Al   Which way do you handle them? (the unemployed)

The mirror relation to the present group is again evident. It is as if, on finding
that the consultant present in the group is not willing to lead them or to
answer their questions directly, group members may discover, in alternative
'consultants', the answers that they desire. The most pressing desires relate to
dealing with the anxieties mentioned earlier, i.e., about the danger of
knowledge and the fears of being observed (and found out!). These anxieties,
subtly present at the onset of the session, become overt after the consultant
intervenes:

Consultant
      The people in the group are worried about the anxiety that's here,
      and how it's going to be coped with initially.
Ca   I don't even understand why I am anxious.
Ha   It's a strange thing. We were talking about when we were having
      coffee, how you get downstairs and have coffee and everyone sits at
      the same table, and everyone talks, and you find too many people
      talking at the one time. And as soon as you get in this situation – it
      happens in any class not just this class – as soon as you get in this
      situation no one wants to talk.
Ge   We're not judged there.
Er   Why do you think we're being judged now?
Ge   I don't know whether we're being judged or not, but I think that
      that's part of the anxiety that we feel.
Fr   Even if you are going to be judged, you are not going to be punished
      for anything you say, or say in your own way.

Ca   You mean judged in the form of, in the sense of being assessed?
Ge   Well I guess what I meant was, that now we're in the company of a
     couple of experts where our psychopathology is going to show up a
     great deal more than it would in the coffee break.

The anxieties have been clearly voiced. They include paranoid fears of being
manipulated ('we are the guinea pig'), of being probed and found wanting
('our psychopathology is going to show up'), and of being judged and
punished. These seem to be common fears among students, and of members
in the initial stages of group formation. Being recorded adds to these general
paranoid feelings, and this is despite the fact that members agreed amongst
themselves to be recorded in order to aid their study.

These anxieties were present in members from the very beginning of the
session. They became intensified in the presence of an authority figure who
seems to fail them by not being dependable enough. In this instance, the group
defence was to find dependency figures amongst themselves (alternative
consultants). The term 'group defence' is used guardedly, however, as this
process of looking outward to other groups and their consultants/leaders
seems to be a necessary and important part of group development in general.
In a sense, the external group acts as a container for projective identifications
(Bion, 1961; Klein, 1946; Ogden, 1979) because the group attempts to work
through its anxieties at a distance. Members do the work via their external
group membership rather than through the present group membership. The
outside group is in the place of the 'other' whose position provides a standard
for the differentiation of an autonomous subjectivity (Lacan, 1949; 1956).

Segment 3   Internal focus and symbiosis

After openly discussing their anxieties, group members move to a discussion
about their own group. Their perceived difficulties centre on entry, and their
anxieties indicate their beliefs about the nature of the group-that-was-joined.
It seems that to become a member means possible exposure to exploitation
and manipulation. Yet they are caught in a dilemma: their presence in the
discussion means that they are already members, at least of something.

Ge   I guess it's our problem about doing it. (the task)
Er   We're not really a group apart from the fact we're all sat round in a
     circle. That's all.
Ge   I think we are a group.
Er   We're a very loose type of group. We're only – to start off, it's a
     fairly artificial group. It's been formed to discuss itself.
Fr   What do you mean artificial?
Er   Just what I said.
De   We've been put in a group.
Er   Yeah.

Ca   No. We haven't been put.
Fr   Not really.
Ca   We're here voluntarily.
Fr   Yes.
De   Oh yes, but the chairs have been placed around and here we are in a group.
Er   Who in the group put the chairs like this?
      (Silence. Fr laughs nervously.)
Ca   Nobody in the group.
Er   Nobody in the group did that I think.

The dialogue indicates that members are unsure about who created the group. On the one hand, they are there voluntarily; on the other hand, they feel they have been formed by the consultant. If no one in the group put the chairs in a circle it must have been her. She is seen as external to the group that is forming in its suspicions, yet she is the initiator of actions in the group-that-is-joined, the artificial group. The group, in attempting to form itself, finds only shared anxieties. Yet to join the consultant's group leaves members helplessly exposed to manipulation.

An interpretation along these lines leads to the first expressions of anger in the group. One member accuses another of observing and writing down those observations. In her accusation she points out that the member indicated had himself previously objected to observers. A third member intervenes and the group moves to discussing how things would improve in the next session after they had all done more reading about groups. A lively debate then ensues about the nature of their task. This leads members to feel pleased with their progress.

De   Yeah 'cos processes are occurring irrespective of what we are talking about so I don't think it's important that we are discussing the group processes at the time, we could do it later and talk about anything. The major stumbling block that we've got is that everybody is so anxious. I think it's. . . .
Ha   We've gone back to that again and that's not a bad thing either. The fact that we're going round in circles doesn't necessarily have to be a bad thing.
Ca   Each time round it's a little bit easier.
Ha   And each time round you begin to recognize it and say: 'Wow, there's a pattern here.' Isn't that a group process in itself? Haven't we achieved a task already?

The process of integrating and becoming a group has clearly moved to a central point within the group itself. However, the integration is tentative and members gain a sense of their own identity in the eyes of the consultant and her task. During this time members are constantly glancing at the consultant.

The atmosphere is tense. Ha's words are an attempt to convince the members, including himself, that they are behaving as they should. It is as if, for the members, the group can exist only if the consultant approves of its existence. Consider the following:

Ge   Isn't it interesting that after the leader (consultant) says something
     .... (indistinct)
Ha   Yeah there's always a period of ... well *that's* shot down. What'll we
     do now?

There is a strong fear that the bad, observing, judgemental consultant will destroy individuals; that she will shoot them down. Ge, however, who often directs attention towards the consultant, identifies anger as being in the members themselves.

Ge   The group processes, to me, seem to have been very cohesive in the
     sense that we were very anxious. That anxiety dissipated a little bit
     and was replaced by anger after something had been made –
     whatever the term is – overt, I suppose, by S (consultant), and
     again we waffled and the anxiety rose again when we were talking
     about me. That's all I can do at the moment. And again S makes
     something overt and immediately there's anger again.

On the whole the group accepts Ge's description, although some members stated they felt more anxious than angry. The attempt to reintegrate some projections of anger and hostility allows for an open discussion of fears about internal issues.

This segment of the transcript has identified the way in which this group internalized the integration process. A comparison with other groups is abandoned for the time being, and members begin to identify their own qualities. The problems addressed are pertinent to the discovery of a symbiotic relationship, i.e., an exploration of the boundary between self and other, and of the other within the group. Examples abound and are best phrased as questions: Whose creation is the group? Who placed the chairs? Who is hostile (the members, or the consultant and observer)? Should the members talk of the future or only be present (in the consultant's presence)?

The distinct boundary between the external observer who is all knowing and judgemental, and the individuals who became members, has blurred. Dangers and benefits are no longer clearly 'out there', i.e., in others outside the group.

Segment 4   Confidentiality

The next clearly identifiable topic is one of confidentiality. Although other groups are referred to, the major focus is internal to the group.

De   I've heard stories about other groups, psychological classes, where
      feelings were pretty intense and some people ended up not talking
      to each other, and I've been nervous about ... I've been sitting here
      waiting for somebody to jump down somebody else's throat and
      cause a problem.
Ha   It'll probably happen.
Ca   That's part of it too, isn't it. I mean I'd like to think that anything
      that happens in the study group is not carried over into the next
      lecture or tomorrow. If we can detach this study group from our
      relationships with each other outside the study group. ...
Er   I think it'd be very hard.
De   That'd be nice.
Er   Well I've seen – I only know about last year's group and what I saw
      ... a few people that I used to see afterwards. There were members
      of that group that they didn't like. Now I don't know whether they
      never liked them at all anyway – could be. I don't even know ... but
      the names they used to (indistinct) about the same person or
      persons just about every week.
Ca   That bears out the point I'm trying to make – that any hostility or
      any emotion at all remains clearly within the group, in my opinion.
      It would be better if we could make some arrangements to keep
      them quite mutual otherwise. ...
Er   It's like shutting off your emotions at 4 o'clock.

It is clear that many of the individuals who have become members have long
been aware of fears about the possible destructiveness of others. The
group-that-was-joined is felt to have a history of violence. (De says: 'I've been
sitting here waiting for somebody to jump down somebody else's throat.') The
anxiety prominent earlier may be understood better in the light of such fears.
However, the group itself can become a forum for such a discussion, and a
container for such awareness, only when it is integrated enough to reflect on
its own nature. It is as if cognitive functions within the group lag behind the
actual emotional experiences that the members have together. This point
requires elaboration.

    In the present case, the anxiety felt by members seems to stem from two
major sources. First is the fear that the consultant will expose members as
generally weak and incompetent. Second is the fear that members will attack
each other. In the group setting, these fears are the basis of early projections
where the consultant is experienced as both powerfully judgemental and
manipulative. It is only after these projections are experienced, discussed and
partially reintegrated that their origins in the fears of members can be openly
examined. Another way of viewing this is to construe the process of
signification (i.e., of giving meaning to experience) as largely retrospective
(Lacan, 1957).

These dynamics are accompanied by differing structural configurations. During the early unintegrated moments, members find commonality in an external group that seems to have a more integrated existence than their own. The image of such a group not only provides a boundary between inside and outside, but also provides for the possibility of wholeness (Lacan, 1949). The possibilities discovered in such a vision lead to an internal focus, and individuals become members of the group-that-is-joined. In becoming members, some individuality is lost through a shaping which emanates from the (perceived) desire of the leader, who is leader of the group-that-is-joined. Or, more simply, members are shaped by the desire of the group itself as it was (or is) conceived by members within history, in this case, from year to year.

Membership of the group-that-is-joined is somewhat problematic for the individual. Vast amounts of experience must be discarded, projected or suppressed, in order to assume a particular member role. Those who are the chief containers of the group's anger or anxiety forget their abilities for compromise or problem solving. These are the dilemmas of the membership individual (Turquet, 1975) or the person caught in groupthink (Janis, 1972). Consequently, those who take on early leadership functions may forget their abilities to follow, and become locked in unresolvable power struggles (Zimbardo, 1969; 1977).

Membership of the group-that-is-joined is evidenced in the symbiosis where an uneasy mistrustful dependency accompanies suspicions about the authorship of group events. During this time, the issues of trust, confidentiality and fear of exposure are at their height. Ca attempts to get others to agree to a norm of confidentiality. In order to persuade she says: 'Surely clinical psychologists or people practising in that sort of area would have to learn skills like that.' In her mind at least, the possibility that the consultant (a clinical psychologist) might not be trusted is barely denied. An interpretation made a few minutes later linked the issue of confidentiality with the earlier fears of being observed.

Segment 5   Repetition

The group members continue by discussing their anxieties once more. They reiterate fears of the tapes, the observers, and of making enemies within the group. Still concerned with the origin of actions, they reconsider Bs, one of the two members considered in segment 2.

Bs I had to talk about me and nobody else has, and I've been waiting for everyone else to.
Ca You had to? Who made you?
Bs Well I guess. . . .
Er Me!
Bs Yeah, he put pressure – yeah right!

Ca   It was your suggestion in the first place. . . .
Er   Right.
Ca   We should talk about ourselves.
Bs   Nobody else has.

There is concern with the question of manipulation, yet, this time round, two members, Ge and De, consistently remind others of their task:

Ge   If the group task is to examine the group process, do we all have a different idea of what a group process is? Is anxiety a group process? Is anger?
De   Why are people so angry? What is it everybody is afraid of?

Whilst returning to discuss anxiety, the idea of being 'shot down' returns:

Ca   I was just feeling that anything I had to say was going to be shot down. I'm just finding it very difficult to say anything at all.
Er   I think that might be a general feeling. People are afraid to start something – everybody else might jump on them.

and later:

De   If somebody makes what somebody else considers a bad observation, it doesn't really matter does it? It might mean the person's being shot down but I don't think it should.
Er   It will probably be, initially. If you say something and somebody says: 'That's a lot of rubbish,' and says something else, and everybody agrees with it, you probably feel a bit silly. But it's not going to last very long. It's not going to make that much difference, I don't think.
Ge   If I understood what Ca was saying, she doesn't mind if someone says: 'That's a load of rubbish.' It's when it's not as overt as that, that it's a problem.

It seems that members are able to voice their anxiety but can go no further. A large segment of time has been spent in repetition, with some elaboration. The symbiosis is in evidence insofar as members have great difficulty in seeing themselves as the authors of their own actions. Further, the relationship with the consultant is still seen as threatening to their self-esteem ('being shot down'). One defence against the paranoid anxieties is humour. The nature of the humour, however, is not that of a life-giving social exchange but a lifeless and barren presence masking an absence, as the next exchange shows:

Ty   I'm just saying what I experienced, you know. That it seems to be a very serious group. Haven't heard much of pregnant jokes, you know. Not much wit.
De   Also people are a bit reluctant to try out their jokes on a new crowd of people.

Ha   (laughs) Without a warm up.
Er   (laughs)
      (pause)
Ca   Like that pause.
Er   Yeah.
      (pause)
Ha   There it goes again. (laughs)
Bs   We could. . . . We'll have to learn some jokes between now and next
      week.
Ty   To fill in the gaps.
Bs   Mmmm.
Ty   So we can fill in the gaps.
      (pause)
Er   Only got ten minutes.

This group seems to end its first session with the members uneasy and unable
to resolve the problems present. The symbiotic phase is still at its height and
there seem to be too few good aspects to the group to support members through
their anxieties. They are waiting for the session to end in order to be released
from the situation. Yet they know that they must return and continue, if they
wish to achieve their individual aims. The session ends with fears of disintegration. The accompanying wish for social comfort through oral gratification
is apparent.

Er   Who's coming back next week?
De   (laughs)
Ca   Why shouldn't we come back.
Er   I'm coming back?
Consultant
      There does seem to be a bit of feeling that the group is
      disintegrating: when Ix left, the fear of people not coming back,
      and you did mention earlier that, if you were a social group, you
      wouldn't come back.
Er   If it were a social group I'd come back with half a dozen cans.
Ha   (laughs) Yeah. Perhaps that's the key.

This group will be discussed more fully at a later stage (Chapter 11 and
Appendix B) when the repetitions and apparent lifelessness in response to
anxiety will become clearer.

Chapter 10

Comparison of groups 1–3 from the cross-sectional study

Thus far, a comparison has been made between early group formation and early infant development, whereby the process of individual integration (Winnicott, 1945) can be seen to occur as the disparate elements, the members, create a new structural entity, the group. A discussion of group 1 indicates that the symbolic leader of the group-that-is-joined plays a major role by providing a centre about which these processes occur. Leadership, in this sense, is seen to provide both containment (Bion, 1970) and partnership (Mahler, 1968) for the developing group. These two aspects of the symbolic leader provide models for two alternative, yet complementary group structures, both of which act to maintain the group in the face of possible disintegration.

The discussion of group 2 delineates more clearly the manner in which the leader/consultant represents the group-that-is-joined, which in itself is symbolically able to provide the functions of containment and partnership. This group clearly acts as a structural entity in the formation of a new group, and its qualities may be realized in the leader and/or internal aspects of the members. A prominent example of the relations between the group-that-is-joined, the leader, and membership qualities, was evidenced in the rising apprehension of a malevolence felt to reside in the observing function. This function was identified as belonging to the leader (as psychologist), the members (as psychology students), and as a central function of the group-that-was-joined, and is commensurate with the observing function discussed by Freud (1914). The relationship of the watching agency to the ego-ideal (outlined in Chapter 8) illuminates Freud's (1921) discussion of groups (Chapters 3 and 5, above). Each member unconsciously seems to adopt the ego-ideal of the leader, becoming linked in a shared identity. According to the present analysis, the group-that-is-joined contains the ego-ideal and the watching agency via the members' projections, and these are later instituted into the group as it forms.

The analysis of group 3 further elaborated the role of the shared ego-ideal and its associated watching agency, felt in this case to be a judgemental and manipulative presence. As with the first two groups, integration occurred primarily at a distance through a mirroring process involving other groups. Gradually this became personalized when the 'locus' of integration moved from an external position to one within the group. Such a position is, moreover, at the intersection of the group-that-was-joined and the emergent group, i.e., at the location of the symbiosis. To continue the geographic metaphor, it is here that the pressing questions of the origins of action are to be found. During the symbiosis with the leader (of the group-that-is-joined), members struggle with questions of manipulation, coercion, power, and the general feeling of being subject both to a hostile force in the group yet feeling outside themselves as individuals. Simultaneously, such struggles mark the formation of a social reality for that group.

Not surprisingly a presence, felt to be in the group yet outside themselves, is experienced by members in a somewhat paranoid fashion. In fact, the emergent nature of their reality does not arise from a single identifiable source, leader or member. As mother and child create the child's reality between them in the space that is possible because human culture provides it, so too do individuals create their own group realities mutually, in that space made possible by the group-that-is-joined. In short, the group that has a history in a particular culture allows a focus, and provides the possible roles for individuals to fill in membership of both this group and the group-to-be-created.

A distinction between 'members' (of these groups) and 'individuals' (who tend to become members of many societal groups) is important when considering the comparison of early group and infant integration. Many groups in society, for example, take already integrated complex individuals as members (i.e., adult members). Any one group may draw on only a limited number of skills, abilities, motives, etc. of the individual. In fact most groups will severely limit the expression of an individual's potentialities, because members stand in a value relation to one another and are defined by their relatedness (see Chapters 2–4). Consequently, individuals rarely feel that they are their 'full' or 'real' selves in any one group. In considering group 3, it was evident, before the commencement of the session, that many individuals were aware of those anxieties which the group as a whole took some time to apprehend. These included fears of being attacked and judged, which served as a starting point for integration. Nonetheless, the group itself was at first unintegrated. Whatever the sophistication of individuals, it is the structure of the group, not its elements, that concerns us here.

There are processes and structures common to the three groups, discernible from the perspective of group integration, personalization (identity) and realization (emergent social reality). These will now be examined and are summarized in Table 1.

Table 1   States inferred from the observation of the first session of three different self-study groups

State: non-integrated
Introductions serve to reflect those aspects of individuals that belong to the role of member of the group-that-is-joined.

Group 1	Group 2	Group 3
Introductions	Introductions	Introductions took place prior to the first session. Initial anxieties about the group-that-was-joined are expressed.

State: mirror state
Integration is apprehended outside the group. Other external groups are discussed and seen to have identity. Some group work on norms, values, etc. may be done by discussing such issues tangentially, as they pertain to the external groups.

Group 1	Group 2	Group 3
Discussion about a group seen on a video tape in a previous year. This group is held as an 'ideal type'.	Discussion about several groups. Emphasis is mainly on delinquent adolescents. The discussion serves to investigate members' ideas on handling aggression, hostility and sexuality.	Discussion about the work of two members with outside groups. Emphasis is on disturbed marriage and the unemployed. The groups of these members seem to represent a unity denied the present group.

State: internal focus, internal division

Integration is attempted within the group. An initial form of group identity occurs. The internal state of the group does, however, contain difference and may be experienced as split (segregated) and chaotic. In contrast, the group-that-is-joined is perceived (in fantasy) as intact.

Group 1	Group 2	Group 3
Members discuss their expectations. Internal disputes appear. Suppressed hostility is evident. There is a myth that the group-that-is-joined is there to 'get things out of'.	Members discuss their own group and how it should develop. Disputes and differences arise between members. The group-that-is-joined is felt to be judgemental and potentially dangerous.	Members openly discuss their anxieties about becoming members of the present group. The group-that-is-joined is perceived to be potentially judgemental and manipulative.

State: symbiosis

Integration is achieved by symbiotic union with the group-that-is-joined through its representatives (usually a leader or, in the present case, a consultant). Group identity is achieved by individuals becoming members.

Group 1	Group 2	Group 3
The symbiosis is evident. 1. One member becomes strongly identified with the consultant. 2. The group acts as if the consultant's comments are commands. 3. There is confusion over who initiated a major issue in the group.	The group acts out the early polarity of action vs. observation raised by the consultant. Members also attempt to identify with the 'good' aspects of both positions. Strong identification with the consultant is indicated.	The distinctive boundary between the external observer (who is all-knowing and judgemental) and the members has blurred. Dangers are seen within the group. Questions of the origin of actions in the group appear.

State: created autonomy

In this state the members attempt to 'hatch' from the symbiosis and create their own group.

Group 1	Group 2	Group 3
Members begin to explore the possibility of becoming a group apart from the group-that-was-joined.	Not observed in first session.	Not observed in first session.

It should be noted that these structures and processes do not refer to developmental stages such as those presented by Bennis and Shepard (1956), Tuckman (1965), or Stock and Lieberman (1962); nor do they correspond exactly to the segments of transcript chosen in the previous chapters; nor do they form a comprehensive list of structures entered by groups in their formative times. They are *states* that may appear in historical sequences, although even this is not postulated as necessary (they are similar to Kleinian 'positions', or Lacanian 'moments').

The importance of conceptualizing these structural organizations as states is most urgently felt when examining group 3. This group, within its first session, repeated much of its initial content. The nature of states allows, even demands, that repetition (not necessarily regressive) may occur when certain associated dynamic conditions occur in the history of the group. Fluctuations from state to state depend upon many factors including the group environment and the conscious and unconscious motives of leaders and members. Most important, however, is the collusive group process where displacement and condensation act to gather and represent the most pressing of membership concerns in a collective fashion (see especially the discussion of group 2, Chapter 8).

Repetition of states may be evidenced in a variety of situations. For example, the symbiosis may be reinstated at those times when the autonomy of members is repressed, as in a group or regime where totalitarian measures dispel the individual members' ability to identify the source of their own feelings or actions. The technique of brainwashing is instituted under such conditions. Similarly, group and membership identity may move from a state of internal confusion to a greater or lesser integration. The history of religious groupings reveals the movement through many states of integration, schism, symbiosis and so on.

Symbiosis may return when members, for internal reasons (e.g., loss of members or failure at an important task), are subjected to intense anxiety, depression or disillusionment. Many returns to fundamentalism, to create anew from an original group-that-was-joined, may be viewed as the result of disillusionment with the autonomy of a long standing group (e.g., Lacan's 'return to Freud' after disillusionment with some forms of modern psycho-analysis, or the return to Islamic fundamentalism in Iran after disillusionment with the Shah's rule). The presence of the state of symbiosis is indicated by the questioning of the authorship of action, values and thoughts. In fact there is doubt about the group's ability to perceive and act independently as a whole. Yet with this state comes the possibility of a new space where new illusions may arise (e.g., the new 'French School' following Lacan). Without that space, states of internal division, or even disintegration, may occur.

Many other states are possible but will not be discussed here. With reference to group integration, however, two others are important. These are the states of disintegration and rebellion. Disintegration differs from un-integration insofar as the latter is a potentially pleasant state if achieved within a 'holding' environment, whilst the former involves the fear of fragmentation in a destructive and anxiety provoking environment.

Rebellion in 'laboratory groups' has been widely discussed (Slater, 1966; Bennis and Shepard, 1956). In the present scheme, a state of rebellion occurs when members actively reject the group-that-was-joined. A new and complexly created autonomy may follow rebellion, although other states are likely, given favorable circumstances.

Part III

The longitudinal qualitative study

This section is concerned with a longitudinal qualitative study of a group of 10 members, one consultant and an observer (12 persons altogether), who met for 14 one-and-a-half hour sessions over a period of 16 weeks. This is reported in Chapter 11 (the theoretical framework for this study includes the material presented in Chapters 2–5).

INTRODUCTION TO PART III

It has already been stressed in Part I, that the overall history of a group (as an entity) shares some characteristics with individual histories. These characteristics are best highlighted when we consider both group and individual as systems (Chapter 2). The group is a complex system of many individual motives, memories and concerns, etc., all of which are potentially available to the group. However, the group-as-a-whole may be understood only in terms of how these interact to produce that coherence that *is* the group system.

Winnicott's ideas in regard to the early experiences of the infant were found to be useful in discussing integration in groups. The other processes described by him as occurring in the infant during its early relatedness to the mother figure are personalization and realization (Winnicott, 1958). These seem pertinent as Winnicott may be describing the processes inherent in the histories of all living human systems, individual and group. Integration, for example, may be understood as a necessary aspect of system unity. From the perspective of the observer it is, perhaps, a major organizational principle allowing for parts to act as a whole and hence exist as a system. In addition, personalization, as a complex psychological process of internalized identity, may resemble group identity. Perhaps, too, realization is bound to our unique symbolic abilities as humans, and cannot be separated from our social and cultural definitions of reality in or out of groups.

It is recognized that the comparison of groups with individuals may be challenged, and an argument has already been presented in Chapter 10 with respect to the distinctions to be drawn between 'persons' and 'group members'. It is also recognized that pre-oedipal processes (e.g., personalization) and oedipal or post-oedipal processes (e.g., identity formation) may not be treated as identical. However, they are comparable and may operate synchronically in, e.g., a family group. In the case of the infant, the mother partner/container herself 'holds' the important social signifiers during the so-called pre-oedipal configuration. It is her role in the duality to introduce the child to these signifiers. The normal mother/child pair is predicated upon the presence of the oedipal configuration (Lacan, 1977), just as the life of the group is predicated upon socially shared significations (of members) from its inception. The hypothesis advanced here is that personalization and identity are both predicated upon similar structural assumptions.

As a general basis for the following analysis, it is assumed that the group is regarded as a living system which has a history, and whose structures and dynamics are both constrained and retrospectively restructured by the members' capacities to structure experience symbolically. Such a general conception allows a framework for the more specific approaches of Winnicott, Lacan, Freud, Bion, Klein, Harré and others. That is, it allows for the specific application of the approaches of both psychoanalytic writers and social psychologists who approach an analysis of groups as emergent systems.

Chapter 11

The longitudinal qualitative study

This chapter describes the structural analysis of a group of 10 student members, a consultant and an observer, over 14 one-and-a-half hour sessions. A structural analysis requires that we segment history into particular moments or states that contain meaning. Moreover, it is the observer who punctuates history (Maturana, 1970), and a group contains many observers who, collectively, give it meaning.

In examining the life of a particular group, certain considerations must enter the process. The observer of group life must segment its history according to certain theoretical principles. Additionally, s/he must consider whether the 'meaning' that is given to each moment, structure or state should arise mainly from his or her own cache of concepts, or should somehow be discovered within the concepts provided by the group members themselves, or both of these means.

THE APPROACH

This analysis will firstly approach the group chosen for study by identifying some major events in the group's history and considering these as central foci, traumas or social episodes (Harré, 1979; Forgas, 1979). These events, which all group members agreed were 'highlights' of the group, may lead to an understanding of the symbolic organization of the group, an organization that is neither obvious nor immediately available consciously to group members. It is this symbolic organization and its manifestations in group structure (i.e., its Imaginary representations) that is analogous to the Unconscious as elaborated by Lacan (1977), and to the symbolic organizations of myth and revealed in the transformations of myth structure outlined by Levi-Strauss (1964). Hence two levels of organization are postulated:

1 The surface level which is recorded in the history of the group and is organized around central foci which may be social episodes or events, but are essentially points of significance to group members. This will be taken to be the level of *group structure*.

2 The underlying *cultural level* of symbolic organizers, i.e., signifiers that are reflected in the events of the surface level.

An explication of the group's central foci should lead to a valid dissection of its history, valid at least in terms of the phenomenology of the group members, and of the group as an emergent entity. By proceeding from the surface level punctuated in this manner, it is hoped that a further examination will lead to insights about the underlying symbolic structure.

Additionally, the concept of group identity will provide a focus for the research. Identity is to be understood here as a result of how the group comes to have its own particular structure, derived from identifications within the ego-ideal and separate from the group-that-is-joined (see Chapter 5).

AIMS

In short, the present study aims to:

1 identify the traumatic or central events which act to punctuate the history of the group (i.e., the social episodes, Harré and Secord, 1972; Harré, 1979);
2 construct the historical states, moments or structures so organized through this punctuation;
3 deduce or infer the underlying symbolic organization of the group;
4 discuss the emerging identity of the group in terms of the states and structures identified;
5 link identity to power, leadership and authority in the group.

THE GROUP

This group has been described elsewhere in this work as group 3 (Chapter 9) although one member left and one new member commenced attending after the second session. The group consisted of 12 people. These were 10 student members (seven women and three men), a female consultant and a male observer. The members' task as a group was to 'study the processes of the group as they occurred'. This group was entitled 'the study group' and constituted an experiential section of a course in 'Group behaviour', which in turn made up an optional unit in a Psychology major within a Bachelor of Arts degree at an Australian College of Advanced Education. The observer was a male member of staff, who also led the group members in a tutorial discussion which constituted another section of the same course. He sat in a corner of the room away from the group, who usually sat on chairs set in a circular formation during the study group sessions.

METHODOLOGY

Chapter 6 discussed the methods considered suitable for the study of groups as well as some methodological problems. It was argued that a descriptive analysis using formal and final causal explanations (Rychlak, 1968; 1977), would best serve the aims outlined above.

It is acknowledged that the task of observing has its own organizing principles which may influence and distort the observation process, e.g., the problem of deciding which entities should be the focus of observations (Chapter 6). However, the present observational task may best be served by an analysis that closely follows the 'text' of the group. This will provide an approach to the group at the surface structural level. Consequently all group sessions were taped and the tapes were transcribed. Frequent reference will be made to these transcripts.

METHODS

The following longitudinal 'case' study will lean heavily on Harré's (1979) methods of identifying episodes, acts and actions. This is because these categories provide a distinctive manner of punctuating and operationalizing the social interpretations required to make sense of behaviours in groups. They offer one means of quantifying complex observations so that meaningful comparisons can be drawn between different segments of the group history. Here the acts and actions concerned are primarily verbal because of the task of the group. The episodes are coherent segments of social interactions, identified as 'wholes' by the participants.

The accounts of group members will also be examined in order to aid an interpretation of the episodes identified. However, in the present study these accounts form part of the verbal acts themselves, and will not be treated as separate. (Appendix B, however, briefly reports on an accompanying study of group member perceptions, which acts as a support to the study presented here.)

This method can be employed only in a framework which considers the specific social dimensions involved; i.e., an analysis of episodes requires a general understanding of what type of episode is being examined. Harré's work is premised upon the theory that social life is both pragmatic and expressive. In terms of group life this could roughly be translated as the task and maintenance dimensions (Bales, 1958) or the work and basic assumption aspects (Bion, 1961), although the emphases implicit in these concepts make some difference.

It is proposed here to examine specifically episodes or foci within the political and emotional dimensions of the group. As outlined in Chapter 5, this is because identifications and identity play a major role in the dynamics of both leader/member and member/member relations, and so an examination of the political (i.e., power and authority) and emotional dimensions of group life is necessary.

The political dimension is, in fact, of paramount importance because it is concerned with the tasks and functions of leadership, and with the relatedness between members on issues of power and authority. Bennis and Shepard (1956) and Tuckman (1965) see authority issues in groups as constituting the first major concerns of members. These concerns are viewed as, firstly, focussed on the members' relations with the leader, and, later, on members' relations with each other.

The first episode to be considered will be treated in greater depth than the later episodes. The reason is that the first episode contains structures and meanings that remain somewhat constant and therefore do not require new descriptions in later episodes where they are often developed further. This reflects a process whereby the group begins by developing a structure that later becomes changed or moderated according to new circumstances, i.e., the group has a history.

ANALYSIS OF THREE MAJOR EPISODES

This section aims at identifying and analysing the surface group structures (see Introduction to Part III).

THE FIRST MAJOR TRAUMATIC EVENT OR EPISODE

The task given to the group members at the outset of their scheduled 14 sessions was to learn about groups by studying the processes and dynamics in their own group as they occurred. Each session was preceded by a theoretical seminar led by the staff member who acted as observer to this, the study group. It was stressed from the beginning, however, that the staff member acting as consultant to the study group was not there actively to direct or guide the group in its task, but would act in the capacity of commentator on the processes of the group as she saw them.

The first session has already been discussed extensively (see Chapter 9) in terms of the process of integration. The first major traumatic event to be discussed took place in session 6. Here one member made a direct and memorable verbal attack on another. This incident was the culmination of tensions that had built up over time, but especially in this and the preceding session. The attack was bitter but somewhat cathartic in that it served to express the suppressed emotions of some members, and to demystify others who were aware of the tension, but unsure as to its cause. A brief resume of the discussion preceding in sessions 5 and 6 is required:

Session 5 began with one member re-introducing a theme of death that had emerged previously (session 4). She then proceeded to talk of trust in the group and of her own fears of the loss of individuality entailed in group life. Other members developed this theme and also talked of their fears of discussing private feelings. In realizing that they were once more discussing problems of being 'shot down', some members expressed dissatisfaction at not yet having solved this problem.

Some half-hearted joking then occurred and one member's preoccupation with aggressive feelings was mentioned. At this stage Ha, a youngish male, spoke up:

Ha I used to think that Ge was the only one who felt it but now I feel I probably feel it too. I mentioned it last time for about the tenth time, about being canned. I don't know if I mentioned it at the time but I'm also worried about the first time I can someone else.

Ca You've been worried about that for a while haven't you?

Ha More and more all the time though.

Ca What's so frightening about the prospect of canning someone?

Ha (hesitatingly) I think it . . . trying not to intellectualize it too much. . . . I think that it's a real fear that I'm going to lash out at someone and the group will think that's going too far – he shouldn't've said that.

Er Are you afraid of hurting someone?

Ha No. I'm not afraid of hurting someone.

De Are you afraid of the group not liking you?

Ha Yeah! I'm afraid of being a shit.

The questioning of Ha continues. There is obviously interest in the possibilities that he presents:

Fr Were you contemplating some particular person? That's probably why you don't want to attack that person. It might represent power.

Ha I don't think that concerns me. I'm concerned I'll think about retaliation but not from the person I'm going to attack.

De From the rest of the group?

Ha It's getting more and more likely isn't it? Now it's the person I'm going to attack.

Er Why don't you do it?

Ha Even now I've still gotta have an excuse. I've got to have something to deal with to do it.

The next fifteen minutes are spent in discussing whether or not Ha should make his attack:

Ix The point is, Ha, that there have been attacks in the group before and they've been coped with, somehow, well or not well – I don't know if everybody coped with it. (speaks louder) If somebody in the group attacks another person something is going to happen.

Maybe not straight away, maybe later. Something's going to happen. But it's not necessarily going to be totally destructive. I'm sure there is a feeling that the group can destroy; that's a feeling. There is a feeling that one can almost destroy the group. That too is a feeling. But in reality those things don't actually happen in that . . . people come back. People continue to survive and perhaps the worst thing that can happen is that someone can leave the group. (silence)
That sounded as if I'm telling you to attack the person. I'm not really. . . .

Ha   You sure are! 'Go get 'em Ha', you said.

Ix   I'm not really.

and later:

Ha   It's the sort of thing that I . . . it's the sort of anger that I would tolerate outside and realize that . . . that it would be quite acceptable not to attack it, you know what I mean.

De   You'd just have to cope with it yourself and not take it out on anyone?

Ha   I wouldn't take it out on anyone in the way I would like to.

Er   You're going to have to do something.

Ix   The group might be waiting for you to, Ha, – to release their tension. We might be waiting for you to do it for us.

Eventually Ha refuses to talk about his anger any more. He says: 'Now I think that if I get angry I'm expected to act like a bloody raving lunatic and not be rational.' It seems that no one is quite sure who Ha wishes to attack and the group is left with a 'mystery' person. Other issues are taken up although Ha's anger and the 'mystery' person are often alluded to.

Session 6 began with Ca asking Al whether she felt depressed. Apparently this followed a discussion during the week, prior to the group meeting. Al hesitated but went on to discuss the basis of her depression. She had felt that she was the object of Ha's anger the week before but also felt that she was being 'supersensitive' about the issue. Although Al expressed the wish to curtail the discussion, Bs and Ix continued to prompt her.

Next the discussion returned to Ha and to the subject of anger. To some members the whole issue was mystifying and frustrating.

Er   Well we're faced with two . . . three choices. We can keep talking about Ha, Ha can talk about himself, or we can forget the whole thing and start something else.

Al   I'm sorry. I wasn't bringing Ha in. . . .

Er   (overriding her and sounding angry) Ha's either going to tell us what he feels, we're going to tell Ha what he feels or we're going to keep going and do something else. All we're doing now is sighing and saying – look you're doing it again! Either Ha's going to tell us or he's not going to tell us as far as I'm concerned. Are you going to tell us or not. . .? We may as well change the bloody subject.

The consultant is also confused and later in the session says:

Consultant
  Yet I've observed a reasonable amount of anger in this group today. I don't think people are so afraid of expressing anger when they feel it. I think there's something else they are afraid of expressing. It doesn't seem to be anger today because there's been snaps backward and forward over many things.
Bs I feel that there's a lot more anger. I don't think much anger is being . . . the degrees of anger have been very contained.
Ix I think the anger's been misplaced too. I think that's one of the problems. People have been misplacing anger since the time we walked into this room.

The consultant also remarks on the lack of obvious sub-groupings. However some members are aware of the sub-groupings present:

Ca The sub-groupings are quite clearly defined outside this room aren't they?
Ha I think they are inside too.
Ca They are inside, only it's not overt.

The situation is clearly understood by some members and not by others and it is in the atmosphere of tension built up by hints and innuendoes, sniping and frustration, that the attack occurs. Ha and Ix explain:

Ha I picked a safe target earlier today.
De What do you mean?
Ix He means he wasn't angry with me and I wasn't angry with him. It was just a setup, a game. It was as (the consultant) said, to prevent being too personal, safeguarding, protecting that which we may damage the most. Because we don't want to be responsible for damaging something that will really break, so we'll just bruise and it will get better.
Ca Yet when Ge did make some direct personal remark that died easily.
Ge Well I think it was seen for what it was, which was supporting to Ha rather than perhaps wanting really to have a go.
Bs Was that what you meant or was it. . . .
Ca When Ge said that Al annoyed her.
Bs Mmmm.
Ge I mean I would have been quite happy to have gone through with that, but it was really said in support of Ha.
Al Well can you go ahead with it now then? I mean I didn't get angry when you said that, I just accepted it.

(Voices all coming in quickly)

Ix   (strongly) You're supersensitive, you're never anxious. You read books but you don't . . . you're not honest about yourself and your feelings. You protect yourself and you delude yourself. So there! You've got it. The whole group's worth!

Other members continue by voicing their own criticisms of Al. Although there is some defence of her by members clearly not included in the attacking sub-group, these do not stem the tide of previously suppressed feelings.

It is as if Ix has provided a model for the release of anger. She acts to disinhibit others (Bandura, 1973; Redl, 1942).

This incident, referred to in the group as the attack on Al, has been described in some detail. It clearly brought to light some of the major sub-groupings and the dynamics between members. At this stage, although membership is not consistent through time, the sub-groups can roughly be identified in the following manner:

Sub-group 1: Ix, Ha, Bs, Ca and Ge, who launched the main critique of Al;
Sub-group 2: Al and Fr, who are friends outside the group and displayed allegiance to each other during the sessions examined;
Sub-group 3: De, Er and Ja, who are grouped mainly on the basis of their neutrality with regard to the previous two sub-groups;
Sub-group 4: The two staff members, who, it is understood, discuss the group after each session.

This incident is the culmination of a major social episode. What are the dynamics at play? Such a question may be approached in a variety of ways and here we can hope to establish only a few of the possibilities supported by the content of the group discussion. Possible hypotheses will be presented along with the evidence from the transcripts.

To begin, there is the simple explanation that some members were annoyed with Al's behaviour in the group. Until this point, presumably out of polite-ness, these members have not mentioned Al's annoying habits. Now, in order to fulfill a self-set task of being 'honest', members finally come to tell Al of her faults. The problem posed in doing this was to avoid the guilt it engendered, e.g., Ha says: 'I'm afraid of being a shit!' The solution to this problem involved an elaborate sub-grouping phenomenon involving partly conscious collusion, explained as follows.

Ha announces one week that he is angry with someone. He is then coaxed by group members, some of whom are later revealed as knowing to whom he refers, and some of whom are confused, or fear that it is them. But Ha refuses to say exactly what he is angry about. The next week sees the 'victim' taunted and prompted to talk of her depression and her vague suspicions that she is the 'mystery person'. The session continues with a discussion about anger, which contains many sarcastic and sometimes bitter snipes between the members of sub-groups 1 and 2. These snipes occur at a covert level (hinted at by Is and Bs: 'there's a lot more anger' and 'the anger's been misplaced too') and are confusing to the staff and to members of sub-group 3. Finally the attack occurs, and in the discussion afterwards it seems that Ix has acted as mouthpiece or seducer (Redl, 1942) for others.

Fr   Who were you speaking for, Ha, then?
Ha   Definitely speaking for me.
Fr   She has been speaking for you?
Ix   I've been speaking for more than Ha.
Fr   So it is possible your feelings are. . . .
Ix   I feel very exposed.
Ha   She's done almost what I asked her to do.
Ca   I think she said before she'd been set up, coaxed. I think she was all those things.

and later,

Ca   She's spoken a lot of things that we've been feeling.

The sub-group members were insistent that Ix's attack had not been planned but seemed to emerge in the session, and that the tensions felt by others were expressed by Ix. As Ca said: 'It was never set up, Al. I mean there was no deliberate attempt to set anyone up to speak for the group. It wasn't formal in any way.'

We are provided now with a second avenue of explanation for the incident. It would seem that members of a sub-group, who had casually discussed Al's behaviour whilst reflecting together on the progress of the group, had each felt annoyed by Al but had been unwilling to express their annoyance individually in the group. The accumulation of tensions, beginning with Ha's pronouncements and ending with Ix's outburst the next week, was the result of these feelings, and eventually, through a process of group collusion, hints and innuendo, a spokesperson emerged which allowed personal criticisms to be made. This explanation of incitement to act in a verbally aggressive manner seems satisfactory, particularly if, in the eyes of other members, Al is considered as a figure who invites attack, i.e., as much a persecutor as a victim, actively annoying other group members. Some little evidence for this process comes from the ease with which Ix changes from being seen as the 'attacker' to being seen as the 'victim'. Consider the following:

Ix leaves the group early saying that she does so because of

'cowardice I guess'.

Later Er says: (speaking strongly)

I feel that Ix was speaking for some members of this group, how they feel about Al, and those members of the group didn't have the guts to say it themselves and she's now . . . she's gone off now and she's gonna feel all the guilt for you, and she's done the axing for you.

'Attacker' and 'victim' are caught in a web of anger and guilt, strongly felt and voiced, and eventually discussed by group members. Yet this explanation requires another. Why is it that Al's annoying behaviours are the cause of so much antipathy, such strong suppressions, and, finally, an outburst that leads to guilt?

Let us consider her 'sins' as voiced by the group members, referring back to the transcripts of earlier sessions for evidence that may account for the strength of the emotions felt.

1. Emphasis on the tape recordings

Accusation in session 6:

Ca   Al most of the times you talk about the group, you talk about it as it is on the tapes, the tapes, the tapes.

Ix   Just listen back Al. It's there if you'll listen to it!

Apart from the irony inherent in Ix's comment, we may note that reference has been made to learning from the tapes by many members other than Al. For example, in session 2 Er declares that when he listened to the tapes he 'got more out of it'. Ca also refers to learning from what is heard on the tapes. In fact in session 2 she has an angry interchange with Ix whom, she claims, sabotages the work of others by speaking so softly that she cannot be heard on the tape. Perhaps by session 6 Ca has forgotten her own insistence on the importance of the tapes.

2. Being unfeeling

The accusation in session 6:

Ge   (accusingly to Al) But you can't come here and not *feel*, Al!

Ix   You protect yourself and you delude yourself.

In previous sessions both Ge and Ix have expressed difficulty in expressing their feelings. They both claim to have many feelings that they cannot always understand.

3. Emphasis on books and an intellectual approach

The accusation in session 6:

Ix   You read books but you're not honest about your feelings!

This accusation was made earlier in a general way about all the group members (session 2).

It seems that by session 6 these group members have rid themselves of these traits (i.e., insisting on the importance of the tapes, being dishonest and confused about their feelings, and referring to books in order to understand the group). They find them now almost exclusively in Al.

There is some unease in this projection, however, especially in Ge:

Ge   I think it's roughly these things Al, but the thing that probably worried me more than anything else is what is there in you that's like me. That makes me angry because there isn't anything in you that I would really like to be part of me. I don't mean that to put you down. I'm just trying to be honest.

Ca   What I think I was trying to say when I said I couldn't listen to you talking about your depression the other day, was because I couldn't identify with you.

Their attempts to distance themselves from Al are clear. Despite Ge's unease and partial awareness of what she is doing, the projective phenomenon is clear. So we can ask with Al: 'Am I the scapegoat again today?', and we can understand, by the present analysis, the strength of the attack on her. She is seen to hold many traits repudiated by others.

The use of Al as a scapegoat to account for repudiated traits and feelings is an hypothesis that seems to fit the observed facts, which are: (a) anger directed to Al by several group members after much tension is aroused by reference to a 'mystery person' villified by Ha; and (b) specific faults attributed to Al were openly discussed, in earlier sessions, as problems also belonging to other members.

But we still have to understand why it is Al who is 'chosen', and these particular traits. Certainly Al does exemplify certain readily observed behaviours in the group. She brings many articles and books into the group, and often refers to authors and the tapes. If other members did this also, as has been observed, they did so more noticeably in the earlier sessions. Why did they stop? Why did Al continue? Once again reference to earlier sessions is required.

Session 2 began with hostile interchanges between members who arrived on time and those who arrived late. The question of leadership arose along with a discussion about the role of the consultant. It seems that much of the early hostility is still present. The discussion centres on whether or not the consultant might 'shoot down' emerging leaders. Ha says: 'We don't want to feel that she's dominating us but we still want to rely on her.' Er says: 'It's amazing that we still see (the consultant) as a figure we're going to have conflict with.' Ge says: 'Why is she still sitting in the group if she's not part of it?' in reply to a query about the consultant's status.

During this discussion Al speaks. She explains how she feels about the consultant's comments to the group.

Al   I felt that we were being led by an expert. I'm not worried about who's sitting behind me. I'm not worried about the tapes. I'm not worried about the staff. I'm here to learn something and I'm here to get the guidance from a consultant.

At this stage it seems that Al does not feel the anxiety and hostility that the others are debating. This alone could make her a candidate for future hostility, but a comment by the consultant must be taken into account. The consultant, in commenting on the discussion about herself, refers members back to their feelings of being judged in session 1 (see Chapter 9). She makes the interpretation that members may be dealing with the anxiety aroused there by reversing roles in this session: 'Now you are able to judge me', she says. As an example in support of her interpretation, she points out how Al was able to judge her (the consultant's) comments in session 1 after listening to the tapes.

Other comments by the consultant have included:

1 a comment about members referring to books in order to understand her role, rather than trying to understand from direct experience (session 1);
2 interpretations (session 4) about the inability of members to 'come alive' in the group. This was based on members talking of the group as being 'artificial', and the people in the group as having roles rather than being 'real people'. These were referred to later by members, and often felt as a criticism of the group.

It seems, then, that these early comments by the consultant may have sealed the fate on the members' distinction between what constituted 'good 'and 'bad' behaviours in the eyes of the consultant. Using Al as an early example may have been an unfortunate choice, but it is likely that her comments and judgements of the consultant stimulated an unconscious collusion in the group (which included Al herself) about the gradual formation of norms of acceptable behaviours, which the consultant was also drawn into. It is around these very issues, i.e., the issues that group members took to be the desires of the consultant (for acceptable behaviours), that Al is attacked.

Consequently the hypothesis now is that Al is 'selected' as scapegoat because she exemplifies those traits perceived as 'bad' by the consultant. It seems to members that the consultant desires them to not have these traits. Hence to avoid the paranoid anxiety felt in session 1, in session 6 they avoid the judgement of being undesirable by repudiating such behaviours and locating them solely in Al. Hence this defence against anxiety becomes a motive force in the development of at least one group structure, the structure of norms. It also delineates and reinforces sub-groupings, and creates the specific roles of 'victim' and 'persecutor'.

The relation of the attack on Al to the establishment of group norms

It is important to look at the manner in which the dominant unspoken laws or norms were implemented in the group. That it is through the medium of language is established so clearly that it is worth detailing.

Ix's attack on Al took the form of an objection to the language that Al used. Take the following:

Ix   I think what it is . . . I think somehow the group's felt, and it isn't really any reflection on you as a person, it's not trying to break you, it's probably trying to say that individuals do affect individuals. Individuals do affect the group. The word supersensitive has been used instead of anxious. Words you've almost denied the group to feel. You've almost denied the group their right to be because of lots of things that they have to be in order to live, to have life. And I think the thing is the group (sighs) in a way wasn't . . . felt the right was taken away because it was a . . . had to protect you because we weren't allowed to . . . they were taboos and they can't be taboos. They're real things. Anxiety is real, it's not supersensitivity. It's anxiety. We all realized that in the first session.

Al   Why weren't these things brought up earlier then?

Ix   Because I'm the only person probably, and as I was in many ways coaxed into it. . . . And now I'll patch it up. It's no real reflection on you. It's the way the group has reacted, felt or whatever, and so perhaps what the group is trying to say is, you don't have to be afraid to use the words anxious, anger or whatever because we're not going to harm you if you use them. We'll harm you if you don't. We'll harm you if you're unreal. We won't harm you if you're real.

This sounds clear. Ix speaks for members of her sub-group who attempt to define the reality of the group from their own perspective, which they feel reflects the view of the consultant, or more specifically, of the leader of the imaginary group-that-was-joined. Al may not agree but she acknowledges: 'OK, that's what you think of me, OK.' The members of the neutral sub-group were angered by the attack but they didn't question the strongly stated assumption about the language to be used. Through this kind of reality defining, Ix becomes a strong contender for leadership of the group-that-is-created.

The picture currently arrived at from an analysis of this social episode is of the group integrated around the figure of the consultant who represents the group-that-was-joined (see Chapter 9). Members who identified strongly with the consultant's position and the perceived task became key members of sub-group 1, or the more neutral sub-group 3. Sub-group 2 consisted of members early identified as fairly dependent on guidance from the consultant.

Al became the attacked scapegoat because (a) she focussed the anger felt by members at perceived attacks on their own traits or behaviours, which by a process of projection became hers alone, and (b) she was believed to be the focus of the consultant's anger at the group, i.e., on many occasions she was seen to be 'holding the group back' (session 6) and 'denying them life', which the 'good' consultant presumably wanted them to have. It is notable that the consultant herself was often accused of stopping the group with her interventions. It seems that sub-group 1 was identified with the 'good' consultant who desired that they live, whereas sub-group 2 was identified with the 'bad' consultant who prevented their progress.

It seems that, within this group, the perceived persecutory elements of the consultant are strongly identified with by members who, in turn, appear to focus their persecution on Al.

The structures involved in episode 1

In identifying the structures involved, it will be useful to re-examine this social episode using Lacanian terms.

As has been mentioned earlier (Chapter 7), the text of the group may be deciphered much as a dream, i.e., through an analysis of its condensations and displacements, or, its processes of metaphor and metonomy (Chapter 3). And if, as Lacan says, 'the symptom *is* a metaphor' (Lacan, 1957, p. 175), we might add that the group structure is a metaphor. This is not to say that the structure of the group is similar to linguistic structures, but that it *is* part of the language of the *social,* if not of its speech.

We may then regard the group units (roles, sub-groups, defensive structures, etc.) as signifiers. As with all signifiers, these have value only in relation to the other signifiers in the system. The roles of 'victim' and 'persecutor', for example, have specific meanings in relation to each other in this group. Additionally, they are 'open to meaning', and it has already been demonstrated how they 'slide' from one member to another. The prime examples are that (a) Al is at one time the 'victim', after having been seen as the 'persecutor', i.e., the member who prevented the group from having life, and that (b) Ix is firstly the 'attacker' of Al, and then later the 'victim' of the other members of her sub-group. Both of these signifiers emanate from their original attachment to the consultant who in sessions 1–4 is often seen as a 'persecutor' mainly by 'stopping the group' through her interventions, thus making a 'victim' of the group.

In order to help decipher these signifiers it is important to turn to an understanding of the authority structure of the group, for this structure encompasses those transformations of signification that are formed within the members' identifications with the leader, and subsequently with each other (Chapter 5). This also encompasses the structure of libidinal transformations seen by Freud (1921) as constituting the basis of group life, and encompasses the line e–I (representing the ego's identifications and the ego-ideal) in Lacan's Schema R (Lacan, 1959, p. 197).

At this stage in the history of the group, the group political structures are focussed on authority with its attendant right to define reality via expertise. Session 1 gives ample evidence that it is the expertise of the staff that the members regard as the basis for the consultant's authority, and even as late as session 8 De says:

> The consultant makes a comment. She's the expert. If she says this is happening therefore it is happening. If we become aware of it we stop doing it. I don't know why we stop doing it because that sort of implies that we shouldn't't've been doing it in the first place.

Thus although the consultant acts as container/partner in the integrative process (seen by many theorists as a pre-oedipal structural configuration in the individual), she also embodies the authority usually seen as proper to the triangulated oedipal structure. This is no contradiction, because what in the individual are seen as pre- and post-oedipal structures may occur concurrently at different group levels (Foulkes, 1964), e.g., at the bodily-integrative level and at the social (political) level. Moreover, in Lacan's view, the oedipal structure is always present in the cultural field (the psychotic being marked by his or her absence from registration in its structure, Lacan, 1959).

Authority is defined from the perspective of the observer. Consequently, the consultant's early interventions in the group were listened to in a particularly selective manner, congruent with the state of the member-as-observer at that time. The overall intent of each statement was often discounted as members searched for directions in defining norms, or, more importantly, for hints of how to avoid the anxiety attendant on early persecutory anxieties. The desires inherent in this relation to authority became structured in the group, perhaps in the ways to be described next.

The trauma evidenced in the episode described did not create the sub-group structure, nor did the sub-groups create the incident in any linear causal manner. The sub-groupings were present prior to session 6. What did occur was a situation that organized the sub-groupings into focus; they became important signifiers in the group process. This is what is meant by the traumatic event being a *central organizer* in the history of the group. The attack on Al organized and defined, in the conscious language of the group, roles and relations that were only nascent previously. Ix, for example, is strongly identified with the consultant in the minds of many group members, not only because she shares her given name (both Ix) but because she claims an ability to speak for the group with the voice of authority. She states the words to be used and no one challenges this. Also, she comes to embody the attack that many members feared but couldn't or wouldn't imagine coming from a staff member, whose role should be to guide and protect them in the learning process. (In this, Ix plays a role similar to that of the 'ship's officer' described by Jaques, 1955. She 'holds' the persecutory aspects of the 'authority'.)

Moreover, if the foregoing account is useful, the incident focussed and organized for this group a mode of defence against persecutory anxiety.

Briefly, the structures thus far delineated are:

1 the particular roles of 'persecutor', 'victim', 'scapegoat' etc.;
2 the structure of the sub-groups, one of which contained a member highly identified with the consultant, and who claimed the right to define the reality of the group via an authorizing language;
3 a mode of organizational defence involving projections, projective identifications, scapegoating and identification with the persecutor/ aggressor (Chapters 3 and 5).

A point to emphasize about the sub-groupings is that, like individuals, they stand as signifiers. They are open to meaning (through their relations with other sub-groups) and to being reconstituted by different members over time. In the case of the present group certain key members came to represent the three major membership sub-groups evidenced, whilst other individuals felt aligned to different sub-groups at different times. De, for example says: 'I found myself vacillating very much between the sub-group Ix outlined and one where I can't feel aligned to anyone or any sub-group at all' (session 9).

This interrelated nature of signification, containment and defence may be illustrated by reference to session 9.

Session 9 was spent in yet another attempt to understand the members' feelings about the consultant. In comparison with earlier discussions on this theme, where members voiced more or less individual feelings and opinions, the focus was now on two dominating sub-groups: those who saw her primarily as good, helpful and rewarding, and those who primarily saw her as bad, punishing and misleading. After much discussion, members concluded that each person felt either way from time to time. The very possibility of this split in relations with the consultant allowed members a choice of alignment, and provided a structural containment for their feelings such that these might be at times acknowledged and at times rejected.

For instance, with regard to the feeling that the consultant may be manipulating the group, Er says:

> I've gone in and out of this manipulation thing. When this group first started I didn't think it was going – No it's not going to happen. And then I thought, Yeah! bloody oath! it is! The group's being manipulated something shocking. And then I went back to saying no, it's not. I don't think that's right, and then – I don't know actually. I still have a deep suspicion that this manipulation does happen. (session 9)

Er is regarded as being in the 'neutral' sub-group during the episode of the attack on Al. He made many attempts to reconcile differences amongst others. In this more neutral role, he was torn between these and a third form of sub-grouping, in which the two sub-groups signified the issue of manipulation.

(i.e., one sub-group saw the consultant as 'leading' the group, the other sub-group saw her as observing and commenting).

The organization of the group

What has developed, then, is an organization that allows for the containment within the group of projections emanating from unacceptable traits and thoughts. This underlying organization produces structures able to signify different things at different times, and which are semi-permeable to membership. As such, they are symbolic structures with signifying values in the group, dependent on the specific history of the group. Additionally, the particular structure of the group during the episode described provides an internal sub-group ego-ideal which allows for individual identity within sub-groups. Sub-group members identify with one another and, most importantly, with seemingly conflicting aspects of the consultant and the group-that-was-joined.

The sub-group structure is closely linked to the defensive structure of the group, and aids members in dealing with the conflicting feelings, images and ideas necessarily aroused in group life. Sub-groups, then, may temporarily signify unwanted traits or desires, as well as providing a structural defence for the group. In this regard they are similar to dreams and neurotic symptoms, described by Freud as having both an expressive and a defensive component. (i.e., they express repressed desires and simultaneously defend against them). Moreover, perhaps a major process of institutionalization may be regarded as a fuller rigidification of group structures whereby roles and sub-groupings become less open to new significations. Even in the case of the present group it can be seen that certain key figures (Ix and Al for example) do not have the same freedom to move between sub-groups as do De and Er.

Summary of the first major episode

In concluding the discussion of the first major episode, it is useful to present a summary using Harré's (1979) terminology; this will allow for comparisons with the analysis of other episodes. Table 2.1 provides a summary of episode 1. The actions and acts listed in this and the following tables do not constitute an exhaustive list of actions and acts of the group, even in relation to the episodes specified. For example, this table emphasizes the unconscious nature of the specific acts identified in the analysis of the episode.

Table 2   Summary of the first major episode in the longitudinal study

Table 2.1 The group structure (social syntax) in terms of episode, actions and acts

Episode	Constitutive actions	Social acts (largely unconscious)
Attack on Al	Expression of Ha's anger. Group interest in Ha's anger. Discussion by sub-group 1 (in café outside group).	Identification of a scapegoat.
	Attempts to get Al to talk. Attack on Al by Ix. Group discussion of Al. Departure of Ix. Expressions of anger and guilt.	One member (Ix) becomes the 'spokesperson' for others.

Table 2.2 The social semantics (the meaning of the episode, actions and acts)

1   Al is attacked on the basis of annoying habits located solely in her after a process of projection.
2   The annoying habits are those identified as 'bad' or 'wrong' in the eyes of the consultant.
3   Al is therefore attacked as the container of (or signifier for) aspects of members that are unacceptable to the Imaginary consultant (i.e., the consultant in the minds of the members, or the consultant in the group's Imaginary register).
4   The processes involved include projections, identifications and displacements. Identification with the consultant (particularly by Ix) serves to deflect and displace feared attacks and persecution.

Table 2.2 provides a summary of episode 1 in terms of meanings (significations) of actions and acts. Neither this, nor similar tables that follow it, purport to produce an exhaustive list of meanings. The meanings identified are those from the psychoanalytically based analysis.

A SECOND MAJOR EPISODE

A second major traumatic event occurred over sessions 9–11. During session 10, three members were absent and were regarded by other members as deliberately attempting to manipulate the group. It eventuated that they were attending a funeral at the time. The episode is characterized by the absence of the members, the anger of the other group members towards them, the discovery by these other members that the three members had a legitimate reason for their absence, and the consequent expression of guilt in the group. The 'missing' members were seen as particularly important in that (a) these three were key members of the previous sub-group 1, which had led the attack on Al; (b) they were known to spend time together outside group sessions; and, in the light of distinctions drawn in session 9, (c) they were perceived as labelling themselves as the sub-group who were 'good' in the eyes of the consultant. These points require elaboration.

Session 9

Session 9 contains quite a long discussion about the sub-groupings experienced during previous sessions. The divisions in the group now centred around three issues:

1 The consultant's usefulness. The group was divided between those who felt they could understand and, to some degree, use the comments, and those who found the consultant confusing.
2 The consultant's manipulation. The group was divided between those who believed that the consultant manipulated or, more mildly, 'ran' the group, and those who believed that she did not.
3 The group's autonomy. The group was divided between those who believed that the group would function better were the consultant not present, and those who disagreed with this idea.

These issues did not form clear cleavage lines between distinct sub-groups because members expressed vacillating and, at times, confused opinions. They are best regarded as positions in the debate which acted as signifiers open to changing membership and changing significations. They acted as central integrating points or nodes around which sub-groups could tentatively form and members could test out alignments.

The following dialogue illustrates the development of these themes:

De   She (the consultant) can't run it unless we want her to.
Ha   Does that mean if she runs it we want her to?
Er   The word really is to manipulate the group. You're saying she doesn't manipulate the group. That's what you're saying. OK But that's what we're talking about. Leading us down here! Leading us this way! Doing that! It's manipulating the group. That's the word to describe it.

Ix responds by refusing to join in a rebellion, and by defining a rebellion itself as dependent, thus portraying any possible rebellion as impotent. Her final words in the next exchange emphasize such impotence.

Er   Whether you want to call that leading or putting us on the right track or manipulating, we're still doing what (the consultant) is telling us to do. Now it gets back to the power we have.
Ix   Doesn't that depend upon your perception. I mean, sure, my

> attitudes change, but to make the point that some observations (the consultant) has made have actually made me think. . . .
>
> Er   I won't dispute that. The argument is about – we almost got off it – you won't accept that we're letting (the consultant) do it, and we could stop her if we wanted to with a concerted effort.
>
> Ix   I won't accept that because (pause) – I won't accept that.
>
> Er   Because you don't want to stop (the consultant).
>
> Ix   Because I think that what goes with that is strong dependency too.
>
> Er   It doesn't negate the fact that we could stop her if everyone wanted to.
>
> Ix   We talk about it. You'll never do it.

The next line of argument put forward by Ix is to refer to the word of (the consultant's) authority:

> Ix   (The consultant) made the comment a few weeks ago, and it ran along the lines that we wouldn't be this group without her, and that is so true. It doesn't mean to say we wouldn't be another group – but we wouldn't be this particular group without her.
>
> De   Yes, but theoretically we could. . . .
>
> Ix   (overriding her) And it moves into survival – the meaning of this group – whether this group has meaning for us.

After some more discussion on manipulation and punishment De once again raises the idea of rebellion:

> De   I see no reason at all why we should be dependent upon (the consultant) in this group. We can go any way we like, and we've spent so long talking about our mummy (said with sarcasm), and I don't know why everybody feels like that. Does anybody else feel that they don't need this dependence? Maybe I'm protesting too much but. . . .
>
> Ha   That's a provocative statement.
>
> De   I don't know. It's a terribly dependent group.

However, Ix seems able to deflect the attack:

> Ix   I'd like to suggest that the idea of good and bad in this group. . . . I don't believe it's absolutely associated with (the consultant). I feel good or achievement associated with members of the group – and some with bad.

She is supported by Bs who engages Al and Fr by saying that they look depressed, and moves the discussion away from De. Ix ends the session by saying that she feels 'shortchanged' by the group because she seems to exert more energy than many of the others.

During the discussion the consultant indicated that one sub-group within the total group was perceiving her as good, and felt themselves to be the recipients of good interpretations, whilst another sub-group saw her as bad, and felt themselves as the recipients of verbal punishments. Furthermore, this latter sub-group felt mystified and unable to decipher her interpretations. In discussing this comment members identified themselves as belonging to one or the other of these sub-groups.

The sub-group of Ix, Bs and Ha came to be regarded, in this session, as supporters of the consultant insofar as they stressed that she was necessary to the group, that her interpretations were stimulating and helpful, and that to prevent her from directing the group would in itself be a sign of dependence.

Session 9 served to group the members in opposition to one another around the issues of manipulation, authority and rebellion. The argument may seem at first to be about the consultant, but it emerges as lodged in the power struggles between members.

Session 10

Session 10 may be understood as containing two aspects of the present episode.

1 An attempt by group members to discuss their feelings about the consultant and each other. This was instigated by one member (Cr) who was later referred to as leader during the early part of this session.
2 A discussion about the three absent members.

The first part of the session consisted of members identifying feelings about themselves in relation to the consultant. For example Er felt manipulated, Ja felt stupid, Ca felt inadequate, Ge felt angry, De felt they would be better off without the consultant and Fr felt concern for the consultant's own feelings. As the discussion proceeded members appeared to be far more relaxed than usual.

The discussion of the 'missing members' then arose and proceeded in the following manner:

1 Anger and envy were aroused:

Ca   The people who aren't here were the ones who were labelled the 'good' group or. . . .
Er   Well, they labelled themselves.
Ca   Yes that's true. I mean I think they saw themselves as the independent sub-group who were getting all the good messages from (the consultant). Most of us weren't.
Fr   There's only (indistinct)
Ge   Sorry Fr. I can't hear you.
Fr   There's only one in particular, who probably, who really feels . . . who's getting all the messages.
Er   (sarcastically) I wonder who that is?

Ja   That she's what Fr?
Fr   I'm not going to mention the name.
Ja   Yeah – that she's what?
Fr   That she seems to get all the messages right. That she's one who for some time has really understood what's going on.

2 The missing members were seen to be manipulating the group by their absence.

Er   Because that's what . . . I might be paranoid again . . . but they're not here because they want to see what the reaction's going to be. I don't want to react to them at all – that's probably a reaction in itself.
Ca   Er, you probably feel a bit . . . at least I don't know but I feel a bit pissed off because I think it's stupid if they have decided not to be here. It's juvenile.
Er   They might have a perfectly good reason but it seems to me if three people are not going to be here . . . it seems hard to think of three genuine reasons that are going to occur on the same day anyway.

3 The 'leader' of the missing members was seen as attempting to take on the consultant's role.

Al   I said that at coffee. I made the observation that Ix, that I felt that Ix seems to mouth words and say it in the same concept as (the consultant).

It is noticeable that these accusations, of a claim to special knowledge, and of the attempt to manipulate, have been attributed previously to the consultant (session 9). It seems that, in session 10, a more relaxed rapport had been established where members were more easily able to discuss their feelings. Positive feelings towards the consultant were experienced, and negative feelings became redirected towards the missing sub-group, who were envied anyway. More correctly, it might be said that redirection of the negative feelings enabled the consultant to be experienced more positively. One did not cause the other; both occurred as part of the group system at that time.

This episode led, in session 11, to some bitter exchanges. The reason for the missing members' absence was revealed: they had attended a funeral together. This naturally aroused guilt in the others although the anger attendant upon this sub-group, and Ix in particular, was still present.

Once more, a summary using Harré's terms is provided.

Table 3   Summary of the second major episode in the longitudinal study

Table 3.1   The group structure (social syntax) in terms of episode, actions and acts

Episode	*Constituting actions*	*Acts* *(largely unconscious)*
Three absent members	1 Sub-groups identified as 'good' or 'bad' in the eyes of the consultant.	Group acts to identify Ix with the consultant.
	2 Three members, absent during session 10, identified as the self-appointed 'good' sub-group.	
	3 Discussion of sub-group.	
	4 Identification of Ix as leader of sub-group.	Group acts to identify Ix as 'bad'.
	5 Anger and envy of the three.	
	6 Dispute between sub-groups in session 11.	

Table 3.2   The social semantics (the meaning of the episode, actions and acts)

1 The absent members were identified as those who felt themselves to be 'good' in the eyes of the consultant, and Ix is identified as their leader.
2 The act of identifying Ix with the consultant was both formed by, and strengthened, the following meanings:
   (a) Ix is able to interpret the consultant's interpretations, i.e., she makes sense of them;
   (b) Ix is seen as speaking like the consultant;
   (c) Ix is seen to receive 'good' from the consultant.
3 The identification of Ix with the consultant enabled the group to retain positive attitudes and feelings for the latter, whilst negative attitudes and feelings were felt towards Ix. She (Ix) acted as a displacement figure by virtue of her similarity to the consultant, and came to embody the 'bad' aspects of the consultant. For example, the debate over whether or not the consultant was manipulative is partially resolved by regarding Ix as manipulative and the consultant as benign.

COMMENTS ON THE ANALYSES OF EPISODES 1 AND 2

The analysis of this second episode reveals a strengthening of those structures discussed earlier. That is, roles and sub-groupings have been strengthened, and the defence of projective identification has been elaborated. The manner by which the sub-groups are open to signification is important. For example, the consultant seems at times to signify that which is the cause of suspicion, worthlessness, anger and helplessness in the members. This creates a high degree of anxiety as she is also seen as the source of power and possible rewards. The availability of sub-groups to signify the former relieves the tension, for a while at least. Moreover, it opens the field for power struggles and the open expression of anger without directly engaging the consultant and risking her wrath.

The group structures seem to be emerging both as direct containers for emotions, thoughts and intentions, and as signifiers for the source of other emotions, thoughts and intentions. The absent sub-group was seen as manipulative *and* as the source or cause of manipulative feelings in others. Hence they are experienced both as Imaginary containers exemplifying split-off aspects of the whole group, and as Symbolic entities giving form to other structures. Furthermore, the structure appears to emerge as a concomitant to cognitive polarities which themselves are the result of the perception of differences within the group, exaggerated by the process of projection. In turn, this projection is understandable as a defence against the anxiety aroused by the feeling of being judged. The resulting splits and, possibly, fragments, became the background for reintegration. Social structure, particularly unconsciously formed or planned structure, may well provide a unifying experience, analogous to the unifications experienced in the imago of the mirror stage. Both are subject to language but not to speech (Lacan, 1957).

Lacan argues that aggressivity is inherent in the unified ego because it contains the diversity brought about by many identifications with others, i.e., it contains the natural confrontation of two (or more) subjectivities (Lacan, 1949). Analogously, such aggressivity as is present in the unified group may partly be due to unification, through a particular structuring that brings with it the tensions that hold its elements in relation to one another. Differentiation brings with it potential inequalities with respect to dimensions that members consider important, e.g., power, status, differential sexual attractiveness, etc. In the present group, the experienced anger and its perceived source seem to shift between signifiers; here it is between consultant and sub-groups. In short, the present analysis specifies the emergence 'at one time' of members' emotions, cognitive polarities and group structures. This 'at one time' phenomenon typifies the emergence of an historical state (Watzlawick et al., 1968).

This state, now identified as *'internal division'*, has certain similarities to Klein's paranoid/schizoid state, typified by splitting, projective identification and the separation of 'good' and 'bad' objects. Ironically, it *emerges from a process of unification*. Superficially, the group seems more divided than earlier when, it could be argued, it was in a totally fragmented state (session 1, see Chapter 9). However, the fragments are united in the process whereby sub-groups use each other in a mirror function and as a container for projections. The anxiety and dread experienced by individuals early in the group's life is transformed into the righteous anger experienced by each of the sub-groups.

Additionally, it is an Imaginary state insofar as it is the imaginary representation, to the members, of the symbolic authority relations in the group.

A THIRD MAJOR EPISODE

Following a suggestion by one of the members, this third episode will be termed 'the breakdown of Ix'. Firstly, let at us look at some introductory material.

Session 11 contained a lengthy argument between the three who were previously absent and the other group members. By the end of the session it was generally agreed that Ix held a powerful position in the group as a whole insofar as she excited strong feelings in many of the other members, feelings both positive and negative. Furthermore, it was agreed that she had played the role of the most outspoken member, and had 'earned' power through her ability to interpret the interpretations of the consultant. Other members' feelings for her ranged from envy and anger through to admiration and protectiveness.

Session 12 contained some angry exchanges. Fr, a close friend of Al and a low participator in the group, stated that she didn't believe Ix was the group leader and that she, herself, had never wanted Ix to be leader. Fr claimed that the consultant was the true leader of the group, and that, although Ix had often attempted to become leader, she was unacceptable because of her hostility (invoking the earlier attack on Al as evidence).

During session 13 this incident was revived:

Fr once more claims that Ix is not an acceptable leader because she is too aggressive and prevents others from being themselves. When Ix denies this Fr says:

Fr   Look around. Look at Al. She was prevented from being herself. She has not talked much for the last few sessions because she was frightened and she would be stupid to expose herself again. And other people admitted that they were glad it was Al because it wasn't themselves. There was the element of fear in here.

Bs   I don't see Ix as being a big monster.

Fr   Yes, because she would never attack you.

Fr goes on to argue for equality in the group and claims that she would be happy to have someone as leader who could unite the group, but that she could not accept someone who divided the group. Ix responds by saying that it isn't necessarily a bad thing for a group to be split. Er then points out that he doesn't think that Ix has split the group. Ix, he says, is accepting Fr's assumption that she, Ix, has split the group. Ix responds angrily in order to reject any suggestion of her agreement with Fr.

The text that refers most directly to the episode of 'the breakdown of Ix' occurs shortly after the abovementioned interchange.

Ix   All this stuff about me being wrong. All these implications. I can't believe I'm the only one who's false at times and wrong at times.

Al   I don't think it's that you're wrong. It's the hostility that you give out.

Ca   I'm sure other people feel hostile but can't express it.

Al   I don't feel envy for hostility. Perhaps we can find out what makes her hostile.
      (depressed laughter)

Ge   I think it's pretty clear why she feels hostile. She's hostile because everybody is telling her she feels hostile.

Al   That's only now.

Ge   But for four weeks.

Ix   (angrily) I'll tell you what! The more you tell me the more I will be. No doubt about it because – boy! do I feel angry.

Ja   We had the example two minutes ago when Er was defending Ix and she jumped at him. Er was defending Ix against what Fr had said.

Ge   Did you really see it as that, Ja?

Ja   Fr said Ix had divided the group and Er said: 'No' he did not see that. He disagreed with that.

Ge   Right. But I don't think that was a defence of Ix.

Ix   (sounds and looks very confused) He said that I agreed. The implication was . . . that I took from Fr's comment . . . that I had been responsible for the group splitting . . . that I had the power to split the group. He didn't agree that I did. That was all.

Er   Ja's right! I was trying to defend you and that's fair dinkum. What it was was that you could not accept me actually being on your side for a change. For I hadn't been on your side for weeks and weeks. You couldn't accept it.

Ja   That's why for the first time since we've been here, I actually felt sorry for Ix, because someone came to her defence, who normally wouldn't, and without listening she immediately thought he's attacking me, and she attacked back. That she's sort of got an inbuilt mode to attack somebody who's attacked her at some other time, says something.

Ha   To be honest I've got to agree with Ja. I thought Er was defending you Ix. Although I've got an idea that if you were already talking about the fact you felt threatened by people and they made you feel hostile, if you added that they hurt your feelings when they did that, they might – it might be more acceptable.

(Ix looks very confused)

Consultant

It does seem that you're working through Ix at the moment. There is the general belief that she is strong enough to take it all. It's as if there is a belief that these things can be worked out through her.

The consultant attempted to interpret the foregoing incident as an attempt by the group to understand hostility and aggression. They did this through an exploration of these emotions in one member, Ix. She had become more angry and hostile while other members described her in that way. Eventually she became extremely confused about how the others felt, and was unable to perceive support for her position even when it was intended. The interchange concluded with her looking frightened and confused. After the consultant's intervention she expressed relief. The consultant's interpretation about group process focussed the discussion away from her directly as the source of anger and hostility. She said that she had felt overwhelmed by the feeling of not being able to rely on her own perceptions and judgements.

During this time all members of the group seemed to be highly engaged with what was occurring.

Once more Harré's format may be employed in an attempt to understand this episode of 'the breakdown of Ix'. Table 4.1 presents a summary of the acts and actions involved.

Thus far, three central or traumatic episodes have been examined. They have been examined in the light of Harré's action/act distinction and also with regard to their semantic status. With regard to the latter, it may be said that the meaning of actions and acts within the group may be derived through an examination of emergent group structures. For example, the sub-group structure of the present group became explicit at the time leading up to the attack on Al, and has been seen as emergent alongside the organization of a group defensive system. The sub-group led by Ix came to signify the attacking aggressive aspects of the group, whilst the more 'neutral' members came to signify doubt (i.e., the vacillations of Er on the question of manipulation), and its partner, hope (i.e., the insistence of De that the group could function without the consultant). The fact that many of these aspects of group life are originally signified by the consultant in her role as leader of the group-that-is-joined, has also been considered.

The next task is to elaborate the historical states or moments identified by the analysis. This task will be aided by the separate consideration of two dimensions: the political and the socio-emotional.

Table 4   Summary of the third major episode in the longitudinal study

Table 4.1   The group structure (social syntax) in terms of episode, actions and acts

Episode	Constitutive actions	Social acts (largely unconscious)
Breakdown of Ix	1 Group agreement that Ix is important.	Ix's power proclaimed.
	2 Fr accuses Ix of being aggressive and hostile and that she split the group and was therefore unacceptable as leader.	Ix's power challenged. Ix accused of having 'bad' qualities.
	3 Fr claims that the consultant is the leader.	Consultant's power is signified.
	4 Er supports Ix, saying he doesn't believe that she split the group. He says that she accepted Fr's view too easily.	Ix supported by Er (who is seen as a powerful independent member).
	5 Ix is angered. Feels attacked.	Ix unable to accept support.
	6 Ja and Ha state that Er was defending Ix.	
	7 Ix becomes confused and inarticulate.	Ix withdraws.
	8 Consultant interprets the process.	Consultant's power is re-established.

Table 4.2 presents a summary of some possible meanings of the actions and acts involved in the episode of 'the breakdown of Ix'.

Table 4.2   The social semantics (the meaning of the episode, actions and acts)

Ix is seen as a potential leader able to challenge the power of the consultant. For some members, however, she represents the threatening and hostile aspects of authority. The events of this episode proceed such that, in exploring this anger and hostility, Ix is pressed beyond her capacity to 'hold' these emotions *and* simultaneously to uphold her leadership. The 'good' consultant is able to hold her power by providing an interpretation that restores Ix to 'sanity'. The complexity of the processes involved is great. The *outcome* is that a possible challenge by the member most identified with the consultant, and who comes to represent her imagined hostility, is curtailed. The benign and positive aspects of authority (including the power to enlighten members) seem to triumph at this point.

ANALYSIS OF THE POLITICAL AND SOCIO-EMOTIONAL DIMENSIONS

This section will be concerned with the aim of identifying underlying symbolic structures with particular emphasis on explanations in the political and socio-emotional dimensions of the group.

The political dimension

Power, or the ability to influence others, derives from several sources, both legitimate or otherwise (see Chapter 5 and Appendix A). Ix, it seems, was given power through her identification with the consultant (referent power), her ability to interpret the consultant's words and, hence, to shape the reality of the group (expert power), and through her initiating the attack on Al, thus confirming the group's defence against persecutory anxieties (authority via endorsement). Perhaps more important than her actually holding power was her signification of both the potential power of members and the hostile power of authority. Her power, for example, was exaggerated during the episode of the absent members and, by session 13, Fr sees her as having the power to 'prevent people from being themselves'. Finally, her power was challenged, and, even with the support of the 'neutral' members, she was unwilling or unable to become fully established as leader. She became confused and withdrew.

After this episode some of the other more neutral members (Er, Ca and Ge) took over some leadership functions for the group.

The historical states associated with the power theme may be identified in the following manner.

1 A state of *defensive preparation* occurred whereby the members unconsciously sought means of defending themselves against feared

attacks by the consultant with respect to their incompetence, their lack of knowledge, and their inability to understand their task without the support of books, notes and tapes. The attack on Al is a culmination of this preparation, and is co-emergent with a structure of sub-groups that act as signifiers of important symbolic polarities within the group.

2 Once established, the sub-groups became engaged in a state of *structured division*. This state bears similarity to the paranoid/schizoid state identified by Klein, insofar as certain characteristics of group life became contained in particular substructures. Gradually the group structures came to be closed to signification. Particular persons or sub-groupings were labelled with or without the agreement of the person or persons concerned. In particular, Ix became closed to signification, as exemplified in the episode of the absent members, and she felt she had little choice to be anything else until she 'broke down'. The rigidity of the signification involved seemed to lead to conflict which culminated in open hostility, the confusion of Ix, and the consequent inability of the group to maintain its dependence on Ix as 'hostile leader'.

3 The state of structured division seemed to end during a brief state of *challenge*, although it seems that the unconscious plan (Gustafson and Cooper, 1979) of many members was to gain reassurance that the positive aspects of authority would overcome its more hostile components. The challenge ended with the breakdown of Ix, and the state which followed was one where the more neutral members shared leadership functions in the group.

Although these states appear to have occurred in a particular historical order, it is not suggested that they are in any sense developmental stages. In fact the history of this group evidences many fluctuations from one state to another even within one or two sessions. What has been discussed is an overview along particular dimensions or manifolds of dimensions (Glaser, 1984) in the history of the group.

The socio-emotional dimension

Although conceptually separate from the political dimension, the structures developed within this dimension may also be seen as centred on the major episodes outlined. In this dimension, the sub-groupings act more as emotional support structures than as containers of power and influence. Clearly the sub-group of Ix, Bs and Ha (the absent members), and the sub-group of Al and Fr, act as friendship groups both inside and outside of the weekly group meetings. Moreover, the support structure is similar for both sub-groups, e.g., session 13 contains the following exchange:

Bs I'm fed up with the attack on Ix.
Ca I'm fed up with Bs supporting Ix.
Bs I don't just support Ix. We're each our own person.

Session 12 had contained an almost identical exchange when Al was accused of always supporting Fr. Fr disagreed saying they were 'both individuals'.

Thus, although these two sub-groups seem to be at opposite poles on the power dimension, they have a position similar to each other on the socio-emotional dimension. This emotional support was highlighted during the episodes of the 'attack on Al', and of the 'absent members'.

The sub-groups also play an important structural role in the processes of projection and projective identification; group problems were located in particular individuals or sets of individuals, and explored by questioning these individuals and observing their reponses. Ix and Al are both given this as a major role, although others also occasionally performed this function.

The socio-emotional states outlined by Bion (1961) and discussed earlier (Chapter 3) were evidenced in the group. Their emergence is notable in connection with the political states identified. For example, Ba. dependency emerged most strongly at those times when existing political structures were threatened or weakened. Ba. fight emerged when the sub-groups were most clearly identified, and they were relatively closed to signification. Ba. pairing (not to be confused with the presence of sub-group pairs) was evident whenever the structures were most open to signification, e.g., when members were exploring the possibility of forging new relationships.

Interpretations given by the consultant about the socio-emotional dimension also seemed to be received differently according to the political state present at the time. One prominent example is that of the interpretation of the group process in terms of projective identification. The consultant often remarked on the way that group members seemed to explore issues of importance to themselves by provoking others and then probing them for feelings. During the state of defensive preparation, these interpretations were received as critical attacks. During the state of structured division, they were received as supportive of one sub-group or another (i.e., the consultant was seen as taking sides or giving the 'good' interpretations to favoured sub-groupings). During the state of challenge, they were received as confirmations of reality, and sometimes as confirmations of guilt and despair (reminiscent of Klein's depressive position).

In terms of historical change, it seems that the political and socio-emotional states identified in this group are closely interrelated. Each state is defined by its culmination in a particular traumatic or memorable episode which in itself shapes the perceptions, memories and accounts of members in particular ways.

THE GROUP SESSIONS AS A DRAMA

In one sense the group sessions constituted a drama (Harré, 1979) which played out an imaginary relation between the consultant and members. Ix was always a strong advocate of the task set by the consultant, and her power was partially derived through her ability to interpret the interpretations of the consultant; when Ix was challenged, it was mainly on these grounds. Her authority, it seems, came from her ability to voice clearly the primary task of the group through an identification with the consultant. In one sense, she best represents the overall group view.

In contrast, the member who continually advocated independence from the consultant was De. However, she was rarely listened to, and her view of the members and staff was often the furthest from the majority view. She perceived others predominantly in terms of their emotionality, rather than in terms of their dominance or activity as such. De, it seems, appeals to an identity based on grounds other than that understood by the majority.

Apparently, the group was uninterested in breaking with their given authority. Their identity as a group is most easily viewed as being formed around an exploration of that authority, and member roles and sub-groupings reflected this. De stated that she could never be aligned to any one sub-group for long. Her role often appeared to be signifying individuality and a break with authority, and it was difficult for this role to find alignment with others in the group.

The importance of dominance and authority provides some support for the theoretical formulations of Freud and his followers. Identification of members with each other, and with the authority figure and her task (the ego-ideal of each group member *qua* member), seems to provide the substantial structural basis for the internal dynamics of the group. Each observable sub-group provided what it thought was a viable rendition of the task. Each offered its own identification with the task and consultant. For example:

1 Al (most prominent member of the Al and Fr sub-group) attempted to achieve the task by reading, taking notes, studying the tapes, and discussing these things. Hers was an identification with the consultant as lecturer/teacher, and the corresponding role in her sub-group tended to be 'student'.
2 Ix (most prominent member of the 'missing' sub-group) attempted to achieve the task by interpreting the ongoing process in a manner similar to the consultant's. For this sub-group the major identification (with the role of consultant) was matched by the role of being the 'good' members (perceived to be 'good' in the eyes of the consultant).
3 Ca and Er (prominent members, respectively, of the 'attacking' and 'neutral' sub-groups of the early sessions) attempted to achieve the task largely by examining their own experiences and by critically questioning the consultant. Additionally, Ge became prominent in a sub-grouping that at times attempted to explore anger and other feelings towards the consultant and other members. The identifications of these members seemed to be with the consultant as 'clinical psychologist'. Corresponding membership roles seemed to be 'client' or 'patient' roles.

Each sub-grouping held varying degrees of attractiveness for the members with relatively less 'fixed' roles. Whilst each in its context signified an alternative manner of achieving the task, it also signified a defence against the anxiety and conflict experienced as 'students', 'good' or 'bad' members, 'clients' and 'patients': Al and Fr were seen by others to retreat into dependency; the 'missing' sub-group as exemplifying fight and flight; Er as 'sitting on the fence', and as being uncommitted to any course of action; and Ge was seen as overly concerned with emotions. For varying amounts of time, each dominant member seemed to signify some perceived aspect of the consultant/staff member's role.

It may be that the major conflict between Ix and Al partially reflected the consultant's own role conflict between teacher (a more didactic role) and consultant (a less directive role). She purported (consciously) to relinquish the role of 'teacher' and assume the role of 'consultant'. In this sense, the group-that-was-joined, with its consultant leader and its experiential method, was itself attempting to create a new identity within an educational institution having a history of didactic teaching. Given the possible identifications with the consultant/teacher, loyalty and the wish to gain approval may have created the need in members to punish defenders of the 'old order'. It may be inevitable that a sub-group signifying the classic teacher–student role relations, supposedly repudiated by the consultant, became the attacked sub-group and was seen to contain relatively less dominant members. Interestingly, Al was not regarded as dominant, yet she did command a strong reaction from others at times, so it might be said that her dominance was unrecognized in the judgements of others. Perhaps she is best described as *prominent* in the group, i.e., as a central person rather than a leader (Redl, 1942).

The group 'drama' was also about matters other than the exploration of identifications with the authority: about issues of sociability, of learning about others as individuals, of learning about groups and the concepts used by psychologists in their study of groups, and of matters of personal interest to the members. However, what has been explored in the longitudinal study is the structural basis of group cohesion and identity. It is concluded that this frames a context, or Imaginary hegemony, which structures the concerns of the group from moment to moment.

CONCLUSIONS FROM THE LONGITUDINAL STUDY

The states identified earlier were seen as culminating in those social events that in themselves act as historical organizers in the accounts or narratives (Harré, 1979) of group members. The complexity of the power that social organization has in affecting social accounts does not rest there. The accounts in themselves act as signifiers within the organization of the group, and hence shape further acts. For example, the middle sessions in the life of this group (sessions 8–11) were notable for the tensions that regularly occurred between members of the sub-groups. These tensions sometimes occurred between members of the sub-group seen as led by Ix, and the sub-group seen as 'dependent', but were more often between the former and the so-called 'neutral' members. They were highlighted by the incident of the absent members. Fr referred to the sub-group structures as evidence of a split in the group (sessions 12 and 13). Others referred to this structure as evidence of a self-perceived 'good' group and another 'bad' or (more accurately) 'confused' group.

Consequently, whatever the actual label used, the accounts of the members about incidents or episodes in the group came to play a role in either changing or consolidating an existing structure. In this way, the accounts themselves became acts. This amount of complexity may be comprehended better by reference to the variety of levels of signification within group life. These have been mentioned but will now be summarized.

1 Group structures may be seen to signify various elements of group life be they, say, political or emotional. For example, amongst other things the sub-groups signify 'goodness' or 'badness', and members at times signify positions such as 'victim' or 'persecutor'. Important is the fact that group structures are *open to signification within the group system*. They are open to meaning whether this be in terms of political or emotional meaning, or in terms of the particular members who are seen to form particular structures (while also remembering that the identification of sub-group membership may at times depend on the perceiver). The degree of openness of group structures depends upon factors relevant to the group as a whole. These include the signifying value of other group structures, and the syntactic relations between structures, i.e., the social rules and dynamics (including defences) that serve to combine the structures.

2 Episodes, acts and actions within group life may act as signifiers within the accounts of individual group members. These episodes are also open to signification within the accounts of the group as a whole. Members modify their accounts according to their interactions and relations with other members, including the accounts of these others.

3 Signification within structures and episodes will also be open within the context of the group's history as a whole. What this means is that the history of the group acts as a constraint on future significations, and also acts retrospectively by influencing members' accounts of the past.

Thus, these structures and episodes, set within an historical sequencing of qualitatively different states, have an existence in the Symbolic order. It would seem that specific roles and sub-groups came particularly to signify those elements of group life surrounding the nature of the task as group members understood it. The task was to study their own processes, in the presence of an 'expert', who was there to comment on those processes in order to aid members. Perception of the task was in a social context, and involved an apprehension of the group-that-was-joined, personified most directly in the consultant. Perceptions, emotions and desires aroused by contact with her, and in contact with each other, came to be signified by the developing group structures. In this sense, the group was able to move from being the group-that-was-joined to a group with its own identity, evidenced in the particularity of the Imaginary representations of group structures and dynamics. The Imaginary representations are embodied in the actual people filling the roles and sub-groups at any one time, and realized in their immediate experience.

By this analysis, the identity of the group is seen as a particularization of its symbolic organization. This particularization or structure is, by nature, open to signification but becomes, through history, crystallized in an Imaginary structure of the group, just as a wish may become crystallized in a neurotic symptom or 'written in the sand of the flesh' (Lacan, 1957, p. 69).

This chapter has dealt with a qualitative longitudinal analysis of a particular group. As a longitudinal study, the emphasis was upon historical changes in the group; as a structural analysis, the emphasis was upon group structures.

It is not suggested that the group structures discussed are present in every group; that is a question for further empirical investigation. Nor is it suggested that the structures exclusively generated the surface structure of the group. What is here claimed, is that the particular structures delineated are living social structures contemporaneous with, and hence aetiologically important to, the behaviours, fantasies, emotions and dialogue experienced and enacted by these group members in the group setting. The *living* nature of the structures is emphasized for two reasons. Firstly, the structures identified are part of a living system. They are both the result of, and an influential pattern for, living beings; and they are tied to those beings insofar as they cannot exist independently of them. Secondly, the structures are identified by the researcher/observer only insofar as they are able to crystallize moments in time. As with a kaleidoscope, we view the picture as a whole only when the motion is stopped. It is then that the structure becomes a signifier, set apart from some aspects of the ongoing group existence (the Real of the group) by its symbolic function, and yet constitutive of the next moment in the history of the group, for the same reason.

The analysis contained in this chapter is based on the theoretical considerations presented in Chapter 5. There the psychoanalytic perspective was employed and special attention was paid to the Freudian and Lacanian analyses of narcissistic libido and its place in the dynamics of group cohesion and identity. Three dimensions of relatedness between group members (elements) were proposed:

1 Direct object relations based on direct or aim-inhibited object libido or aggressive wishes, i.e., relations of sentiment;
2 Relations of identification, either libidinal or aggressive;
3 Relations of a common defensive stance (e.g., Bion's basic assumption cultures).

These were seen to correspond broadly to the socio-emotional, task and defensive dimensions frequently noted in the literature on groups.

Following Freud (1921), the relations of identification were regarded as central to the cohesion and identity of the group. These relations are expressed through the authority and power structures in the group, i.e., through the political dimension, and through their connections with the major group tasks.

Although the identity of a group may be approached from external reference points, that is, from the point of view of other groups within an intergroup context, the emphasis here has been on an internal structural perspective.

The stated task of the present group was for members to study their own dynamics as a group. In order to do this, the members joined a group. The legitimate leader of the group-that-was-joined was the consultant. Many members wished her to remain the leader. She held legitimate authority and seemed best able to do the task. It is also evident from the analysis of the sessions that the members were able to split off, unconsciously, those aspects of the consultant that they feared. These persecutory aspects seemed to derive originally from the fears of the members themselves, and were then projected into another dominant member, Ix.

Chapter 12

Conclusions and implications for future research

This chapter will attempt briefly to review the major theoretical arguments and findings of the present research and to point towards a few implications for future consideration.

The research was reported within a general systems framework (Chapter 2). This helped guide a series of studies, involving group properties viewed as emerging from a system of interrelated parts. The most general aim of these studies was to describe the structural organization of the particular groups studied.

Psychoanalytic theory was used as a specific theoretical framework (in particular, theories of Freud, 1921; Winnicott, 1958; Mahler, 1968; Bion, 1961; Foulkes, 1964; and Lacan, 1977). This framework guided the more specific aims of describing structures in terms of group integration and identity. It also guided an analysis of particular group structures, e.g., power, leadership and authority; socio-emotional and task relations; and group defence structures (Chapter 5).

However, before describing the empirical work, an argument for the use of 'transindividual' concepts was advanced, supported by a review of some theories that utilize such concepts (Chapters 3, 4 and 5). In particular, the concept of identification taken from Freud (1921) was considered as a major transindividual process. It is through identifications that the group comes to exist. Furthermore, these identifications are within the symbolic structure of the group. That is, individuals identify with aspects of other group members as they are related to themselves in the group system as a whole. Characteristics of the leader, *qua* leader, for example, are those chosen for identification.

Following this, an argument was made for the use of descriptive research methods (Chapter 6). The methods of participant observation, episode analysis, and a structural analysis of interactions and dialogue were regarded as most appropriate for the aims of the research reported.

The empirical work consisted of two major studies, summarized below:

1. A CROSS-SECTIONAL STUDY OF THE FIRST SESSION OF EACH OF THREE DIFFERENT GROUPS

The cross-sectional study reported in Chapters 8–11 looked at some structures involved in the integration of groups within their first meetings. These structures seemed to act as points of reference for the integration processes. For example, a 'mirror state' was identified where the group appeared to be momentarily integrated through a process of apparent similarity with other groups (an external point of reference), and a state of 'symbiosis' was identified where a point of reference for integration seemed to be located in a symbiotic relation between members and the leader of the group-that-was-joined. Other states identified were states of internal focus and of created autonomy.

During the process of integration, it seemed that the leader (consultant) provided a focus for the emergence of a new systemic entity through her position as (symbolic) leader of the group-that-was-joined. This symbolic position, or signifier, appeared to provide a link between the existent social structure (of groups that may be joined) and the newly emergent group. In addition it enabled the leader to act, at different times, as 'container' and 'partner' in the process (Chapters 4 and 7–10).

Implications

Many studies have indicated that certain leadership styles are more effective than others in some situations (Lewin et al., 1939; Lippett, 1939; Weber, 1947; Etzioni, 1961; Bales, 1958; 1970; Wong, 1981; Bass, 1981; Hollander, 1985). The aspects of these situations include group size and structure, the nature of the task and the personality of the leader.

The present work has argued for the identification of group 'states' (of integration). Group states, it seems, constitute a particular structuring of the group's systemic organization, and may need to be included amongst those situations that modify the leader role within the group system (e.g., leader's behaviour, effectiveness, and relatedness to the group members). Although 'effectiveness' has not been measured in the present study, it may be that, whilst structured in certain states, groups constrain the meanings, and consequently the effects, that leaders may have in the group. This is done, for example, by anticipatory or retrospective significations (Chapters 3 and 6). It would seem that knowledge of such states and their constraining effects would aid members and leaders in a realistic appraisal of possible courses of future action. For example, group members may be able to decide whether they require a more containing or a more partnership type of leadership for the immediate future (Chapter 8). Leaders may be able to modify their own behaviours, for instance, their interventions (Yalom, 1975; Morran and Hulse, 1984; Wong, 1981), according to the needs that members have during particular states of integration.

2. A LONGITUDINAL STUDY

A longitudinal study examined a group in terms of some important social episodes. These episodes consisted of sequences of social action and dialogue which were identified as important to group members, and were remembered by members as 'incidents' in the life of the group. As such, they have been termed 'traumatic' incidents, and have been viewed as structural organizers for the group (Chapter 11).

From this study, it seemed that the group structure was constituted in terms of members' identifications with the symbolic leader (consultant). The particular structural elements that emerged (e.g., roles, sub-groups, defensive structures) may be seen in the context of the group members' attempts to deal with their anxieties and desires in relation to the consultant and the tasks that she represents (Chapter 11). The emergent structures seemed to constrain further group structures and relations between members. For example, the other group members' relations to Ix appear to be largely structured by her seeming to represent certain of the consultant's characteristics.

The Lacanian concept of 'signifier' was used to discuss the results. For example, it was noted in this study that the group structures were 'open to signification'. This meant that new meanings could be applied to the structures as new social actions and relationships emerged. It also indicated that the structures acted symbolically (i.e., as signifiers) in the group. Consequently, they were also 'open to meaning' in a second sense of being open to membership (within the constraints of group norms). For example, the roles of 'persecutor' and 'victim' were taken by different members at different times.

The role of 'leader' was seen as a major element or signifier in the group system. The group seemed to gain identity through the members' identifications with aspects of this signifier.

Implications

The use of Lacanian concepts, e.g., the Symbolic and Imaginary registers, 'signifier' and 'signified', allows us to understand the group as a system emergent from the relations of its particular members within a more general cultural milieu. There are two major implications. (a) The structures discussed are not regarded as the result of any pre-determined developmental schema, but appear to have arisen from the attempts of these particular members to work together. For example, the particular roles identified have specific meanings, open to change, in the context of this group. Understanding the changing significations attributed to group elements and structures in particular groups may aid group members, leaders and consultants to more realistically achieve group aims. (b) However, the structures discussed may also be seen in terms of the Symbolic order shared by the members as participants in a common linguistic and cultural population. Alongside their particular meanings in a group, these structures also seem to represent a more general organization of the group. This organization might be seen as the 'symbolic group', perhaps identified by Freud as the primal horde, but also clearly evident in the expectations and fantasies of group members about the group-that-was-joined. It seems that there is a symbolic group that acts to constrain, rather than determine, the particular structures of the group-that-is-formed.

The application of Lacanian concepts in future studies may allow for a clearer understanding of the relations between the abstract and general 'symbolic' group organization and its particular or more concretized structurings throughout the life of a variety of different groups.

In addition to general theoretical applications, the specific results of this study are indirectly applicable to other groups. For example, it may be that the question of female authority requires further exploration, especially in terms of possible 'splitting' mechanisms and partial identifications made by members. Such processes may be viewed as derived from common deep-seated views of women gained through early experience (Dinnerstein, 1976) or through social values (Long, 1989). Additionally, the structural relation between the consultant, Ix and the other members suggests a need for the further examination of relations between (perceived) leaders and their (perceived) immediate subordinates (Jaques, 1955; Scott, 1981).

Additionally, further exploration of the meaning of group membership may be required. It may be that the attribution of the membership role brings with it a far less distinct set of social directives than the leadership role. For example, followers have been viewed as linked to leaders by their identifications within basic assumption behaviours (Little, 1980), or as unconsciously colluding members of groups whose judgements are consequently unrealistic (Main, 1975; Janis, 1972). These (negative) aspects of followers often seemed to pervade the views that members had of themselves and each other in the present studies. However, decision-making groups require interdependently working members. An understanding of this requirement of the 'work group', is as important as an understanding of the functioning of irrational 'basic assumption' groups (Bion, 1961; Turquet, 1974). Such an understanding might be achieved through further descriptive studies that focus on effective working groups in a variety of situations.

Appendices

APPENDIX A: LEADERSHIP AND AUTHORITY

The terms 'authority' and 'leader' have been used many times in this work. This appendix will attempt to explore the meaning of these terms in order to clarify some discussions in the main text.

PERSONAL AND IMPERSONAL BASES OF LEADERSHIP AND AUTHORITY

Leadership and authority have been viewed in many different ways, the two not always being clearly distinguished. The following discussion identifies two major characterizations found in the literature.

1 Leadership and authority have both been described in terms of *personal characteristics*.
2 Leadership and authority have also been viewed as *role characteristics*.

These two aspects seem to be poles of a personal vs. role continuum. For example, Weber (1947) discusses three types of authority whose claims to legitimacy are based respectively on rational, traditional and charismatic grounds. Charismatic authority, in this case, is based on the perceived personal abilities of the leader whilst rational (legal) authority is based on the more impersonal aspects of the 'office' or role held by the leader. Traditional authority seems to hold a central position on this dimension as it is seen to combine 'personal' and 'official' status, insofar as the allegiance of followers is to a particular person with traditional rights of office.

Others distinguish between leadership and authority. For example, Bierstedt (1950) emphasized the personal nature of leadership as compared to the impersonal basis of authority. However, Rice (1965) links leadership with personal power and with authority derived from a task.

Leadership may also be viewed as pertaining to a role that itself relates to other roles in the group system (Hills, 1968; Gibb, 1968; Rice, 1969; Katz and Kahn, 1978; Bass, 1981; Hollander, 1985). In this view leadership is a *position* potentially open to any group member. This definition is similar to Weber's definition of rational or legal authority. The position belongs to the group rather than to the individual. Byrt (1978) points out that leadership is predominantly treated in research as leadership of groups, rather than of individuals.

To others, this 'positional leadership' refers to the leader's 'authority' which in turn derives from the situation or task of the group (Follett, 1941; Bion, 1961; Rice, 1965; De Board, 1978). For example, Follett believes that leadership is aided by the depersonalization of authority. This depersonalization derives from 'the law of the situation' (p. 154) which, if obeyed, minimizes conflict in organizations. Bion believes that the authority of the work group leader derives from the overt task of the work group. In this case, members agree that the leader is best able to lead them in their task. However, such authority is not always rational. The basic assumption group leader (Bion, 1961) gains authority via his or her unconscious collusion with other members (Janis, 1972; De Board, 1978).

THE BASES OF POWER

A useful way of viewing authority and leadership is to see them in the context of power. Schopler (1965) views power as the ability to influence others, although he notes that the many definitions of power reported in the literature vary in the emphases that they place on different aspects of the influence process. Field theory, for example, emphasizes the amount of force that one individual may place on a segment of another's life space. This force may be resisted in a variety of ways and the power of the first individual may be seen in terms of overcoming resistances (Cartwright, 1959). The important aspect of this view of power is not so much the behavioural outcome as the interplay of forces between actors. In contrast, the decision-making framework (Dahl, 1957) emphasizes changes in behaviour or in the probabilities of outcomes given particular influences. Power in this case is the ability to influence and change possible outcomes.

Schopler lists several bases of power (taken from French and Raven, 1959). These are:

1 Legitimate power or authority (i.e., power dependent on the prior socialization of the individuals concerned and their belief in the legitimacy of the powerful person(s)).
2 Coercive power (i.e., dependent on the ability to punish or force others).
3 Reward power (i.e., dependent on the ability to reward others).
4 Referent power (i.e., based on the individual's ability to command identifications). This includes charismatic power.
5 Expert power (i.e., based on expertise).

In this scheme authority is one of several types of power. The bases for other types may include personal power, however such power is usually gained from one's position or role in the group. For example, the power to give rewards may depend on one's economic power or one's social prestige in society. Even the brute strength involved in some forms of coercive power depends on the number of others willing to support, or at least not to oppose, the coercion. Power bases, it seems, are more or less personal and power seems to be related to the group context within which it occurs.

This idea of context is important to many modern theories of authority. Legitimation may be seen as an aspect of context. Hollander (1985), for example, indicates that leaders who usurp power and remain unlegitimated have less influence than elected leaders and will be more likely to use coercive power.

LEGITIMATION

Legitimation of power may come from different sources. Scott (1981) describes two sources, the first of these being 'authorization' from superiors in a social hierachy, and the second being 'endorsement' from inferiors. Commonly these represent authority by imposition and authority by election. Needless to say, this is at the conscious level. Authority bestowed via irrational or unconscious processes may best be seen in terms of collusive processes between various sub-groupings of members within a group (Main, 1975; Turquet, 1975).

The relation of power to context is emphasized by those who distinguish between task and maintenance leaders (Johnson and Johnson, 1987). These leaders are seen to derive their power from the corresponding task and maintenance functions within the group. To these authors, the task functions are those related to the primary work of the group and the maintenance functions are related to the social functioning of the group (Chapter 12). Following Bales (1958), Etzioni (1961) uses the terms 'instrumental' and 'expressive' to describe these types of leadership functions. In a given group or organization different persons may become instrumental or expressive leaders.

ASPECTS OF LEADERSHIP

It seems from the above that leadership might usefully be regarded as consisting of several aspects which are expressed differently in different situations.

1 *The personal vs. impersonal dimension.* This is a dimension that differentiates, e.g., 'charismatic' with 'positional' leadership. It also seems to differentiate leadership as a personal quality from leadership as a series of impersonal skills. Personal leadership qualities, however, are based on

personal power which is difficult to maintain over time and distance unless an organizational structure with its own impersonal power structure develops as a support (Blau, 1974). Severe difficulties often accrue to family or charismatically led organizations when their leader leaves because the prior power base, being personal, is not readily transferable.

2 *A dimension based on group functions*. This dimension is related to the first dimension. It is, however, an elaboration of the 'positional leadership' pole. It contrasts, e.g., instrumental leadership with expressive leadership (Bales, 1958; Etzioni, 1961); political leadership with emotional leadership (Chapter 10); or 'containing' with 'partnership' functions. Although these examples are dichotomous, there is no reason to expect all group functions are ordered in this manner. The mother, father, child functions in the family group provide a triadic model.

3 *The dimension of legitimacy vs. illegitimacy*. This dimension contrasts, e.g., Weber's three types of legitimate authority with leaders who usurp power by other means. Processes of legitimation may vary from group to group and between different functions within the group. For example, a religious leader may receive legitimation in a manner quite different from a secular leader. The process of legitimation authorizes the leader to act on behalf of other group members and is an important aspect of group cohesion (Kellerman, 1981).

4 *A dimension of conscious vs. unconscious leadership*. This dimension refers to the degree to which a leader is consciously selected as leader on the basis of some specifiable criteria. It contrasts, e.g., the work group leader with the basic assumption leader (Bion, 1961), or the legitimate authority with the 'central person' who acts to draw together several unconscious thoughts or desires held by group members (Redl, 1942).

CONTRASTING THEORETICAL FORMULATIONS

The present work focusses on psychoanalytic explanations. These may be compared with some recent formulations in attribution theory. For example, Pfeffer (1977) argues that observers attribute many aspects of the group system to those identified as leaders who are in turn seen to cause social consequences such as group performance. This enables complex social processes to be located in one source, i.e., the leader, where they may be dealt with as if they are due to personality traits. It may be that members, as observers, attribute many aspects of the group's performance to the leader who is consequently blamed or idealized. Pfeffer argues that this process may result in the leader's becoming a symbol for certain group processes. However, this view sees the leader's symbolization as an outcome of attributions rather than a basis for them. The present work argues that members or followers attribute certain characteristics to their leaders because the leader provides a signification or imaginary representation of the signifier 'authority'.

By this view, the definition of leadership simply in terms of function is not sufficient. When the consciously operating work group predominates we may expect our leaders to fulfill rational functions. However, the leader also fulfills a role in the unconscious mythology of the group and this may be non-congruent with the conscious group functions.

APPENDIX B: A REPORT ON A STUDY OF GROUP MEMBERS' PERCEPTIONS OF EACH OTHER

The research to be described draws upon an analysis of groups formed for the purpose of learning about group structures and dynamics. They took the form of a self-analytic learning group (Mann, 1966) and were conducted according to the 'Tavistock' style of group (Rice, 1965; McLeish et al., 1973; De Board, 1978). In these groups, the participants are given the task of learning about group structures and processes by examining the ongoing dynamics of their own group, as they occur. The staff member or consultant present has the role of aiding the participants or members in their task. S/he does this by means of interpretations about group processes. These interpretations are developed from his or her own experiences within the group.

The theoretical bases for these groups are largely psychoanalytic and have been strongly influenced by the work of Bion (1961). For example, unconscious processes are examined and the relations of member to consultant and of member to member are seen to include transference phenomena.

Basically group members are free to conduct the group as they wish, given their primary task of learning. The consultant aids them in the task and interprets resistances to the task. The members usually discuss a great many themes, e.g., personalisms, relationships, ways of approaching the task, the consultant's role, the members' roles, leadership, emotions, the group mind, evaluation of progress, etc.

The group to be described consisted of 10 members (seven females and three males), a female consultant and a male staff observer. This group is described in detail in Chapters 7 and 11 of this book. Notable in the dynamics of the group were three major incidents:

1 The scapegoating of one female member which culminated in a strong verbal attack by another female who was said to speak for other members. Structurally associated with this incident was the establishment of sub-groups. These sub-groups were not totally stable but had some core members.
2 A verbal attack on the latter female and other members of what was seen as her sub-group, in their absence and predicated on reasons for their absence that proved to be groundless.
3 A seeming 'breakdown' of this same female in the face of what she felt to be impossible demands by other group members and her apparent 'rescue' by the consultant.

These incidents were interpreted (see Chapter 10) in terms of differential identifications of members with aspects of the consultant. It seemed that the female (designated here as Ix) came to be identified in the group with the perceived attacking aspects of the consultant. The constructive supportive aspects of the consultant were felt by members to be in danger of being depleted by the attacking aspects so they were split off and located in Ix. Both aspects of the consultant were seen to originate primarily in member projections established early in the history of the group. The angry and destructive impulses of group members (from whatever source, but structurally from the death drive in response to their resistances against learning from experience, Bion, 1961) became located in Ix, directed against Al and eventually against Ix herself.

This plainly Kleinian interpretation, arrived at only after much hard work within the group, can be conceptualized within a Lacanian context. The consultant is legitimized and represents the Symbolic leader. Her legitimation comes from three sources: authorization from the institution; endorsement by the members; and via the myth of the group-that-is-joined (i.e., by unconsciously attesting to the myth that the group existed before the members joined and that they joined it as the consultant's group; see Chapter 4). This myth engages those processes whereby the consultant is instituted as the Symbolic leader, the keeper of the task and the anchoring signifier of the group. Membership identifications centre around her role (Freud, 1921) and are partial. Different members identify with different aspects of the consultant (Long, 1991).

Members' perceptions of each other were studied after the last session. These were elicited by means of Kelly's (1955) role repertory test. In this method members were able to make comparisons between all group members, including themselves, the consultant and the observer. The comparisons were made freely on the basis of any criteria that they wished. In this way the constructs used by the members themselves were elicited, rather than any provided by the researcher.

A quantitative analysis involved those statistical methods that operate on quantifying relationships of co-variance and extracting the underlying factors (factor analysis, Cattell, 1978) or dimensions (multidimensional scaling, Torgerson, 1952; Shepard, 1962, 1974; Kruskal and Wish, 1978; Schiffman et al., 1982) that economically describe those relationships (Snyder et al., 1985). Modern methods of analysing repertory grid data (Kelly, 1955; Bannister and Mair, 1968; Bell, 1984; Slater, 1977; Rathod, 1981; and Yorke, 1985) are grounded in such methods. Forgas (1979) recommends MDS methods for the analysis of social perceptions.

Hence, the data was analysed by means of: (a) principal components factor analysis of individual subject data; (b) individual differences multidimensional scaling analyses of the data as a whole using the ALSCAL programme for individual differences MDS (Takane et al., 1977; Young and Lewyckyj, 1979).

This latter method has the advantage of representing the collective judgements of members about members (i.e., their perceptions of each other) as points in multidimensional space, hence providing a directly interpretable 'picture' of members along pertinent dimensions. In addition the method provides information on the degree to which particular judgements weight the overall solution. In simple terms, it provides information on the degree of influence any one member has on giving a pooled picture of how members are perceived. The individual factor analyses of individual members' perceptions, together with interviews with these members, were used in coming to a final interpretation of the solutions.

A three dimensional MDS solution was chosen as this seemed to best account for the variance in the data (Coxon, 1982). The three dimensions, necessarily bipolar, were interpreted as:

1 dominant (active) vs. passive;
2 masculine vs. feminine;
3 stable vs. emotive.

The three dimensions may be represented by two diagrams which view dimensions 1 and 2 for those high on dimension 3 separately from those low on dimension 3.

Eight quadrants are identified in these figures. Quadrants 1 and 5 contain the members of cluster A (one of two major clusters identified in a cluster analysis, Everitt, 1980). This cluster identifies those who held leadership-type positions in the group. Some leaders, it seems, were seen as more stable (the staff members and Er, a male), whilst others (Ix, Ca and Ge, all females) were seen as more emotive. Ix's position as an emotive leader supports the analysis of her close identification with the consultant mentioned in Chapter 10. She

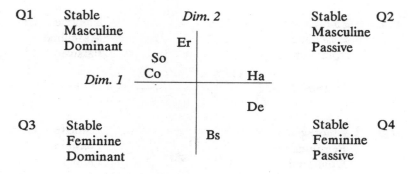

Figure 1   Spatial representation of elements (group 3 members) high on dimension 3, in the 1x2 plane of the three-dimensional group space

tended to be seen as containing those aspects of the Symbolic leader, or the original leader of the group-that-was-joined, that were viewed negatively by members. She tended to be construed as containing the aggressive, angry and judgemental aspects of the consultant along with her more positive capacities to interpret, understand and define group culture. The position that Ix holds might be viewed as an 'hystericized' position, that is, a position from which she, like an hysterical symptom (of the group), unconsciously 'joins in the conversation' (Freud and Breuer, 1974) and is seen by the group as prime interlocuter with the Other, who is in this case located in the leader.

Quadrants 2 and 6 contain the two rather more passive males, one of whom was seen as more stable (Ha, seen as a follower of Ix in the sub-group of three described in the last chapter), the other as more emotional (Ja, seen as a rather isolated individual).

Quadrants 4 and 8 contain the more passive females. Al and Fr, the friends subjected to much of the hostility voiced by Ix, and at times by Ca and Ge, are contained in quadrant 8.

It seems that in this group, leaders are seen to be of three major types:

1 dominant, masculine and stable;
2 dominant, masculine and emotive;
3 dominant, feminine and emotive.

From a consideration of the data, it seems that the most dominant/active members are also seen to be more emotive. This seems to hold for the more passive followers as well as for the leaders. Put another way, the more emotive members are seen to be relatively more dominant. Additionally, males are seen to be less emotive than females. The perception of leadership relates, it seems, to *all three dimensions*.

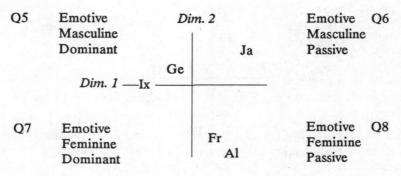

Figure 2 Spatial representation of elements (group 3 members) low on dimension 3, in the 1x2 plane of the three-dimensional group space

Interestingly, although there is a conceptual space for dominant feminine persons, no members definitely fit the positions available in quadrants 3 and 7 (Ix comes closest to this role in quadrant 7). It is as if, in this group, female leaders are conceptualized by either a shift toward the masculine or towards the less stable, more emotional (hysterical) position (i.e., a position of uncertainty about gender). The strong, stable, feminine position seems to remain unfilled. This could be because:

1 members are unable to see actual strong, stable feminine leaders for what they are, and they tend to view them as more 'masculine' or 'hysterical' than they are;
2 members, by some unconscious collusive process, may not allow the role of dominant stable feminine leader to be filled, even by women;
3 the women available to fill the role in this group are in fact more masculine or more emotional than the position.

It is quite possible, even probable, that all three points are interrelated and reflect an interrelatedness in the culture at large. The present study cannot separate out their differential effects, and, in a culture where subjects are exposed to their interrelatedness from birth onward, it would be difficult to do so. One would need to find a measure of masculinity/femininity that was free from the constructions of members of a culture, and since masculinity/femininity is a cultural construct this is impossible. We can rely only on the construct of male/female, knowing that we have a conceptual space for masculine females and feminine males, and have a variety of correlated constructions, under the rubric of gender, some of which have little or nothing to do with the possession of a penis, or of an xx or xy chromosome pattern, but which have a lot to do with the way in which sexual difference is symbolized. The fact that the penis is often equated with the phallic symbol, that great organizer of kinship and culture (Levi-Strauss, 1949), and of family and sanity (Lacan, 1977), is perhaps the ultimate reason why the female authority is necessarily masculinized or neuroticized, particularly in a culture where many have not progressed past the phallic phase nor entered full psychological maturity.

The group described gives one example of dynamics experienced by the author in other groups that have not yet been explored in such a systematic fashion. Other groups analysed by means of this method (i.e., an MDS analysis of member perceptions) have produced results that indicate:

1 that the role of leader, whether consultant, seminar leader or 'ideal leader', is more clearly signified than the role of member and that the role 'ideal member' is more closely identified with the role of leader than with other member roles;
2 that the masculine–feminine dimension is not identical to the passive active dimension (at least in the Imaginary register).

This latter point is of interest given Sayers' (1986) reading of Freud. It may indicate that the symbolic structuring of sexual identity around the oedipal complex allows more flexibility in our understanding of gender than would first seem apparent. In fact Freud (1931) moves toward a view of active feminine sexuality in the phallic phase, although such trends in the mature woman are designated by him as 'masculine'.

References

Note: Where a reference is given for a book or article in other than its first publication, and where the original date is cited in the text, this original date appears at the end of the reference. All dates cited in the text can be found at the end of the appropriate reference.

Abraham, K. *Selected Papers on Psychoanalysis*. London: Hogarth Press, 1927.

Adorno, T.W., Frenkel-Brunswik, E., Levinson, D.J. and Sanford, R.N. *The Authoritarian Personality*. New York: W.W. Norton and Company Inc., (1969) 1950.

Allport, G.W. 'The General and the Unique in Psychological Science'. *Journal of Personality*, *30*, pp. 405–421, 1962.

Allport, G.W. *Pattern and Growth in Personality*. London: Holt, Rinehart and Winston, 1961.

Allport, G.W. 'The Historical Background of Social Psychology'. In G. Lindzey and E. Aronson (eds). *The Handbook of Social Psychology* Vol.1. New York: Random House (3rd Edn) 1985.

Amidon, E.J. and Hough, J.B. (eds) *Interaction Analysis: Theory, Research and Application*. Reading, Mass: Addison-Wesley, 1967.

Argyle, M. 'Personality and Social Behaviour'. In R. Harré (ed.). *Personality*. Oxford: Basil Blackwell, 1976.

Bachelard, G. *The New Scientific Mind*. Paris: Presses Universitaires de France, 1934.

Back, K.W. *Beyond Words*. New York: Russell Sage Foundation, 1972.

Bain, A. 'Presenting Problems in Social Consultancy'. *Human Relations*, pp. 643–657, 1981.

Bales, R.F. *Interaction Process Analysis: A Method for the Study of Small Groups*. Reading, Mass: Addison-Wesley, 1950.

Bales, R.F. 'Task Roles and Social Roles in Problem- Solving Groups'. In E.E. Maccoby, T.M. Newcomb and E.L. Hartley (eds). *Readings in Social Psychology*. New York: Holt, 1958.

Bales, R.F. *Personality and Interpersonal Behaviour*. New York: Holt, 1970.

Bandura, A. *Aggression: A Social Learning Analysis*. Englewood Cliffs, New Jersey: Prentice Hall, 1973.

Bannister, D. and Mair, J.M.M. *The Evaluation of Personal Constructs*. New York: Academic Press, 1968.

Bass, B.M. *Stodgdill's Handbook of Leadership: A Survey of Theory and Research*. New York: Free Press, (Rev. Edn) 1981.

Bateson, G. 'The Logical Categories of Learning and Communication'. In G. Bateson. *Steps to an Ecology of Mind: Collected Essays in Anthropology, Psychiatry, Evolution and Epistemology*. Frogmore, Herts: Granada Publishing, (1973) 1968.

Bateson, G. 'Redundancy and Coding'. (1968) In G. Bateson. *Steps to an Ecology of Mind: Collected Essays in Anthropology, Psychiatry, Evolution and Epistemology.* Frogmore, Herts: Granada Publishing, 1973.

Bateson, G. *Steps to an Ecology of Mind: Collected Essays in Anthropology, Psychiatry, Evolution and Epistemology.* Frogmore, Herts: Granada Publishing, 1973.

Bell, R. 'The Analysis of Multiple Repertory Grids'. Paper delivered to the 2nd Australasian Personal Construct Psychology Conference. Woolongong, Australia: 1984.

Bennis, W.G. and Shepard, H.A. 'A Theory of Group Development'. *Human Relations, 9,* pp. 415–437, 1956.

Bierstedt, R. 'An Analysis of Social Power'. *American Sociological Review, 15,* pp. 730–738, 1950.

Billig, M. *Social Psychology and Intergroup Relations.* London: Academic Press, 1976.

Billig, M. *Fascists: A Social Psychological View of the National Front.* London: Harcourt, Brace & Jovanovitch, 1978.

Bion, W.R. *Experiences in Groups.* London: Tavistock Publications, 1961.

Bion, W.R. 'Language and the Schizophrenic'. (1965) In M. Klein, P. Heimann and R. Money-Kyrle (eds). *New Directions in Psychoanalysis.* London: Karnac Books, 1977.

Bion, W.R. *Attention and Interpretation: A Scientific Approach to Insight in Psychoanalysis and Groups.* London: Tavistock Publications, 1970.

Blau, P.M. *On the Nature of Organizations.* New York: Wiley & Sons, 1974.

Bowers, D.G. and Seashore, S. 'Changing the Structure and Functioning of an Organization'. In W.M. Evan (ed.). *Organizational Experiments: Laboratory and Field Research.* New York: Harper & Row, 1971.

Boyd, R.D. 'A Matrix Model of the Small Group'. *Small Group Behaviour, 14,* No. 4, pp. 405–418, 1983.

Boyd, R.D. 'A Matrix Model of the Small Group Part 2'. *Small Group Behaviour, 15,* No. 2, pp. 233–250, 1984.

Breakwell, G.M. (ed.). *Threatened Identities.* New York: Wiley & Sons, 1983.

Byrt, W.J. *Leaders and Leadership.* Melbourne: Sun Books, 1978.

Caramazza, A. and Zurif, E.B. 'Dissociation of Algorithmic and Heuristic Processes in Language Comprehension: Evidence from Aphasia'. *Brain and Language, 3,* pp. 572–582, 1976.

Carroll, J.D. and Chang, J.J. 'Analysis of Individual Differences in Multidimensional Scaling Via an N-Way Generalization of "Eckart-Young" Decomposition'. *Psychometrika, 35,* No. 3, pp. 283–319, 1970.

Cartwright, D. 'Power: A Neglected Variable in Social Psychology'. In D. Cartwright (ed.). *Studies in Social Power.* Ann Arbor, Michigan: Institute for Social Research, 1959.

Cattell, R.B. *The Scientific Analysis of Personality.* Harmondsworth: Penguin, 1965.

Cattell, R.B. *Factor Analysis in Behavioural and Life Sciences.* New York: Plenum Press, 1978.

Cattell, R.B. and Kline, P. *The Scientific Analysis of Personality and Motivation.* New York: Academic Press, 1977.

Cherns, A.B. and Clark, P.A. 'Task and Organization: Military and Civilian'. In E.J. Miller (ed.). *Task and Organization.* London: Tavistock Publications, 1976.

Chomsky, N. *Aspects of the Theory of Syntax.* The Hague: Mouton, 1965.

Chomsky, N. *Language and Mind.* New York: Harcourt, Brace & Jovanovich, 1968.

Cissna, K.N. 'Phases in Group Development: The Negative Element'. *Small Group Behaviour, 15,* No.1, pp. 3–32, 1984.

Clark, P.A. *Action Research and Organization Change.* London: Harper & Row, 1972.

Cooley, C.H. *Human Nature and the Social Order.* New York: Schocken, 1964.

Cooper, L. and Gustafason, J.P. 'Family–Group Development: Planning in Organizations'. *Human Relations, 34,* No. 8, pp. 705–730, 1981.

Coxon, A.P.M. *The User's Guide to Multidimensional Scaling*. London: Heinemann, 1982.

Dahl, R.A. 'The Concept of Power'. *Behavioural Science, 2*, pp. 201–218, 1957.

Davis, M. and Wallbridge, D. *Boundary and Space: An Introduction to the Work of D.W. Winnicott*. Harmondsworth: Penguin, 1983.

De Board, R. *The Psychoanalysis of Organizations: A Psychoanalytic Approach to Behaviour in Groups and Organizations*. London: Tavistock Publications, 1978.

Deleuze, G. and Guattari, F. *Anti-Oedipus Capitalism and Schizophrenia*. St Paul: University of Minnesota, 1983.

Dell, P.F. 'Beyond Homeostasis: Toward a Concept of Coherence'. *Family Process, 21*, No. 2, pp. 21–41, 1982.

Dell, P.F. and Goolishian, H.A. 'Order Through Fluctuation: An Evolutionary Epistemology for Human Systems'. *Australian Journal of Family Therapy, 2*, No. 4, pp. 175–184, 1981.

Dinnerstein, D. *The Rocking of the Cradle and The Ruling of the World*. New York: Harper & Row, 1976.

Doise, W. *Groups and Individuals: Explanations in Social Psychology*. Cambridge: Cambridge University Press, 1978.

Donzelot, J. *The Policing of Families*. New York: Pantheon Books, 1979.

Drescher, S., Burlingame, G. and Fuhriman, A. 'Cohesion: An Odyssey in Empirical Understanding'. *Small Group Behaviour, 16*, No. 1, pp. 3–30, 1985.

Emery, F.E. *Systems Thinking*. Harmondsworth: Penguin, 1969.

Emery, F.E. and Trist, E.L. 'The Causal Texture of Organization Environments'. *Human Relations, 18*, pp. 21–32, 1965.

Emery, F.E. and Trist, E.L. 'Socio-Technical Systems'. In F.E. Emery (ed.). *Systems Thinking*. Harmondsworth: Penguin, 1969.

Erikson, E.H. *Childhood and Society*. New York: Norton, 1950.

Erikson, E.H. *Identity, Youth and Crisis*. New York: Norton, 1968.

Etzioni, A. *A Comparative Analysis of Complex Organizations: On Power, Involvement and Their Correlates*. New York: Free Press, (Revised and Enlarged Edn) 1961.

Everitt, B. *Cluster Analysis*. London: Heinemann Educational Books, (2nd Edn) 1980.

Fairbairn, W.R.D. *Psychoanalytic Studies of the Personality*. London: Tavistock Publications, 1952.

Fenichel, O. *The Psychoanalytic Theory of Neurosis*. New York: Norton, 1945.

Ferenczi, S. *Contributions to Psychoanalysis*. Boston: Richard Badger, (1962) 1916.

Follett, M.P. 'The Giving of Orders'. In D.S. Pugh (ed.). *Organization Theory*. Harmondsworth: Penguin, (1971) 1941.

Forgas, J.P. *Social Episodes: The Study of Interaction Routines*. London: Academic Press, 1979.

Forgas, J.P. 'Episode Cognition: Internal Representations of Interaction Routines'. In L. Berkowitz (ed.). *Advances in Experimental Social Psychology*. New York: Academic Press, 1982.

Forgas, J.P. 'Cognitive Representations of Interaction Episodes'. *Australian Journal of Psychology, 35*, No. 2, pp. 145–163, 1983.

Foucault, M. *The Order of Things: An Archaeology of the Human Sciences*. London: Tavistock Publications, (1970) 1966.

Foulkes, S.H. *Therapeutic Group Analysis*. New York: International Universities Press, 1964.

French, J.R.P. and Raven, B. 'The Bases of Social Power'. In D. Cartwright (ed.). *Studies in Social Power*. Ann Arbor, Michigan: Institute for Social Research, 1959.

Freud, A. *The Ego and the Mechanisms of Defence*. New York: International Universities Press, 1946.

Freud, S. *The Interpretation of Dreams*. Harmondsworth: Penguin, (1975) 1900.

Freud, S. 'On Narcissism: An Introduction'. *Standard Edition Vol. XIV*. pp. 73–102. London: Hogarth Press, (1957) 1914.

Freud, S. 'Instincts and Their Vicissitudes'. *Standard Edition Vol. XIV*, pp. 117–140. London: Hogarth Press, (1957) 1915.

Freud, S. *Beyond the Pleasure Principle*. London: Hogarth Press and Institute of Psycho-Analysis, (1974) 1920.

Freud, S. *Group Psychology and the Analysis of the Ego*. London: Hogarth Press and Institute of Psycho-Analysis, (1949) 1921.

Freud, S. 'The Ego and the Id'. *Standard Edition Vol. XIX*, pp. 3–172. London: Hogarth Press, (1957) 1923.

Freud, S. 'The Dissolution of the Oedipus Complex'. *Standard Edition Vol. XIX*, pp. 173–182. London: Hogarth Press, (1957) 1924a.

Freud, S. 'Loss of Reality in Neurosis and Psychosis'. *Standard Edition Vol. XIX*, pp. 183–190. London: Hogarth Press, (1957) 1924b.

Freud, S. 'Address to the Society of B'nai B'rith'. *Standard Edition Vol. XX*, p. 273. London: Hogarth Press, (1959) 1926.

Freud, S. 'Female Sexuality'. *Standard Edition Vol. XXI*, pp. 225–243, London: Hogarth Press, (1961) 1931.

Freud, S. and Breuer, J. *Studies in Hysteria* (1895) in the Pelican Freud, Vol. 3, Harmondsworth: Penguin, 1974.

Friedrichs, J. and Ludtke, H. *Participant Observation: Theory and Practice*. Lexington, Mass: Saxon House/Lexington Books, 1975.

Fromm, E. *The Crisis of Psychoanalysis: Essays on Freud, Marx and Social Psychology*. Harmondsworth: Penguin, 1970.

Geist, P. and Chandler, T. 'Account Analysis of Influence in Group Decision Making'. *Communication Monographs*, *51*, No. 1, pp. 67–78, 1984.

Gemmill, G. 'The Mythology of the Leader Role in Small Groups'. *Small Group Behaviour*, *17*, No. 1, pp. 41–50, 1986.

Gibb, C.A. 'Leadership'. In G. Lindzey and E. Aronson (eds). *The Handbook of Social Psychology* Vol. 2. Reading, Mass: Addison-Wesley, (2nd Edn) 1968.

Gibbard, G.S., Hartman, J.J. and Mann, R.D. (eds). *Analysis of Groups: Contributions to Theory, Research and Practice*. San Francisco: Jossey Bass, 1974.

Gilmore, T.N. and Krantz, J. 'Projective Identification in the Consulting Relationship: Exploring the Unconscious Dimensions of a Client System'. *Human Relations*, *38*, No. 12, pp. 1159–1177, 1985.

Glaser, S. 'Once More Unto the System'. *Human Relations*, *37*, No. 6, pp. 473–490, 1984.

Goffman, E. *The Presentation of Self in Everyday Life*. Harmondsworth: Penguin, 1971.

Gordon, R.L. *Interviewing: Strategy, Techniques and Tactics*. Homewood, Illinois: Dorsey Press, (Rev. Edn) 1975.

Grigg, R. 'Jakobson et Lacan: Sur Metaphore et Metonomie'. *Ornicar?*, No. 35, Winter, pp. 12–34, 1985–6.

Grolnick, S.A. 'Dreams and Dreaming as Transitional Phenomena'. In S.A. Grolnick, L. Barkin and W. Muensterberger (eds). *Between Fantasy and Reality: Transitional Objects and Transitional Phenomena*. New York: Jason Aronson, 1978.

Grolnick, S.A., Barkin, L. and Muensterberger, W. (eds). *Between Fantasy and Reality: Transitional Objects and Transitional Phenomena*. New York: Jason Aronson, 1978.

Grotstein, J. *Splitting and Projective Identification*. New York: Jason Aronson, 1981.

Gustafson, J.P. and Cooper, L. 'Unconscious Planning in Small Groups'. *Human Relations*, *32*, No. 12, pp. 1039–64, 1979.

Hall, A.D. and Fagen, R.E. 'Definition of a System'. In *Systems Engineering*. New York: Bell Telephone Laboratories, 1955.

Hamilton, V. *Narcissus and Oedipus: The Children of Psychoanalysis*. Harmondsworth: Penguin, 1979.

Harré, R. *Social Being: A Theory for Social Psychology*. Totowa, New Jersey: Rowman & Littlefield, 1979.

Harré, R. *The Analysis of Action*. Cambridge: Cambridge University Press, 1982.

Harré, R. *Personal Being: A Theory for Individual Psychology*. Oxford: Basil Blackwell, 1983.

Harré, R. 'Social Elements as Mind'. *British Journal of Medical Psychology*, *57*, 127–135, 1984.

Harré, R. and Secord, P.F. *The Explanation of Social Behaviour*. Oxford: Basil Blackwell, 1972.

Hartman, J.J. and Gibbard, G.S. (1974) 'Anxiety, Boundary Evolution and Social Change'. In G.S. Gibbard, J.J. Hartman and R.D. Mann (eds). *Analysis of Groups: Contributions to Theory, Research and Practice*. San Francisco: Jossey Bass, 1974.

Hills, R.J. *Toward a Science of Organization*. Eugene, Oregon: Univ. of Oregon Press, 1968.

Hoffman, L. 'Deviation-Amplification Processes in Natural Groups'. In J. Haley (ed.). *Changing Families*. New York: Grune & Stratton, 1971.

Hollander, E.P. 'Leadership and Power'. In G. Lindzey and E. Aronson (eds). *The Handbook of Social Psychology* Vol. 2. New York: Random House, (3rd Edn) 1985.

Horney, K. *New Ways in Psychoanalysis*. New York: Norton, (1966) 1939.

Horwitz, L. 'Projective Identification in Dyads and Groups'. *International Journal of Group Psychotherapy*, *33*, No. 3, pp. 259–279, 1983.

Jakobson, R. 'Towards a Linguistic Typology of Aphasic Impairments'. In A.V.S. de Rueck and M. O'Connor (eds). *Ciba Foundation Symposium on Disorders of Language*. London: Churchill, 1964.

Jakobson, R. and Halle, M. *Fundamentals of Language*. Second Revised Edition. The Hague: Mouton, (1975) 1956.

James, H. (ed.) *The Letters of William James* Vol. 1. Boston: Atlantic Monthly, 1920.

James, W. *The Principles of Psychology*. Authorized Edition. New York: Dover Publications, (1950) 1918.

Janis, I.L. *Victims of Groupthink: A Psychological Study of Foreign Policy Decisions and Fiascos*. Boston: Houghton Mifflin, 1972.

Jaques, E. 'Social Systems as a Defence Against Persecutory and Depressive Anxiety'. In M. Klein, P. Heimann, and R. Money-Kyrle (eds). *New Directions in Psychoanalysis*. London: Tavistock, 1955.

Johnson, D.W. and Johnson, F.P. *Joining Together: Group Theory and Group Skills*. Englewood Cliffs, New Jersey: Prentice Hall, 1987 (3rd Edn).

Jung, C.J. 'The Archetypes and the Collective Unconscious'. *The Collected Works*, Vol. 9 Pt 1 (2nd Edn), Translated by R.F.C. Hull London: Routledge & Kegan Paul, (1968) 1954.

Kagan, J. 'The Concept of Identification'. *Psychological Review*, *65*, No. 5, pp. 296–305, 1958.

Katz, D. and Kahn, R.L. *The Social Psychology of Organizations*. New York: Wiley & Sons, (2nd Edn) 1978.

Kellerman, H. 'The Deep Structures of Group Cohesion'. In H. Kellerman (ed.). *Group Cohesion: Theoretical and Clinical Perspectives*. New York: Grune & Stratton, 1981.

Kelly, G. *The Psychology of Personal Constructs*. 2 Vols. New York: Norton, 1955.

Kernberg, O. *Object Relations Theory and Clinical Psychoanalysis*. New York: Jason Aronson, 1976.

Kets de Vries, M.F.R. 'Narcissism and Leadership: An Object Relations Perspective'. *Human Relations*, *38*, No. 6, pp. 583–601, 1985.

Kissen, M. 'From Group Dynamics to Group Psychoanalysis: Therapeutic Applications of Group Dynamic Understanding'. In M. Kissen. *From Group Dynamics to Group Psychoanalysis*. New York: Wiley & Sons, 1976a.

Kissen, M. *From Group Dynamics to Group Psychoanalysis*. New York: Wiley & Sons, 1976b.

Klein, M. 'Love, Guilt and Reparation'. In *Love, Guilt and Reparation and Other Works 1921–1945*. London: Hogarth Press and Institute of Psycho-Analysis, (1975) 1937.

Klein, M. 'Notes on Some Schizoid Mechanisms'. In M. Klein (ed.). *Developments in Psychoanalysis*. London: Hogarth Press, 1946.

Klein, M. 'Psycho-Analytic Play Technique: History and Significance'. In M. Klein, P. Heimann and R. Money-Kyrle (eds). *New Directions in Psychoanalysis: The Significance of Infant Conflict in the Pattern of Adult Behaviour*. London: Tavistock Publications, (1977) 1955.

Klein, M. *Envy and Gratitude and Other Works 1946–1963*. London: Hogarth Press and Institute of Psycho-Analysis, 1975.

Knorr, K. 'Social Scientific Method or What Do We Make of the Distinction Between the Natural and Social Sciences'. In M. Brenner (ed.). *Social Method and Social Life*. New York: Academic Press, 1981.

Kohut, H. *The Analysis of Self*. New York: International Universities Press, 1971.

Kohut, H. *The Restoration of the Self*. New York: International Universities Press, 1977.

Kretch, D. In J.R. Royce (ed.). *Toward Unification in Psychology*. Toronto: University of Toronto Press, 1970.

Kruskal, J.B. 'Multidimensional Scaling by Optimizing Goodness of Fit to a Nonmetric Hypothesis'. *Psychometrika*, *29*, No. 1, pp. 1–27, 1964.

Kruskal, J.B. and Wish, M. *Multidimensional Scaling*. Beverly Hills: Sage Publications, 1978.

Kuhn, T.S. *The Structure of Scientific Revolutions*. Chicago: University of Chicago Press, 1962.

Kurzweil, E. *The Age of Structuralism: Levi-Strauss to Foucault*. New York: Columbia University Press, 1980.

Lacan, J. 'Aggressivity in Psychoanalysis'. In *Ecrits*. London: Tavistock Publications, (1977) 1948.

Lacan, J. 'The Mirror Stage as Formative of the Function of the I'. In *Ecrits*. London: Tavistock Publications, (1977) 1949.

Lacan, J. 'Some Reflections on the Ego'. *International Journal of Psychoanalysis*, *34*, pp. 11–17, 1953a.

Lacan, J. 'The Function and Field of Speech and Language in Psychoanalysis'. Report to the Rome Congress held at the Instituto di Psicologia della Universita di Roma. In *Ecrits*. London: Tavistock Publications, (1977) 1953b.

Lacan, J. 'The Agency of the Letter in the Unconscious or Reason Since Freud'. In *Ecrits*. London: Tavistock Publications, (1977) 1957.

Lacan, J. 'On a Question Preliminary to Any Possible Treatment of Psychosis'. In *Ecrits*. London: Tavistock Publications, (1977) 1959.

Lacan, J. *Ecrits*. London: Tavistock Publications, 1977.

Lacan, J. *Four Fundamental Concepts of Psycho-Analysis*. Harmondsworth: Penguin, 1979.

Laing, R.D. *The Divided Self*. Harmondsworth: Penguin, 1975.

Landfield, A.W. and Schmittdiel, R. 'The Interpersonal Transaction Group: Evolving Measurements in the Pursuit of Theory'. In J. Adams-Webber and J.C. Mancuso (eds). *Applications of Personal Construct Theory*. New York: Academic Press, 1983.

Lasch, C. *The Culture of Narcissism: American Life in an Age of Diminishing Expectations*. New York: Norton, 1979.

Lawrence, W.G. (ed.). *Exploring Individual and Organizational Boundaries: A Tavistock Open Systems Approach*. New York: Wiley & Sons, 1979.

Le Bon, G. *The Crowd: A Study of the Popular Mind*. London: Fisher Unwin, 1920.
Lecourt, D. *Marxism and Epistemology: Bachelard, Canguilhem and Foucault*. Translated by Ben Brewster. London: New London Books, (1975) 1969.
Lemaire, A. *Jacques Lacan*. London: Routledge & Kegan Paul, 1977.
Levi-Strauss, C. *The Elementary Structures of Kinship*. London: Eyre & Spottiswoode, (English Edition of Revised Edition) (1969) 1949.
Levi-Strauss, C. *The Raw and The Cooked: An Introduction to a Science of Mythology* Vol. 1. London: Harper & Row, (1969) 1964.
Lewin, K. 'Group Decision and Social Change'. In E. Maccoby, T. Newcombe and E. Hartley (eds). *Readings in Social Psychology*. New York: Holt Reinhart, 1958.
Lewin, K., Lippett, R. and White, R.K. 'Patterns of Aggressive Behaviour in Experimentally Created "Social Climates" '. *International Journal of Social Psychology*, *10*, pp. 271–299, 1939.
Likert, R. 'The Principle of Supportive Relationships'. In D.S. Pugh (ed.). *Organization Theory*. Harmondsworth: Penguin, (1971) 1961.
Lindzey, G. and Aronson, E. *The Handbook of Social Psychology*. New York: Random House, (3rd Edn, 2 Vols) 1985.
Linebarger, M.C., Schwartz, M.F. and Saffran, E.M. 'Sensitivity to Grammatical Structure in So-Called Agrammatic Aphasics'. *Cognition*, *13*, pp. 361–392, 1983.
Lippett, R. 'Field Theory and Experiment in Social Psychology: Autocratic and Democratic Group Atmospheres'. *American Journal of Sociology*, *45*, pp. 26–49, 1939.
Little, G. 'Leaders, Followers and the Self'. Paper presented at a conference Psychohistorical Meanings of Leadership, Chicago. June 1980.
Long, S.D. 'The Signifier and the Group'. Paper delivered at the conference Psychoanalysis and Language, Melbourne. July 1987.
Long, S.D. 'Leadership and Gender: A Psychoanalytic Perspective'. *Analysis*, 1, No. 1, pp. 103–16, 1989.
Long, S.D. 'The Signifier and the Group'. *Human Relations*, *44*, No. 4, 1991.
McDougall, W. *The Group Mind*. Cambridge: Cambridge University Press, 1920.
McLeish, J., Matheson, W. and Park, J. *The Psychology of the Learning Group*. New York: Hutchinson, 1973.
Mahler, M. *On Human Symbiosis and the Vicissitudes of Individuation*. New York: International Universities Press, 1968.
Mahler, M.S., Pine, F. and Bergman, A. *The Psychological Birth of the Human Infant*. New York: Basic Books, 1975.
Main, T. 'Some Psychodynamics of Large Groups'. In L. Kreeger (ed.). *The Large Group*. London: Constable, 1975.
Malin, A. and Grotstein, J.S. 'Projective Identification in the Therapeutic Process'. *International Journal of Psychoanalysis*, *47*, No. 26, pp. 26–31, 1966.
Mann, R.D. 'The Development of the Member–Trainer Relationship in Self Analytic Groups'. *Human Relations*, *19*, pp. 85–115, 1966.
Mann, R.D. 'The Identity of the Group Researcher'. In G.S. Gibbard, J.J. Hartmann and R.D. Mann (eds). *Analysis of Groups: Contributions to Theory, Research and Practice*. San Francisco: Jossey Bass, 1974.
Marsh, P., Rosser, E. and Harré, R. *The Rules of Disorder*. London: Routledge & Kegan Paul, 1978.
Martin, Jr, E.A. and Fawcett Hill, W. 'Toward a Theory of Group Development: Six Phases of Therapy Group Development'. In M. Kissen (ed.). *From Group Dynamics to Group Psychoanalysis*. London: Wiley & Sons, (1976) 1957.
Maslow, A.H. *The Further Reaches of Human Nature*. Harmondsworth: Penguin, 1977.
Maturana, H.R. 'Biology of Cognition'. In H.R. Maturana and F.J. Varela. *Autopoiesis*

and Cognition: The Realization of the Living. Dordrecht, Holland: D. Reidel, (1980) 1970.

Maturana, H.R. and Varela, F.J. 'Autopoiesis: The Organization of the Living'. In H.R. Maturana and F.J. Varela. *Autopoiesis and Cognition: The Realization of the Living.* Dordrecht, Holland: D. Reidel, (1980) 1972.

Maturana, H.R. and Varela, F.J. *Autopoiesis and Cognition: The Realization of the Living.* Dordrecht, Holland: D. Reidel, 1980.

Mead, G.H. *Mind, Self and Society.* Chicago: University of Chicago Press, 1934.

Menzies, I.P.M. 'The Functioning of Social Systems as a Defence Against Anxiety: A Report on the Study of a Nursing Service of a General Hospital'. *Tavistock Pamphlet 3.* London: Tavistock Institute, 1970.

Merleau-Ponty, M. *Phenomenology of Perception.* London: Routledge & Kegan Paul, 1962.

Miel, J. 'Jacques Lacan and the Structure of the Unconscious'. In J. Ehrmann (ed.). *Structuralism.* New York: Anchor Books, 1970.

Milgram, S. *Obedience to Authority.* New York: Harper & Row, 1974.

Miller, E.J. (ed.). *Task and Organization.* New York: Wiley & Sons, 1976.

Miller, E.J. and Rice, A.K. *Systems of Organization.* London: Tavistock Publications, 1967.

Miller, E.J. 'Autonomy, Dependency and Organizational Change'. In D. Towell and C. Harries (eds). *Innovation in Patient Care.* London: Croom Helm, 1979.

Mills, T.M. 'Observation'. In G.S. Gibbard, J.J. Hartmann and R.D. Mann (eds). *Analysis of Groups: Contributions to Theory, Research and Practice.* San Francisco: Jossey Bass, (1974) 1967.

Minuchin, S. *Families and Family Therapy.* Cambridge, Mass.: Harvard University Press, 1974.

Minuchin, S. *Family Therapy Techniques.* Cambridge, Mass.: Harvard University Press, 1981.

Misiak, H. and Sexton, V.S. *Phenomenological, Existential and Humanistic Psychologies: A Historical Survey.* New York: Grune & Stratton, 1973.

Morran, D.K. and Hulse, D. 'Group Leader and Member Reactions to Selected Intervention Statements'. *Small Group Behaviour, 15,* No. 2, pp. 278–288, 1984.

Morrison, A.P. 'On Projective Identification in Couples' Groups'. *International Journal of Group Psychotherapy, 36,* No. 1. January 1986.

Muller, J.P. and Richardson, W.J. *Lacan and Language: A Reader's Guide to Ecrits.* New York: International Universities Press, 1982.

Neumann, E. Von. *The Origins and History of Consciousness.* New York: Pantheon, 1954.

Ogden, T.H. 'On Projective Identification'. *International Journal of Psychoanalysis, 60,* pp. 357–373, 1979.

Pfeffer, J. 'The Ambiguity of Leadership'. In M.W. McCall, Jr, and M.M. Lombardo (eds). *Leadership: Where Else Can We Go?* Durham, North Carolina: Duke University Press, 1977.

Pfeffer, J. *Power in Organizations.* Marshfield, Mass.: Pitman, 1981.

Pfeffer, J. 'Organizations and Organization Theory'. In G. Lindzey and E. Aronson (eds). *The Handbook of Social Psychology* Vol. 1. New York: Random House, (3rd Edn) 1985.

Rainwater, L. 'Crucible of Identity: The Negro Lower-Class Family'. In G. Handel (ed.). *The Psychosocial Interior of the Family: A Sourcebook for the Study of Whole Families.* New York: Aldine, (2nd Edn) (1967) 1966.

Rathod, P. 'Methods for the Analysis of Rep Grid Data'. In H. Bonarius, R. Holland and

S. Rosenberg (eds). *Personal Construct Psychology: Recent Advances in Theory and Practice*. London: Macmillan, 1981.

Redl, F. 'Group Emotion and Leadership'. *Psychiatry*, *5*, pp. 573–596, 1942.

Reich, W. *Character Analysis*. New York: Wiley & Sons, 1963.

Rice, A.K. *The Enterprise and its Environment*. London: Tavistock Publications, 1963.

Rice, A.K. *Learning for Leadership: Interpersonal and Intergroup Relations*. London: Tavistock Publications, 1965.

Rice, A.K. 'Individual, Group and Intergroup Processes'. In E.J. Miller (ed.). *Task and Organization*. New York: Wiley & Sons, (1976) 1969.

Rice, A.K. *The Modern University*. London: Tavistock Publications, 1970.

Richards, L. *Having Families: Marriage, Parenthood and Social Pressure in Australia*. Melbourne: Social Change Research Unit, Dept of Sociology, La Trobe University, 1978.

Rieff, P. *Freud: The Mind of The Moralist*. Chicago: University of Chicago Press, (3rd Edn) (1979) 1959.

Rieff, P. *The Triumph of the Therapeutic*. Harmondsworth: Penguin, 1966.

Rieff, P. 'Sacred Order – What Pictures Reveal and Conceal'. Lecture given as part of a series under the auspices of the Seminar on the Sociology of Culture, in conjunction with the National Gallery of Victoria, Melbourne, Australia, 4 August 1982.

Rioch, M. 'The Work of Wilfred Bion on Groups'. *Psychiatry*, *33*, pp. 56–66, 1970.

Rogers, C.R. *On Becoming a Person: A Therapist's View of Psychotherapy*. London: Constable, 1967.

Rychlak, J.F. *A Philosophy of Science for Personality Theory*. Boston: Houghton Mifflin, 1968.

Rychlak, J.F. *The Psychology of Rigorous Humanism*. New York: Wiley & Sons, 1977.

Sandler, J. *Projection, Identification and Projective Identification*, London: Karnac, 1989.

Saussure, F. de. *Course in General Linguistics*. Glasgow: Collins, (1974) 1959.

Sayers, J. *Sexual Contradictions: Psychology, Psychoanalysis and Feminism*. London: Tavistock Publications, 1986.

Scheidlinger, S. 'The Concept of Regression in Group Psychotherapy'. In M. Kissen (ed.). *From Group Dynamics to Group Psychoanalysis*. New York: Wiley & Sons, 1976.

Schiffman, S.S., Reynolds, M.L. and Young, F.W. *Introduction to Multidimensional Scaling: Theory, Method and Applications*. London: Academic Press, 1982.

Schlachet, P.J. 'The Concept of Group Space'. *International Journal of Group Psychotherapy*, *36*, No. 1, January 1986.

Schoeck, H. *Envy: A Theory of Social Behaviour*. New York: Harcourt, Brace & World, 1966.

Schopler, J. 'Social Power'. In L. Berkowitz (ed.). *Advances in Experimental Social Psychology* Vol. 2. New York: Academic Press, 1965.

Schutz, W. *Firo: A Three Dimensional Theory of Interpersonal Behaviour*. New York: Holt, Rinehart & Winston, 1958.

Schutz, W. *Joy: Expanding Human Awareness*. New York: Grove Press, 1967.

Scott, W.R. *Organizations: Rational, Natural and Open Systems*. Englewood Cliffs, New Jersey: Prentice Hall, 1981.

Segal, H. *Klein*. London: Collins, 1979.

Shambaugh, P.W. 'The Mythic Structure of Bion's Groups'. *Human Relations*, *38*, No. 10, pp. 937–951, 1986.

Shepard, R.N. 'The Analysis of Proximities: Multidimensional Scaling With an Unknown Distance Function'. *Psychometrika*, *27*, No. 2, pp. 125–245, 1962.

Shepard, R.N. 'Representation of Structure in Similarity Data: Problems and Prospects'. *Psychometrika*, *39*, No. 4, pp. 373–421, 1974.

Sherif, M. and Sherif, C. *Social Psychology*. New York: Harper & Row, 1969.

Shorter, E. *The Making of the Modern Family*. New York: Basic Books, 1975.

Slater, P. *Dimensions of Intrapersonal Space*. 2 Vols. London: Wiley & Sons, 1977.

Slater, P.E. *Microcosm: Structural, Psychological and Religious Evolution in Groups*. New York: Wiley & Sons, 1966.

Smith, K.K. *Groups in Conflict*. Dubuque, Iowa: Kendall/Hunt Publishing Company, 1982.

Snyder, C.W., Jr, Law, H.G. and Hattie, J.A. 'Overview of Multimode Analytic Methods'. In H.G. Law, C.W. Snyder, Jr, J.A. Hattie and R.P. McDonald (eds). *Research Methods for Multimode Data Analysis*. New York: Praeger Scientific, 1985.

Sommerhoff, G. 'The Abstract Characteristics of Living Systems'. In F.E. Emery. *Systems Thinking*. Harmondsworth: Penguin, 1969.

Stewart, C.J. and Cash, W.B. *Interviewing Principles and Practices*. Dubuque, Iowa: William C. Brown Publishers, (4th Edn) 1985.

Stock, D. and Lieberman, M.A. 'Methodological Issues in the Assessment of Total-Group Phenomena in Group Therapy'. In G.S. Gibbard, J.J. Hartmann and R.D. Mann (eds). *Analysis of Groups: Contributions to Theory, Research and Practice*. San Francisco: Jossey Bass, (1974) 1962.

Sullivan, H.S. 'The Illusion of Personal Individuality'. *Psychiatry, 13*, pp. 317–332, 1950.

Sullivan, H.S. *The Interpersonal Theory of Psychiatry*. William Alanson White Psychiatric Foundation. New York: Norton, 1953.

Takane, Y., Young, F.W. and deLeeuw, J. 'Non-Metric Individual Differences Multidimensional Scaling: An Alternative Least Squares Measure with Optimal Scaling Features'. *Psychometrika, 42*, pp. 7–67, 1977.

Thibaut, J.W. and Kelley, H.H. *The Social Psychology of Groups*. New York: Wiley & Sons, 1959.

Torgerson, W.S. 'Multidimensional Scaling: 1. Theory and Method'. *Psychometrika, 17*, pp. 401–419, 1952.

Trist, E.L. and Bamforth, K.W. 'Some Social and Psychological Consequences of the Longwall Method of Coal-Getting'. *Human Relations, 4*, No. 1, pp. 6–24, 1951.

Trotter, W. *Instincts of the Herd in Peace and War*. London: Fisher Unwin, 1916.

Tuckman, B.W. 'Developmental Sequence in Small Groups'. *Psychological Bulletin, 63*, pp. 384–399, 1965.

Turner, J.C., Hogg, M.A., Oakes, P.J., Reicher, S.D. and Wetherell, M.S. *Rediscovering the Social Group*. Oxford: Basil Blackwell, 1987.

Turquet, P. 'Leadership: The Individual and the Group'. In G.S. Gibbard, J.J. Hartman and R.D. Mann (eds). *Analysis of Groups: Contributions to Theory, Research and Practice*. San Francisco: Jossey Bass, 1974.

Turquet, P. 'Threats to Identity in the Large Group'. In L. Kreeger (ed.). *The Large Group: Dynamics and Therapy*. London: Constable, 1975.

Van de Geer, J.P. *Introduction to Multivariate Analysis for the Social Sciences*. San Francisco: W.H. Freeman, 1971.

Von Bertalanffy, L. 'The Theory of Open Systems in Physics and Biology'. In F.E. Emery (ed.). *Systems Thinking*. Harmondsworth: Penguin, (1969) 1950.

Watzlawick, P., Beavin, J.H. and Jackson, M.D. *Pragmatics of Human Communication: A Study of Interaction Patterns, Pathologies, and Paradoxes*. London: Faber & Faber, 1968.

Watzlawick, P., Weakland, J. and Fisch, R. *Change: Principles of Problem Solving and Problem Resolution*. New York: Norton, 1974.

Weber, M. 'Legitimate Authority and Bureaucracy'. In D.S. Pugh (ed.). *Organization Theory*. Harmondsworth: Penguin, (1971) 1947.

Whitehead, A.N. and Russell, B. *Principia Mathematica*. (3 Vols) Cambridge: Cambridge University Press, (2nd Edn) 1963.

Whyte, W.F. *Street Corner Society*. Chicago: University of Chicago Press, 1943.

Wilden, A. *System and Structure: Essays in Communication and Exchange*. London: Tavistock, (2nd Edn) 1980.

Wilden, A. *The Rules are No Game: The Strategy of Communication*. London: Routledge & Kegan Paul, 1987.

Winnicott, D.W. 'Primitive Emotional Development'. In D.W. Winnicott. *Collected Papers: Through Paediatrics to Psychoanalysis*. London: Tavistock Publications, (1958) 1945.

Winnicott, D.W. 'Transitional Objects and Transitional Phenomena'. In D.W. Winnicott. *Collected Papers: Through Paediatrics to Psychoanalysis*. London: Tavistock Publications, (1958) 1951.

Winnicott, D.W. *Collected Papers: Through Paediatrics to Psychoanalysis*. London: Tavistock Publications, 1958.

Winnicott, D.W. *Playing and Reality*. London: Tavistock Publications, 1971.

Wisdom, J.O. 'Situational Individualism and the Emergent Group-Properties'. In R. Borger and F. Cioffi (eds). *Explanation in the Behavioural Sciences*. Cambridge: Cambridge University Press, 1970.

Wong, N. 'The Application of Object-Relations Theory to an Understanding of Group Cohesion'. In H. Kellerman (ed.). *Group Cohesion: Theoretical and Clinical Perspectives*. New York: Grune & Stratton, 1981.

Yalom, I.D. *The Theory and Practice of Group Psychotherapy*. New York: Basic Books, 1975.

Yorke, D.M. 'Administration, Analysis and Assumption: Some Aspects of Validity'. In N. Beail (ed.). *Repertory Grid Technique and Personal Constructs: Applications in Clinical and Educational Settings*. Beckenham, Kent: Croom Helm, 1985.

Young, F.W. 'Scaling'. *Annual Review of Psychology, 35*, pp. 55–81, 1984.

Young, F.W. and Lewyckyj, R. *ALSCAL-4 User's Guide*. Cary, North Carolina: Data Analysis and Theory Associates, (2nd Edn) 1979.

Zimbardo, P.G. 'The Human Choice: Individuation, Reason and Order Versus Deindividuation, Impulse and Chaos'. In W.J. Arnold and D. Levine (eds). *Nebraska Symposium on Motivation*. Lincoln: University of Nebraska Press, 1969.

Zimbardo, P.G. *Influencing Attitudes and Changing Behaviour: An Introduction to Method, Theory and Applications of Social Control and Personal Power*. Reading, Mass.: Addison-Wesley, (2nd Edn) 1977.

Zukier, H. 'Freud and Development: The Developmental Dimensions of Psychoanalytic Theory'. *Social Research, 52*, No. 1., pp. 3–41, Spring 1985.

Name index

Allport, G.W. 18, 21, 22, 47

Bachelard, G. 16
Bales, R.F. 77, 181
Bateson, G. 10
Bennis, W.G. 84, 135, 142
Bierstedt, R. 179
Billig, M. 18, 19, 22, 30, 47, 87
Bion, W.R. 14, 22, 24, 28–31, 32, 38, 56,
    71, 84, 86, 87, 92, 95, 121, 138, 169,
    175, 180, 183, 184
Boyd, R.D. 84
Breakwell, G.M. 69, 74
Byrt, W.J. 180

Chomsky, N. 10
Cissna, K.N. 112
Cooper, L. 86

Deleuze, G. 41
Dell, P.F. 10
Doise, W. 47
Donzelot, J. 23

Emery, F.E. 10
Erikson, E.H. 3, 57, 59–64
Etzioni, A. 181

Fagen, R.E. 9, 11
Ferenczi, S. 27
Follett, M.P. 180
Forgas, J.P. 4, 78, 81, 87, 184
Foucault, M. 23
Foulkes, S.H. 22, 24, 37–9, 47, 48, 86,
    175
Freud, A. 68
Freud, S. 3, 18, 19, 22, 24, 25–6, 29, 31,
    33, 39, 40, 44, 45, 46, 52, 57, 59, 61,
    62, 63, 64–8, 71, 87, 107, 109, 122,
    131, 138, 170, 174, 175, 188

Gibbard, G.S. 54, 84
Glaser, S. 75, 81, 87, 91
Goffman, E. 46
Goolishian, H.A. 10
Grotstein, J.S. 28
Guattari, F. 41
Gustafason, J.P. 86

Hall, A.D. 9, 11
Halle, M. 41, 42, 43
Harré, R. 3, 57, 58–9, 79, 80, 81, 86, 87,
    138, 141, 155, 160, 165
Hoffman, L. 10
Hollander, E.P. 181
Horney, K. 46

Jakobson, R. 41, 42, 43, 44, 63
James, W. 46, 59, 61
Jaques, E. 69, 153
Jung, C.J. 39, 47

Kagan, J. 64
Kahn, R.L. 10
Katz, D. 10
Kellerman, H. 70
Kelly, G. 184
Kernberg, O. 62
Klein, W. 24, 26–8, 33, 39, 84, 116, 138,
    162, 168
Kohut, H. 62

Lacan, J. 3, 16, 19, 20, 24, 31, 40–7, 48,
    57, 59, 61–4, 67, 71, 84, 86, 87, 92, 93,
    138, 139, 152, 153, 162, 175
Laing, R.D. 46

Le Bon, G. 65
Levi-Strauss, C. 63, 83, 139
Lieberman, M.A. 135
Lorenz, K.Z. 18

McDougall, W. 65
Mahler, M. 3, 49, 52–4, 83, 87, 96, 98,
    107, 175
Malin, A. 28
Marsh, P. 84, 87
Maturana, H.R. 10, 36
Melbourne, Australia 91, 120, 140
Menzies, I.P.M. 69
Merlieau-Ponty, M. 12, 81
Milgram, S. 20, 21
Minuchin, S. 10
Money-Kyrle, R. 18

Neumann, E. Von 31

Pfeffer, J. 182

Rainwater, L. 19
Redl, F. 26, 86
Rice, A.K. 86, 179
Rieff, P. 26, 71, 72
Russell, B. 76
Rychlak, J.F. 76, 79

Saussure, F. de 41, 43, 63
Sayers, J. 188

Schoeck, H. 116
Schopler, J. 180
Schutz, W. 55, 78
Scott, W.R. 74, 181
Shepard, R.N. 84, 135, 142
Slater, P.E. 22, 24, 26, 30, 31–7, 38, 84,
    87
Society of B'nai B'rith 59
Sommerhoff, G. 10, 75, 82
Stock, D. 135
Storr, A. 18
Sullivan, H.S. 59, 60, 62

Tavistock school 10, 85, 183
Trist, E.L. 10
Trotter, W. 65, 66
Tuckman, B.W. 135, 142
Turner, J.C. 20, 21
Turquet, P. 16

Varela, F.J. 10, 36
Von Bertalaffny, L. 10, 75

Watzlewick, P. 11, 14
Weber, M. 179, 180, 182
Whitehead, A.N. 76
Wilden, A. 15
Winnicott, D.W. 3, 39, 49, 50–1, 53, 54,
    81, 83, 86, 92, 93, 95, 99, 107, 137,
    138, 175

Subject index

accounts 80
action 141, 155, 172, 177; research model 77
acts 80, 141, 155, 172
aggressivity 111, 115, 116, 143, 162, 186
anger 144, 146, 147, 148, 149, 150, 162–3
anxiety 29, 32, 64, 95, 120–4, 130, 135, 150, 154, 162–3
articulating differences 9
attack 142, 146, 147, 148, 165, 184
attributes 9, 82
authority 3, 4, 5, 31, 57, 71–4, 119, 124, 140, 142, 152, 153, 163, 167, 168, 170, 174, 175, 179–83; female 178, 186–7; interdictory 71–2; structure see group structure; see also leadership
autonomy, repression of 135

basic assumption group 28, 29, 31, 32, 178; see also groups
bodily level of experience 48
boundary: development of 50, 94, 96, 101, 128; transactions 11, 32, 33, 34, 37, 38
brainwashing 135

case study methods 2
causal methods 4
cell, as a system 11
central organizer 153
challenge, state of 169
class, definition of 11
clinical approach 2
closed systems see systems
cognitive polarities 162
cohesion see group cohesion
collective: psychology 39; unconscious 47
communication networks 38
condensation, of dreams 109

confidentiality 126–8
consciousness 24
constraint 76
consultant 116, 117, 119, 121, 123, 149, 150, 153, 157, 160, 162, 170, 171, 173, 174, 184; /group duality 101, 119
containers see leadership
conventional meaning 80
counterdependence 104
cross-sectional study 84, 91–106, 131–6, 176
cultural level 140

data problem 79
defensive: behaviour 95; preparation 167, 169; relations 173
delusions, of being noticed 115
dependency group 29, 32, 33
depressive position 27–8, 146, 169
desertion, fear of 104
despair 169
developmental: processes 33, 35, 53; regression see regression; stages 135; see also group development
diachronic see developmental 33
differentation 162
dimensional manifolds 81
displacement 111
dominance 170, 171; see also authority
drama, group sessions as 169, 171
dread 163
dreams 45, 109, 155
dual task 119
dynamics, group 29, 31, 85, 91, 141, 142, 146, 170, 173, 174, 183, 187

ego 25, 40, 45, 59, 61, 62, 63, 65, 67; -control processes 26; development

60; ideal 65, 70, 115, 122, 131; unified 162
egocentricity 112
emergent social reality *see* realization
emotions 162, 172
empirical approach 2, 4
energy 29
entities 9, 85; study of 78, 82
episodes 80, 84, 141, 142–56, 156–63, 163–7, 168, 172, 177; analysis of 175
experimenter myth *see* myth
exploratory approach 2

fantasy *see* phantasy
first order change 12, 13
flight/fight group 29, 32, 33
foreclosure 46
fragmentation 163, 164
free association 37, 38
Freudian theory 25–6, 29, 37
Frommian theory 33

general systems theory *see* systems theory
Gestalt 62
good: /bad duality 103, 172; -enough -mother 99
grid methods 78, 87
group 54–6, 66; analysis 92; behaviour 141, 150; catalyst 101; cohesion 1, 3, 112, 174; comparison 133; complex dependencies 92; concepts 2; defensive system 165, 175; development 34, 49, 135; differentiation 103; discussion 98; disintegration 130, 135; division 134; dynamics *see* dynamics; effectiveness 176; emergent properties of 1; entity 93; evolution of 32; expectations of 95; formation of 66, 131; fragmentation 136; interaction 172; levels of operation 39; matrix 38, 39; mind 38; nucleus 108; occupation 38; organization *see* structure; outcomes 87, 92; phenomena 2, 21, 22; preoccupation 38; primary task of 25, 119; processes 26, 91, 142, 183; properties 175; research *see* research methodology; revolt 31; splitting *see* fragmentation; states 176; study of 91–106, 141–2; as system 9–13, 75, 92, 137, 177; -that is joined 106,

115–16, 124, 128, 132, 151, 155, 165, 172, 176, 184; theory 12, 22–5; therapy 37; -to-be-created 132, 151; un-integration 135; working definition of 72–3
guilt 29, 109, 110, 148, 156, 169

hatching phase 53–4, 101, 105, 134
helplessness 162
heuristics, for systems mapping 81
hierarchical ordering 13
historical changes 173
hostility 95, 165

id 40
identification 3, 61, 64, 116, 141, 170, 175; relations 173, 174
identity 3, 57, 58, 59, 60, 62, 63, 68, 72, 74, 99, 101, 105, 137, 138, 140, 141, 174, 175; development of *see* individuation; formation 60, 70; illusion of 64; psychological 48; social 1, 70; *see also* personalization
illusion 51, 54, 101
imaginary: field 31; hegemony 171; register *see* registers; representation 163; *see also* leadership
impressionistic approach 2
independence, from group 104
individual 1, 2, 11; development 49; illusory nature of 59; level 18, 20, 22; psychology 39, 66; *see also* transindividual
individuality 143, 170
individuation 33, 52, 53, 55, 101
infant: development 50, 51, 101, 131; integration 106, 131, 132; /mother dyad 121
integrating point *see* nodes
integration: group 95, 101, 103, 108, 122, 128, 132, 135, 136, 175; psychological 3, 24, 48, 49, 50, 55, 57, 62, 63, 95, 99, 108, 116, 137, 162, 176
intergroup identity 69–71, 174
interpersonal: level 18–19; relations 39; traits 78
intersubjectivity 63
interviewing 77
intrapersonal object relations 39
introjective identification 26, 27, 29

jouissance 62
judgement, by others 126, 132, 150, 162

key members 157
kingship 34, 35
Kleinian theory 26–8, 30, 32, 35, 121, 135, 184

Lacanian: concepts 40, 177, 178, 184;
    moments 135
language 41, 42, 45, 76, 81, 185, 162;
    levels of 15; metalanguage 15; object
    15
leadership 3, 4, 5, 25, 57, 71–4, 93, 95,
    101, 105, 106, 110, 123, 124, 128, 140,
    142, 149, 151, 163–5, 167–8, 171,
    174, 175, 176, 177, 179–83;
    containing 162, 176; partnership 176;
    symbolic 106, 184, 186; see also
    authority
legitimation 73, 74, 181, 182
libidinal transformations see transform-
    ations
libido 3, 60, 64, 65, 66, 67, 68, 69, 173;
    theory 69, 70
linguistics see language
logical types, theory 15
longitudinal qualitative study 5, 84,
    137–8, 139–74, 177–8

malevolence, group 115, 116, 118, 119
manipulation, group 129, 131, 154, 157,
    160, 162
MDS methods 87, 184–5
measurement: characteristics 79; in
    research 78–82; theory 82
member, definition of 11
mental images level of experience 48
metaphor 44
metasystemic concepts 12
methodology, for research 77
metonomy 44
mirror: mechanism 112, 113; relation
    123, 132; stage 41, 45, 62, 93, 95, 133,
    162, 163, 176
mother/child bond 3, 106, 132
multi-dimensionality 39
mystery person 146
myth: experimenter 55; societal 29, 30,
    31, 33, 54; structure 139; see also
    primal horde myth
mythical leader 106

narcissism 46, 57, 62, 64, 65, 66
narcissistic libido see libido
naturalistic observation 4

neurotic symptoms 155
nodes 157
non-hierarchical relations 13–18

object: language see language; libido see
    libido; relations 173
oedipal structure 64, 71, 138, 153, 188
open: to meaning 152; systems see
    systems
other see unconscious

pairing group 29, 32, 33
paradigmatic relations 42, 47; see also
    psychoanalytic
paradox of reciprocal systemic relations
    16, 85; see also semantic paradoxes
paranoid/schizoid state 162, 168
patterning 2; internal 10
persecutor 115, 150, 152, 153, 154, 172,
    177
personality theory 24
personalization 50, 103, 132, 137, 138;
    see also identity
phantasy 31, 32, 33, 54
phenomenology 12, 81, 140
pleasure principle 46
political dimension 23, 142, 167–8, 169,
    172, 174
power 3–5, 140, 142, 162, 163, 167, 169,
    174, 175, 180–1
precedent meanings 76
preconscious 97
primal horde myth 25, 26, 31, 34
primordial level of experience 39, 48
projection 26, 114, 162–3, 169, 184
projective identification 27, 28, 29, 30,
    154, 162, 169
psyche-individuals 38
psychoanalysis 37, 47
psychoanalytic: paradigm 20, 47;
    perspective 23; theory 4, 22, 175
psychological: identity 3, 70;
    methodology 77–8
psychology 21; group 2, 22–5, 28, 37, 47,
    66; social 1, 47, 60, 66
psychopathology 124
psychotherapy 23

qualitative analysis 86–7
quantitative analysis 87, 184

real register see registers

reality: adaptation *see* realization; principle 46
realization 50, 132, 137
rebellion 56, 99, 101, 135, 136, 157, 158
reciprocal: causation 1; relations 2, 14
registers of experience 19, 40, 47; imaginary 45–6, 48, 62, 64, 177; real 46–7, 48, 64; symbolic 19, 41–5, 48, 64, 82, 177
regression, developmental 34, 35, 37, 38, 39
reification 62
reintrojection 104
relatedness, of individuals 68
relations 71; of identification 173
relationships 9, 71
religion 23, 31
remissive authority 71, 72
repertory grid *see* grid methods; *see also* role construct
repetition 128–30, 135
research: methodology 75–87, 91–106, 141–2, 175; ideographic 2; observational 2, 77
role construct repertory tests 78
roles 1, 42, 162, 172; membership 178

Saussurian symbolism 31
scapegoat 150, 154, 183
Schema R 152
schism 1
schizoid position 27
second order change 13
self-analytic learning group 85–6, 183
self-mastery 64; *see also* identity
semantic: antimonies 14; paradoxes 16
signification 127, 138, 154, 155, 162, 168, 169, 172
signifiers 41–3, 140, 152, 154, 157, 162, 168, 171, 172, 173, 177
sliding 152
social: action *see* action; construction of data 79; determination 1; inheritance 59; interactions 4, 141; interpretations 141; level 19–20; processes 1, 60; psychology *see* psychology; structure 162
socio-emotional dimensions 167, 168–9
sociological theory 21
sophisticated work group 29
spatial representation 186
splitting 27, 162, 174, 178

structural: analysis 139, 152; organizers 177
structure, group 5, 29, 92, 113, 119, 139, 152, 155, 162, 170, 172, 173, 175, 177, 178, 183
structured division 168, 169
sub-groupings 153–5, 157, 159, 162, 165, 168–9, 172, 174, 183
subjectivity, of individual 47
substantive theory 82
superego 40, 70
superordinate system 13
symbiosis 52–3, 96–105, 116–19, 124–6, 129, 134, 135, 176
symbolic 63, 64, 139; authority 163; entities 162; explanation 31; leader *see* leadership; order 172; organization 140; polarities 168; register *see* registers; significance 82; structures 140; systems 59, 61, 82
symbolization 80; cultural 106, 137
synchronic shifts 33
syntagmatic relations 42
systemic: analysis 11; organization 4; living cell 11
systems: approach 9–13; closed 11–12; definition of 11; /environment relations 11; open 11–12; study of 77–87; theory framework 2, 4, 9–48

teleology of causation 76
temporal regression *see* regression
tension, group 144, 145, 147, 149, 162, 171–2
third eye, of envy 116
transference 37; level 48; phenomena 86
transformations 152
transgressive authority 71, 72
transindividual: concepts 75, 175; level 2, 3, 4, 19, 24, 41; phenomena 37, 47; processes 26, 28, 30, 40, 47, 57, 69, 73, 175; *see also* individual
transpersonal level 19
traumatic event 142, 153, 165, 177

unconscious 139, 182; collective 47; formulations 101; processes 29, 30, 40, 45, 86, 109, 174, 183
undifferentiation, state of 33
unity *see* wholeness

valency 29, 81

victim 148, 150, 152, 154, 172, 177

watching agency 131
wholeness, individual 16, 24, 57, 62, 64,
93, 128, 137, 141, 162–3
work group 28, 29, 30, 178; *see also*
groups
worthlessness 162